by Canoe and Dog Train

Yours
very Faithfully
Egerton R. Young

by Canoe and Dog Train

Among The
Cree And Saulteaux Indians

BY

Egerton Ryerson Young

(Missionary)

With An Introduction By
Mark Guy Pearse

"Out of the darkness of night
The world rolls into the light,
It is daybreak everywhere,"
— Longfellow.

Toronto:
William Briggs,
Wesley Buildings.
Montreal: C.W. Coats. Halifax: S.F. Huestis.

Entered according to Act of the Parliament of Canada, in the year one thousand eight hundred and ninety, by WILLIAM BRIGGS, Book Steward of the Methodist Book and Publishing House, Toronto, at the Department of Agriculture.

Printed 1890
First Re-print — April 1991
Second Re-print —November 1991
Third re-print — August 1992
Revised and Edited by
Northern Canada Evangelical Mission Inc.
Box 3030
Prince Albert, Saskatchewan
S6V 7V4

ISBN No. 0-920731-34-1

by Canoe and Dog Train

Among The
Cree And Saulteaux Indians

"Dog Train at full speed."

To The
Faithful And Loving Wife

Who so cheerfully and uncomplainingly for years
Shared the hardships and toils
Of some of the most trying mission fields;
Whose courage never faltered,
And
Whose zeal abated not, even when often in peril
From hunger, bitter cold, and savage men;

This volume is dedicated,
By her affectionate
Husband.

CONTENTS

Page
Introduction 1

CHAPTER I
Indian evangelization —New records of work done — Heroic efforts — The Puritans — Brainerd — President Grant's humane policy 4

CHAPTER II
Work in Canada — William Case — James Evans and his co-laborers in the great lone land, with sketches of Revs. Peter Jones, John Sunday, and Henry Steinheur 9

CHAPTER III
The summons to the Indian work — The decision — The valedictory services — Dr. Punshon — The departure Leaving Hamilton — St. Catharine's — Milwaukee custom—house delays — Mississippi — St. Paul's — On the prairies — Frontier settlers — Narrow escape from shooting one of our school teachers — Sioux Indians and their wars — Saved by our flag — Varied experiences 29

CHAPTER IV
Still on the route — Fort Garry — Breaking up of our party of missionaries — Lower Fort — Hospitable Hudson's Bay officials — Peculiarities — Fourteen Days in a little open boat on stormy Lake Winnipeg — Strange experiences — Happy Christian Indian boatmen —In peril by waters 45

CHAPTER V
Arrival at Norway House — Our new home — Rev. Charles Stringfellow — Thunderstorm — Rev. James Evans — Syllabic characters invented — Difficulties overcome — Help from English Wesleyan Missionary Society — Extensive use of the syllabic characters — The people, Christian and otherwise — Learning lessons by dear experience — The hungry woman — The man with the two ducks — Our first Sabbath in our new field — Sunday School and Sabbath services — Family altars 59

CHAPTER VI
Constant progress — Woman's sad condition without Christ — Illustrations — Wondrous changes produced by Christianity — Illustrations — New Year's Day Christian festival — The aged and feeble ones first remembered — Closing thanksgiving services 69

CHAPTER VII

Oxford House Mission — Visited by canoe — Description of this useful craft — Indian skill — Oxford Lake — Dr. Taylor — Edward Papanekis — Still on the trail by birch canoe — Narrow escape from being crushed by the ice — On stormy Lake Winnipeg — Pioneering farther north — Successes — "Show us the Father, and it suffices us" — Christ accepted in the place of idols 78

CHAPTER VIII

The wild north land — The two methods of travel, by canoe and dog train — The native dogs — St. Bernard and Newfoundland dogs — The dog sleds — The guide — The dog drivers — The long journeys — Night traveling — Wondrous visions of the night 99

CHAPTER IX

On the trail with the dogs to fields ripe for the reaper — The place — The trip — The winter camp — The bitter cold — Enduring hardness — Death shaking hands with us — Many days on the trail 112

CHAPTER X

Nelson River — A demonstrative welcome — First religious service — A four hour sermon — The Chief's eloquent reply — The old man with grandchildren in his wigwam — "Our Father" — "Then we are brothers" — "Yes" — "Then why is the white brother so long time in coming with the gospel to his Indian brother?" — Glorious successes .. 129

CHAPTER XI

A welcome accession — The Rev. John Semmens — A devoted young missionary — First to reside at Nelson River — In labor and in peril often — In journeys often by dog trains together — The centenarian Christian — William Papanekis — His godly life and wondrous translation 139

CHAPTER XII

Rev. James Evans, the peerless missionary — His journeys by canoe and dog train — The Cree syllabic characters, his invention — Lord Dufferin's words concerning him — His successes — His trials — Accidental shooting of his interpreter — Surrendering himself to the avengers — Adopted into a Chipewyan family — Visit to England — Sudden death 152

CHAPTER XIII

Sowing and reaping — Beautiful incident — "Help me to be a Christian!" — Thirty years between the sowing and the reaping — Sorrowing, yet stubborn, Indians induced to yield by the expression, "I know where your children are!" 167

CHAPTER XIV

On the trail to Sandy Bar — Sleeping on the ice — Thievish Eskimo dogs — Narrow escape of Jack — Joyous welcome — Society formed — Benjamin Cameron, once a cannibal, now a lay helper — Plum-pudding — A striking instance of honesty 180

CHAPTER XV

An Indian lovefeast — Many witnesses — Sweet songs of Zion — The Lord's Supper — Memoir of William Memotas, the devoted Christian 190

CHAPTER XVI

Varied duties — Christianity must precede civilization —Illustrations — Experimental farming — Ploughing with dogs — Abundance of fish — Visits from far off Indians — Some come to disturb — Many sincere inquirers after the truth — "Where is the missionary?" — Beren's River Mission begun — Timothy Bear — Peril on the ice 204

CHAPTER XVII

Smallpox pestilence — Heroic conduct of Christian Indians — Whites supplied with provisions by Indians — The guide, Samuel Papanekis — His triumphant death — Nancy, the happy widow — In poverty, yet rejoicing 218

CHAPTER XVIII

A race for life in a blizzard storm — Saved by the marvelous intelligence of Jack — "Where is the old man, whose head was like the snowdrift?" 234

CHAPTER XIX

Work outside the pulpit — Polygamy and its evils — Family rearrangements — Dangerous work at times — Practical pastoral duties — A fish sermon — Five men won to Christ 247

CHAPTER XX

Exploring new fields — The gospel before treaties — Big Tom's noble spirit of self-sacrifice 265

CHAPTER XXI

A mission among the Saulteaux established — Nelly's death — Missionary anniversaries attended — Rev. Thomas Crosby — Travelling adventures — More working with dogs — Our new home — Visit from a chieftainess — Closing words 279

LIST OF ILLUSTRATIONS

Portrait Of The Author	ii
Dog train At Full Speed	vi
Rev. John Sunday	19
Rev. Henry Steinheur	23
Jonas, Samson, Pakan	27
Portrait Of Mrs. Young	31
Rev. William Young	34
A Prairie Scene	39
Roving Indians And Metis	47
An Indian Canoe Brigade	56
Fat Ducks	64
"Many A Duck Was Shot By These Young Indian Maidens"	74
Taking The Bark From The Trees For Canoe Making	80
"As The Doctor Was An Enthusiastic Fisherman"	87
"With His Light Canoe He Can Go Almost Everywhere"	101
"Here The Black Bears Are Very Numerous"	127
"We Exchanged Our Black Clothes For Our Leather Suits"	141
"We Have Looked Death In The Face Together Many Times"	148

"No River Seemed Too Rapid, And No Lake Too Stormy" 154
Cree Syllabic Alphabet 164
The Lord's Prayer 165
"Some Came In Their Small Canoes" 207
I. Nothing But The Hind Quarter Of A Wild Cat For Breakfast. Off Looking For Game 215
II. Six Hundred Yards Is A Long Shot, But Wild Cat Is Poor Food, And So We Will Try For Something Better 216
III. Come, Share With Me Our Savory Venison 217
Dog train With Mail 221
Rev. Edward Papanekis And Family 222
Fishing Through The Ice 229
Christian Indian's Barn, Scugog Mission 233
Indian Ceremonies At A Dog Feast 236
Sea River Falls, Near Norway House 263
Indian Council 267
A Young Indian With His Canoe At The Foot Of The Rude Water Slide 274
Toiling Along On Snowshoes Through The Woods 287

INTRODUCTION

My friend, Mr Egerton R. Young, has asked me to write a few words of preface to his book. Although he needs no words of mine to introduce him to the people "at home," as the Canadians call the motherland, I very gladly comply with his request.

It was on a sunny day in the early part of May, 1887, that I met Mr. Young away at Meaford on the shores of Georgian Bay. We passed the river, crowded with boys and men snatching with leaded hooks at the mullet that were swarming in shoals from Lake Huron, along by the wharves to the water's edge, and there on the pebble ridge we sat and talked. A simple, honest, straight forward Methodist preacher, one felt at home with him at once. I found that he had been a missionary for many years among the Cree and Saulteaux Indians away in "the lone land." I had but to ask a question here and there and sat entranced; the people, the country, the cold, the dogs, the bears, the whole surroundings of the life began to live before me, and with many a wild scene of adventure, and many a wonderful story of conversion. That afternoon sped away, for me, much too quickly, and ever since it has hung up in "the chambers of my imagery," among its most vivid and most treasured pictures.

I went with him to his house and made the acquaintance of Mrs. Young, his brave and devoted wife, and the children. I stood on a mat of some fur which interested me. "What is this?" I asked. My host laughed "A silver-grey wolf: a mad fellow that wanted to make a meal of my boy Eddie, and but for God's mercy would have."

And then began another story how that as with elephants and buffaloes and all creatures that are gregarious there is often one that for some reason or want of it lives alone, and is of all its kind the most mischievous and most dangerous often, perhaps generally, mad; in this case it was a wolf. The Indians were in the forest cutting wood for the winter, and the little lad with his train of dogs enjoyed the drive in the sledge to and fro, bringing home the load of wood, or racing back in the empty sledge. It was as the boy was returning that out of the forest rushed the fierce beast, and raced beside him, trying to reach him on the pile, while the frightened dogs galloped furiously to the Mission House. A moment's delay, an upset, and the wolf must have had the lad, but in God's providence he reached home in safety. A little afterward the wolf was killed, and here was its silver fur resting in front of the fireplace. Everything suggested some new question, and that led to some new story. At last I had to leave for my service, and then home by a long row across the lake. But before we parted I got a promise that Mr. Young would come to England and tell the people "at home" the story of his mission.

I felt that he could do for us a work that needed to be done, and that few could do, in renewing the popular interest in foreign missionary enterprise. I had hoped that the Missionary Society might have utilized him for deputation work, and have sent him through the country on this errand. This hope, however, has not been fulfilled. But not the less service has been rendered by Mr. and Mrs. Young, as they have gone from place to place interesting and thrilling tens of thousands by the records of their great success and of God's blessing among the Indians.

It is said that "men who make history do not write it." Years among the dog trains and birch canoes do not afford much room for practicing the art of writing, especially when six months had to intervene before receiving any communication from the "world of letters." If Mr. Young's written narrative has not the force and charm of his spoken addresses, is it not true of everything that is worth hearing when it loses the voice of the speaker? But in spite of this we are quite sure that thousands will be thankful to have in a permanent form that which Mr. Young has given them here; and that very many others will be glad to read what they could not hear. My earnest wish is that the book may have the circulation it deserves; my prayer is that it may be made the blessing which its author desires.

Mark Guy Pearse.

CHAPTER I

Indian Evangelization — Few records of work done — Heroic efforts — The Puritans — Brainerd — President Grant's humane policy.

"Gather the harvest in:
The fields are white, and long ago ye heard,
Ringing across the world, the Master's word:
'Leave no such fruitage to the lord of sin;
Gather the harvest in'."

The question of evangelizing the Indian tribes of North America is one that has been more or less prominent before the Christian churches for many years. In the prosecution of this work some of the noblest of God's heroes have been engaged, some of the greatest hardship and suffering have been endured, and some of the grandest trophies have been won.

It is to be regretted that Indian missionary biographies are so limited. But few are the "abiding records," in book form, of those men of heroic mold, who have devoted themselves to this department of missionary toil.

While we rejoice that we have the biographies of Eliot, Brainerd, and a few others of the early missionaries, who so nobly toiled, and not in vain, among the people of the forest, we cannot but regret that so little has been published of such Indian missionaries as Evans, Rundle, McDougall, Steinheur, and others, whose daring, patience, endurance, and successful toil would make their biographies as thrillingly interesting and as valuable to the church as those of Carey, Judson, Hunt, or Morrison.

These missionaries to the aborigines of the American continent deserve all the more credit from the fact that their lives and energies were devoted to the benefit of what is generally considered a vanishing people, a dying race. For the Indian, in too many instances, the gospel of bullets has been preached more loudly than the gospel of love. More laws have been enacted to legislate him out of existence, than to lift him up into the condition of a loyal citizen, and the enjoyment of a consistent Christianity. Very humiliating is the fact, that there are in these so-called Christian lands many who, forgetting the doctrine of the universal brotherhood of humanity, and also that of the universality of the atonement, have become so dwarfed and prejudiced in their minds concerning the Indian as to leave him completely outside the pale of humanity, and utterly beyond the reach of God's mercy.

It is a cause of thankfulness, that while ignorance, or terror, or ambition, or greed, has caused too many to have such views, many others have differed, and have gone to work to do the Indians good; and their lives have not been complete failures. Apart from the efforts made by the priests who accompanied Cortez, Pizarro, and other military adventurers, very early in the sixteenth century, priests were laboring in Florida, and in the Rio Grande country, for the conversion of the natives, and they counted their converts by thousands long before any considerable settlement of English-speaking people had been formed on the Continent. Then, in the following century, the story of the labors and hardships of the Jesuits, and other organizations of the Church of Rome, among the Hurons of Canada, the Iroquois of New York, the Abenakis of Maine, and various other tribes, as narrated in the eloquent pages of Parkman's fascinating histories, reads more like a thrilling romance than as the sober recital of actual facts.

In the first settlements in Maryland, the conversion of the Indians was a subject that at once attracted attention; and the laborers did not toil in vain. In the Charter given to the band of adventurers, who, in the year 1607, fixed upon Virginia as their home, these words occur. They were ordered to "use all proper means to draw the Indian people to the true knowledge and service of God."

Within a year after the arrival of the Pilgrim Fathers at Plymouth Rock, one of the elders, a Mr. Cushman, in writing back to his friends in England, referred to "the tractable disposition of the Indian youths, and the possibility of doing them much good." Those grand and sturdy people, who for conscience' sake had come out into the wilderness, had themselves declared that they had come to America for weighty and solid reasons, among which was this that they might be used for the "propagation and advancing of the gospel and kingdom of Christ." In their conscientious way they set about the fulfillment of these designs. Of the wonderful revivals among the Indians, under the labors of the Revs. David and John Brainerd, a good deal has been written. Their consecrated zeal and great successes fired anew the hearts of such glorious men as the Wesleys, Whitefield, and Jonathan Edwards. An eminent writer has declared that "the work of God among the Indians at that period was perhaps without parallel in missions since the days of the apostles." David Brainerd, in writing of the wondrous work, said: "The power of God seemed to descend upon the Indians like a mighty rushing wind, and with astonishing energy bore down all before it. Marvelous were the results. Old men and women were in deep distress for their souls, and the most stubborn hearts were compelled to bow, and thousands were happily converted to God."

So deeply impressed was John Wesley with Brainerd's work among the Indians, that we find in the fifth volume of his Works the following question and answer:

Question: "What can be done in order to revive the work of God where it is decayed?"

Answer: "Let every preacher read carefully over the 'Life of David Brainerd,' etc."

To follow and record, with any degree of completeness, the work carried on by the churches among these "wards of the nations," would be interesting and a labor of love, but it would occupy volumes. Suffice it to say, ere we begin to make fuller mention of the Canada work, of which we have some personal knowledge, that the churches of the United States are carrying on a grand enterprise with increasing vigor and encouraging success. Excellent schools, like those at Carlisle, in Pennsylvania and Hampton Institute, in Virginia, are developing noble Christian men and women, who are giving fresh impetus to the blessed work of lifting up these remnants of once mighty tribes to the enjoyment of true religion and to a higher plane of civilization. It is also an encouraging sign of the times, that the government of the mightiest republic the world ever saw is waking up to its responsibility, and, as if to atone for the misdeeds of its agents and the sad blunders of the past, is entering on a new career, resolved that justice, although long delayed, shall yet be meted out to its Indian subjects.

The "blood-and-iron" policy was a disgrace to American civilization and to our common Christianity. The effort to make the Indian "decent by force" has been a complete failure. The force of honest, straight forward example will do vastly more. By right thinking people General Grant deserves ever to be held in kindly remembrance for his "peace policy." When so-called friends urged him to make a change in it, his reply was characteristic of the man, and worthy to be remembered: "If the present policy towards Indians can be improved in any way, I will always be ready to receive suggestions on the subject. I do not believe our Creator ever placed different races of men on this earth with a view to having the stronger exert all his energies in the extermination of the weaker. If any change takes place in the Indian policy of the Government while I hold my present office, it will be on the humanitarian side of the question."

CHAPTER II
Work in Canada — William Case — James Evans and his co-laborers in the great lone land, with sketches of Revs. Peter Jones, John Sunday, and Henry Steinheur.

For many years the Methodist Church of Canada has taken a deep interest in the spiritual welfare of the Indian tribes of the great Dominion. For a long time its efforts were but feeble, and the results proportionally small. In the year 1823 an impetus was given to the work by the conversion of an Indian lad, who afterwards became the Rev. Peter Jones, a devoted and successful missionary to his own people. When this Indian lad first stood up in a fellowship meeting, and told the simple story of his conversion, the presiding elder, the Rev. William Case, shouted out, "Glory to God! Now is the door opened for the work of conversion in his nation."

The report of what was going on in the old province of Upper Canada fired the hearts of the parent Wesleyan Missionary Society in England; in the year 1840 they sent out, to what was then known as the Hudson's Bay Territories, the Rev. Messrs. Barnley, Rundle, and others, to be under the superintendence of the Rev. James Evans, who had been labouring in Upper Canada, but who left his successful work, and hurried away to assume, as desired, the leadership of that heroic band which, with apostolic zeal, was about to enter into the very heart of this then unknown region.

Mr. Evans, with his family, travelled all the way from Thunder Bay, on Lake Superior, to Norway House in a birch bark canoe, a distance of many hundreds of miles. His library and household effects had to be shipped to London, England, and then re-shipped on the Hudson's Bay Company's vessel to York Factory, on the western side of Hudson's Bay.

From this port they were carried in open boats up a dangerous, toilsome route of over five hundred miles. Scores of times they had to be unloaded and carried on men's shoulders round the falls, or rapids, of treacherous, dangerous rivers, until finally they reached their owner, after having crossed the Atlantic twice, and travelled altogether a distance of some twelve thousand miles; many months having been taken to perform a journey which now, by the aid of rail and steamer, can be made in five days.

Grandly and well did Evans, Rundle and Barnley toil. Their names, in that great land, are still fragrant as the breath of heaven. Their heroic deeds live on, their faithful words are not forgotten; and to this day there still remain many Indians who were rescued from sin by their faithful labours; and the "church triumphant" holds a goodly company who have finished their course with joy.

In 1854, the Indian Missions in the North-West Territories were transferred from the English Wesleyan to the Canadian Methodist Church. The appointments for that year were as follows:

Norway House, Lake Winnipeg, — Thomas Hurlburt.
Oxford House, — Robert Brooking.
Lac La Pluie, — Allen Salt.
Edmonton and Rocky Mountains, — Henry Steinheur.

Thomas Hurlburt was of a family that gave five sons to the Methodist ministry. He entered the ministry in 1829, and devoted the greater part of his long ministerial life to the evangelization and civilization of the Indians, a work in which he was very successful.

Robert Brooking also deserves honourable mention. Before coming to America, Mr. Brooking was a missionary of the English Wesleyan Church.

For years he lived and laboured in Ashantee, on the west coast of Africa. His health failing in the excessive heat of that field of labour, he returned home, and after his restoration, came to Canada, and devoted himself to the Indian work. Strange to say, he was now sent to the coldest field in the world. He has given more than thirty years of faithful service to the Indian work, and now, after long years of self-denying toil, is enjoying a happy and contented old age, patiently waiting until the summons shall be heard to "come up higher."

Allen Salt, the third name on the 1854 list of appointments for the great lone land, is a pure Indian, one of the first converts of missionary toil. He is a man of commanding appearance and pleasing address. He has proved himself to be a most trust-worthy and useful brother, respected by the whites, and a blessing to his own people.

Henry Steinheur, the last of the four, was also a pure-blooded Indian. His name has been a household word for many years in and beyond Canadian Methodism.

A poor neglected Indian boy, he was found by one of the missionaries, and induced to attend a mission school. His progress in his studies was rapid, and his life became pure and consistent. A fuller record of him will be found farther on. He now rests from his labours. Two noble sons have taken up his mantle, and are giving promise of doing valiant service for the Master.

Time and space would fail us, if we should attempt to enumerate the long list of good men and true, who have given their lives to this blessed work.

Dr. Egerton Ryerson stated, when "in age and feebleness extreme," at the Brampton Conference, in 1883, that the happiest year in his life was that of 1826, when he was stationed at the Credit as a missionary, and preached and toiled a good deal among the Indians.

Who, that ever knew, can forget Sha-wun-dais, the Rev. John Sunday, the Indian orator and the Christian gentleman? How fresh and spontaneous his wit! How gentle his spirit! How overwhelming, at times his appeals for missions! Then there was Solomon Waldron, who cheerfully gave the best years of his life to the Indian work; and scores of others, whose record is on high, and whom any church might feel honoured to claim as her sons.

> "They climbed the steep ascent of heaven,
> Through peril, toil and pain.
> O God, to us may grace be given
> To follow in their train!"

Before beginning my own personal narrative, I will here give brief sketches of three successful native Indian missionaries — Peter Jones, John Sunday, and Henry Steinheur.

The Rev. Peter Jones

Peter Jones was born on the heights of Burlington Bay, Canada West, January 1st, 1802. He was brought up by his Indian mother in the customs and ways of her people. For fourteen years he lived and wandered about the woods with the Indians in Canada and the United States.

He suffered many hardships in that kind of life. His name was Kah-ke-wa-quon-a-by, which means "Sacred waving feathers." Like all other Indian lads, he was taught to use the bow and arrows, and afterwards became expert with the gun, and was a good canoe man and fisherman.

In 1816 he had the advantages of an English

school, and was taught to read and write. After this he settled among the Mohawk Indians. In 1820 he began to attend church, and to think favourably about the Christian religion. But when he saw the whites get drunk, quarrel, fight, cheat the poor Indians, he thought the Indian's religion was the best. Though a wild youth, he never fell into the vice of drunkenness. In 1823 he became acquainted with Seth Crawford, an earnest Christian worker, and one who had taken a deep interest in the spiritual welfare of the Indians. His piety and sympathy for them made a deep impression on the mind of Peter Jones.

Soon after, a camp meeting was held in the township of Ancaster by the early Methodists of those days. Many were drawn by curiosity to visit this gathering. Among the rest this young Indian and his sister, Mary, came to see how the Methodists worshipped the Great Spirit in the wilderness.

William Case, who was afterwards justly called "The Apostle of the Indian work in Canada," had the general oversight of the camp meeting. With him were associated a number of ministers, who alternately delivered pointed and powerful discourses from the preacher's stand to the large multitudes who gathered in from many miles around. Generally three sermons were preached each day, after which prayer and inquiry meetings were held, at which the unconverted were exhorted to a personal acceptance of Christ. Peter Jones' own description of the scene is as follows:

"On arriving at the encampment I was immediately struck with the solemnity of the people, several of whom were engaged in singing and prayer. Some strange feeling came over my mind, and I was led to believe that the Supreme Being was in the midst of His people, who were now engaged in worshipping Him.

"We pitched our tent upon the ground allotted to us; it was made of coarse linen cloth. The encampment contained about two acres, enclosed by a brush fence. The tents were pitched within this circle; all the underbrush was taken away, whilst the larger trees were left standing, forming a most beautiful shade. There were three gates leading into the encampment. During each night the whole place was illuminated with fire stands, which had a very imposing appearance among the trees and leaves. The people came from different parts of the country, some ten, some twenty, and some even fifty miles, in their wagons, with their sons and daughters, for the purpose of presenting them to the Lord for conversion. I should judge there were about a thousand persons on the ground.

"At the sound of the horn we went and took our seats in front of the stand, from which a sermon was delivered. After this there was a prayer meeting, in which all who felt disposed took part in exhorting and praying for penitents. The next day, Saturday, 2nd of June, several sermons were preached, and prayer meetings were held during the intervals.

"By this time I began to feel very sick in my heart, but did not make my feelings known. On Sabbath, there was a great concourse of people who came from the adjoining settlements, and many discourses were delivered, some of which deeply impressed my mind, as I could understand most of what was said. I thought the 'black-coats' knew all that was in my heart, and that I was the person addressed. The burden of my soul began still to increase, and my heart said, 'What must I do to be saved?', for I saw myself to be in the gall of bitterness and in the bond of iniquity. The more I understood the plan of salvation by our Lord Jesus Christ, the more I was convinced of the truth of the Christian religion and of my need of salvation. In spite of my old Indian heart, tears flowed down my cheeks at the remembrance of my sins. I saw many of the white people powerfully awakened, and heard them crying aloud for mercy, while others stood and gazed, and some even laughed and mocked. The meeting continued all Monday, and several discourses were delivered from the stand. My convictions at this time were deep and powerful. During the preaching I wept much. This, however, I endeavoured to conceal by holding down my head behind the shoulders of the people. I felt anxious that no one might see me weeping like an old woman, as all my countrymen consider this beneath the dignity of an Indian brave. In the afternoon of this day my sorrow and anguish of soul greatly increased, and I felt as if I should sink down to hell for my sins, which I saw to be very great, and exceedingly offensive to the Great Spirit. I was fully convinced that if I did not find mercy from the Lord Jesus, of whom I heard much, I certainly should be lost forever. I thought, if I could only get the good people to pray for me at their prayer meetings, I should soon find relief to my mind, but had not sufficient courage to make my desires known. O, what a mercy that Christ did not forsake me when my heart was so slow to acknowledge Him as my Lord and Saviour! Towards evening I retired into the solitary wilderness to try to pray to the Great Spirit. I knelt down by the side of a fallen tree. The rattling of the leaves over my head with the wind made me uneasy. I retired further back into the woods, and then wrestled with God in prayer, who helped me to resolve that I would go back to the camp and get the people of God to pray for me. I went, but when I arrived at the meeting, my fearful heart again began to hesitate. I stood by the side of a tree, considering what I must do, whether I should give up seeking the Lord altogether, or not.

"It was now about dusk. While I was thus

hesitating as to what to do, a good old man, named Reynolds, came to me and said, 'Do you wish to obtain religion and serve the Lord?' I replied, 'Yes.' He then said, 'Do you desire the people of God to pray for you?' I told him I did, and that was what I had desired. He then led me into the prayer meeting. I fell upon my knees, and began as well as I could to call upon the name of the Lord. The old man prayed for me, and exhorted me to believe on our Lord Jesus Christ, who, he said, had died for Indians as well as for white people. Several of the preachers prayed for me. When I first began to pray, my heart was soft and tender, and I shed many tears; but, strange to say, some time after my heart got as hard as a stone. I tried to look up, but the heavens seemed like brass. I then began to say to myself, 'There is no mercy for a poor Indian.' I felt myself an outcast, a sinner bound for hell. About midnight I got so fatigued and discouraged, that I retired from our prayer meeting and went to our tent, where I immediately fell asleep. I know not how long I had slept when I was awakened by the Rev. E. Stoney and G. Ferguson, who had missed me at the prayer meeting, and had come with a light to search for me. Mr. Stoney said to me, 'Arise, Peter, and go with us to the prayer meeting, and get your soul converted. Your sister Mary has already obtained the Spirit of adoption, and you must also seek the same blessing.'

"When I heard that my sister was converted and had found peace (not knowing before that she was even so much as seeking the Lord), I sprang up and went with the two good men, determining that if there was still mercy left for me, I would seek until I found it. On arriving at the prayer meeting, I found my sister apparently as happy as she could be. She came to me and began to weep over me and to exhort me to give my heart to God, telling me how she had found the Lord. These words came with power to my poor sinking heart, and I fell upon my knees and cried to God for mercy. My sister prayed for me, as well as other good people, and especially Mr. Stoney, whose zeal for my salvation I shall never forget. At the dawn of day I was enabled to cast myself wholly upon the Lord, and to claim the atoning blood of Jesus, as my all-sufficient Saviour, who had borne all my sins in His own body on the cross. That very instant my burden was removed, joy unspeakable filled my heart, and I could say, 'Abba, Father.'

"The love of God being now shed abroad in my heart, I loved Him intensely, and praised Him in the midst of the people. Everything now appeared in a new light, and all the works of God seemed to unite with me in uttering the praises of the Lord. The people, the trees of the woods, the gentle winds, the warbling notes of the birds, and the approaching sun, all declared the power and goodness of the Great Spirit. And what was I that I should not raise my voice in giving glory to God, who had done such great things for me!

"My heart was now drawn out in love and compassion for all people, especially for my parents, brothers, sisters, and countrymen, for whose conversion I prayed, that they might also find this great salvation. I now believed with all my heart in God the Father, Son, and Holy Ghost, and gladly renounced the world, the flesh, and the devil. I cannot describe my feelings at this time. I was a wonder to myself. O, the goodness of God in giving His only begotten Son to die for me, and thus to make me His child by the Spirit of adoption! May I never forget the great things He has done for me on the glorious morning of the 5th day of June, 1823!

"Before the meeting closed on this Tuesday a fellowship meeting was held. The Rev. W. Case requested all those who had experienced the blessing of justification to stand up, and a goodly number rose, among whom were my sister Mary and myself. When Elder Case recognized me, he exclaimed, 'Glory to God! There stands a son of Augustus Jones, of the Grand River, among the converts. Now the door is opened for the work of conversion among his nation!'

"The meeting being closed, we returned home; and with tears told our parents what the Lord had done for us. Our simple story affected them much; they wept, and said they were glad that we had given our hearts to God, and exhorted us to persevere in the good way.

"A few days after this the evil spirit tempted me to doubt the reality of the change wrought in my soul by the Holy Spirit, but this seemed only to urge me to seek the Lord with greater diligence. I searched the Scriptures, prayed much, and waited for a clearer manifestation of His work on my heart. One day I retired to a grove to pray, and while thus engaged, all my doubts and fears were dispersed, and I was enabled to receive the witness of the Spirit bearing witness with my spirit that I was a child of God, that I had passed from death unto life, and that of a truth a good work was begun in my heart."

The Rev. John Sunday

One of the most remarkable conversions among the Indians of Canada was that of John Sunday, who afterwards was so well known and justly beloved in Canada and England. For many years after his conversion he was employed as a missionary among his own people, and hundreds were converted through his instrumentality. He was very much sought after to attend Missionary Anniversaries. Immense crowds gathered wherever he was announced to speak. There was at times a marvellous pathos in his addresses, and his audiences were often moved to tears as well as charmed with his quaint humour. He lived a consistent and godly life, and

Rev. John Sunday

afforded a glorious testimony of the gospel's power to lift up and save a drunken, lost Indian.

The account of John Sunday's conversion, which he himself wrote after he had gone to school and acquired a partial knowledge of the English language, is so intensely interesting that we give it here in his own quaint broken English, which will give a fair idea of his way of expressing himself in his inimitable addresses.

"Brother Scott want me that I shall write my conviction about nine years ago. First is, we had camped at Mr. James Howard's place one morning. I go to Mr. Howard to get some whiskey; so I did get it some. After I took it, that fire-water, I feel very happy. By and by, James Farmer he says to me, 'Do you want go see them preachers at Belleville? They want see all Indians.' I say to him, 'Why they want see Indians for?' He says to me, 'Them are preachers talk about God.' So I went home to my wigwam to tell others; and we took some our blankets. We hire with them, Mr. Howard with his team, to take us at Belleville. We got there about nine o'clock. We have no chance to go in the meeting house; so we went to the wood pile; so we sit there all day in the wood pile, until about five o'clock in the evening. By and by them came out from meeting house; so we went to them, and shake hands with them. About seven o'clock in the evening went to meeting; I want to hear them very much, what they will say to us. By and by one of them rose up talk to us; he begin talk about God, and soul, and body; he says this: 'All mankind is only two ways we have got to go when we come to die; one is broad way, and other is narrow way. All the wicked white men, and wicked Indians, and drunkards go there; but the good white people shall go in the narrow way; but if the Indians also become good, and serve the Lord, they can go in that narrow way.' Then now I begin think myself; I begin feel bad in my heart. This is, I think, I am one to go in that broad way, because I had hard drink last night. My father and my mother had taught me this ever since when I was little boy, 'All the Indians shall go where sun set, but the white people go in the Ish-peming,' That I had trouble in my heart. Next morning again they had talk to us; so they went off from us. As soon as they went off, some them Indian says, 'Let us get some more whiskey to drink it. What them men say unto us, we shall not do so; we must do our own way.' So they went to get more whiskey. So I take it little with them; and immediately after I had drunk it, I went home, me and Moses. Is about seven miles to our house. All way along the road I thinking about these two ways. Four nights I do not sleep much. On Saturday we all went to Belleville again. There I saw Brother Case. He says to me, 'How you like Peter Jones' talk?' I say unto him, 'Four nights I do not sleep much.' And he began to talk about religion of Jesus Christ. Oh, I feel very bad again; I thought this, 'I am one of devil his men, because I so wicked.'

"On next Monday we all went home again. That night I thought I would try pray: this is first I ever did intent to pray. I do not know how to pray—my heart is too hard—I cannot say but few words; I say this: 'Oh Lord, I am wicked, I am wicked man, take me out from that everlasting fire and dark place.' Next morning I went in the woods to pray; no peace in my heart yet. By and by I went to other Indians to tell them about what the men had said unto us at Belleville; so I went home again. By and by we went to cross the Bay on Sahgegwin Island. So Indians come there on island. By and by we begin have prayer meeting in the evening, and in the morning. I talk with them all time. I had boy about six years old; by and by he got sick, and died. I felt very bad. I thought this, 'I better not stop to pray to God;' I went to Belleville to all them Methodist men to come on Sahgegwin Island to pray for us. I asked one of them Methodist men for glass of beer to comfort in my heart. That man say to me, 'Beer is not good for you; better for you to have Good Spirit in your heart.' None them they do not want to come on our wigwam. So I went home without glass of beer. So we have prayer meeting. None of us had religion yet. By and by I went to quarterly meeting at Mr. Ketcheson. I saw one man and one woman shouting; I thought they were drunk. I thought this, 'They cannot be drunk, because is them Christian: must be something in them.' Brother Belton he preached that day: he says this, 'If any man be great sinner, Lord will forgive him, if only believe in Him.' I thought this, 'If I do well, maybe God will forgive me.' About one week after this, another quarterly meeting at Seventown, Mr. Dinge's barn. In the morning they have love feast; they give each other little bread and water; they give us some too, that piece and bread and water. I do not know what they do it for. When I took it, the bread had stop in my throat, and choke me. Oh how I feel in my heart! I feel very sick in my heart. I think this, 'Surely I belong to devil, because the Lord bread choke me: I know how that Great Spirit is angry with me.' I think this again, 'I do not know what must I do to be save my soul from that everlasting fire.' I thought, 'I will try again.' Take another piece and bread not that the Lord bread, but some I got at a house. I did swallow it down. I feel worse again, because I swallowed down that bread. Oh how I feel in my heart! I feel like this—if I in under the water.

"In afternoon we went to prayer meeting in the Old House, about five o'clock, and Peter Jones says to us, 'Let us lift up our hearts to God.' I look at him; I do not understand him. I think this, 'If I do this—take my heart out of my body, I shall be died,' However, I kneel down to pray to God. I do not know what to say to ask for religion; I only say this: 'Oh, Keshamunedo, shahnanemeshim!' 'Oh Lord, have mercy on me, poor sinner!' By and by, the good Lord He pour His Spirit upon my poor wretched heart; then I shout and happy in my heart. I feel very light, and after prayer meeting I went to tell Peter Jones how I feel in my heart. I say to him this, 'I feel something in my heart.' Peter says to me, 'Lord bless you now.' Oh how glad in my heart! I look around, and look over other side a Bay, and look up, and look in the woods; the same is everything NEW to me. I hope I got religion that day. I thank the Great Spirit what He done for me. I want to be like the man which built his house upon a rock. Amen."

Mr. Sunday lived for many years a godly, consistent life, beloved by all who knew him, either in England or Canada, and then died at a good old age. His end was joyous and triumphant. His body rests in the beautiful little cemetery at Alnwick, near Rice Lake, close by all that is mortal of the Rev. William Case, his beloved spiritual father.

The Rev. Henry Steinheur

One of the most devoted and successful native Indian missionaries was the Rev. Henry Steinheur.

When a poor little child, wretched and neglected, he was picked up by the Rev. William Case, who patiently cared for the lad, and not only taught him the simple truths of Christianity, but also laid the foundation of an English education, which afterwards became so extensive that many a white man might honestly have envied him.

As the boy was observed to be the possessor of a very musical voice, Mr. Case selected him to be one of a little company of native children with whom he travelled extensively through various parts of the Northern States, where, before large audiences, they sang their sweet Indian hymns and gave addresses, and thus showed to the people what could be done by the Indians, who, by too many, were only considered as unmitigated evils, as quickly as possible to be legislated out of existence.

In one of the cities visited by Mr. Case and his

Indian boys, a gentleman named Henry Steinheur became so interested in one of the bright, clever little Indian lads that he made an offer to Mr. Case that if the little fellow, who was as yet only known by his native name, would take his name, he would pay all the expense incurred in his securing a first-class education. Such an offer was not to be despised, and so, from that time forward, this Indian lad was known as Henry Steinheur.

When the lecturing tour was ended, after some preparatory work in the Mission school, Henry was

Rev. Henry Steinheur

sent to Victoria College in the town of Cobourg, Canada. Here he remained for some years. He was not only a first class student, but also a consistent, devoted Christian. Such was his progress in his studies that he showed that the Indian mind is as capable as any other to receive and retain a first class education.

With great pleasure, many years after his college

days were over, I heard him preach a capital sermon before a large congregation containing many ministers. Before reading his text in English Mr. Steinheur read it in Greek, in a way that pleased the most learned Greek scholars present, although even then he had just come in from a far off Indian Mission, where for years he had only heard the native dialect spoken.

After his college life was ended, he devoted himself most thoroughly to missionary work among his own people, and for over forty years was the same modest, unassuming, useful, godly missionary. When I went to Norway House I found that, although he had been away for years, his name was "like ointment poured forth." Many were the loving inquiries made of me concerning him, and many assured me that he had been the instrument in God's hand of leading them out of the dense darkness of their old sinful lives into the blessed light of the gospel.

He spent the last years of his useful life among the Cree Indians at White Fish Lake and other Missions in the great Saskatchewan country of the Canadian north-west. He triumphantly passed from labour to reward, realizing in his closing hours the sustaining power of that gospel which he had faithfully and lovingly preached to others. Two sons have followed in his footsteps.

The following incident, which I had from the lips of Mr. Steinheur, will give some idea of the steadfastness of some of the Indian converts. At one of the Missions in the Saskatchewan country the Rev. William Rundle was very much owned of God in the conversion of a band of Indians. Circumstances made it necessary for Mr. Rundle to return to England, where, at Wolverhampton, in a happy old age, he, at the time of my writing, still lives. For several years the Indians at that place were never once visited by a missionary or teacher. After many days of weary travelling over the prairies, Mr. Steinheur reached that lonely western Indian village. He told me that the hour for camping overtook him several miles from the village, but so anxious was he to be with the people among whom he had come to labour, and to end his journey of ten weeks, that he could not bear the idea of camping so near them; so he pushed on in the evening twilight, ahead of his party, to the spot where he saw the wigwam village on the prairies. When he drew near to the outermost wigwam, which was a large one, he heard singing, and great indeed was his surprise to find that instead of it being the monotonous droning of the pagan medicine man or conjurer, it was a good Christian tune, and one with which he was very familiar.

Soon the singing ceased, and then after a little pause, a clear manly voice began to pray. For a time the prayer seemed to be all thanksgiving; and then there went up an urgent request from the earnest one praying: "Lord, send us another missionary like Rundle. Lord, send us a missionary to teach us out of Thy word more about Thy self and Thy Son Jesus." Mr. Steinheur said he was thrilled and delighted, and so he lifted up the hanging tanned leather skin door and quietly entered in and bowed down with them in prayer. When they arose he told them who he was, and that he had come to dwell among them as their missionary. Great indeed was their joy and excitement. They crowded around him, and some of them kissed him, and all welcomed him with shouts, and tears of gladness, as though he had just come down from heaven to dwell among them.

Anxious to know as to the people's steadfastness and integrity through all those years of neglect, when the Church had left them alone, surrounded by pagan tribes, without a missionary or religious teacher, I said to Mr. Steinheur, "Tell me, my brother, in what state did you find them as regards their religious life,

Jonas, Samson, Pakan

the observance of the Sabbath, and their religious services?"

"Brother Young," said he, "It was just like a Conference change of ministers. It seemed to me as though my predecessor had only been gone two or three weeks. They had remembered the Sabbath days and had kept them. They had not neglected any of their religious services, and they were living as consistent lives as God's dear children anywhere."

The accompanying portraits are of three of the Christian Indians from those western missions. Jonas is a Mountain Stoney, Samson and Pakan are Crees. Pakan is the chief, a worthy successor of Maskepetoon, who was so foully murdered by Nah-doos, the Blackfoot chief, and the story of whose marvellous conversion has thrilled so many hearts. At a camp fire on the western prairies, Maskepetoon heard the beautiful chapter which contains the Saviour's prayer for His murderers: "Father, forgive them; for they know not what they do." By the faithful missionary this was held up as the example which must be followed by all those who would be real Christians. The warlike chief listened in amazement to these requirements, so opposite to the revengeful spirit of the lost. But, after he had pondered them over, he decided to accept them, and showed the genuineness of his conversion a few days after by forgiving the murderer of his only son.

CHAPTER III

The summons to the Indian work — The decision — The valedictory services — Dr. Punshon — The departure — Leaving Hamilton — St. Catharine's — Mil-waukee custom-house delays — Mississippi — St. Paul's — On the prairies — Frontier settlers — Narrow escape from shooting one of our school teachers — Sioux Indians and their wars — Saved by our flag — Varied experiences.

Several letters were handed into my study, where I sat at work among my books.

I was then pastor of a church in the city of Hamilton. Showers of blessing had been descending upon us, and over a hundred and forty new members had but recently been received into the church. I had availed myself of the Christmas holidays by getting married, and now was back again with my beloved, when these letters were handed in. With only one of them have we at present anything to do. As near as I can remember, it read as follows:

Mission Rooms, Toronto, 1868
Rev. Egerton R. Young.

Dear Brother, At a large and influential meeting of the Missionary Committee, held yesterday, it was unanimously decided to ask you to go as a missionary to the Indian tribes at Norway House, and in the North West Territories north of Lake Winnipeg. An early answer signifying your acceptance of this will much oblige,

Yours affectionately,
E. Wood,
L. Taylor

I read the letter, and then handed it, without comment, across the table to Mrs. Young, the bride of but a few days, for her perusal. She read it over carefully, and then, after a quiet moment, as was quite natural, asked, "What does this mean?" "I can hardly tell," I replied; "but it is evident that it means a good deal."

"Have you volunteered to go as a missionary to that far off land?", she asked.

"Why, no. Much as I love, and deeply interested as I have ever been in the missionary work of our Church, I have not made the first move in this direction. Years ago I used to think I would love to go to a foreign field, but lately, as the Lord has been blessing us here in the home work, and has given us such a glorious revival, I should have thought it like running away from duty to have volunteered for any other field."

"Well, here is this letter; what are you going to do about it?"

"That is just what I would like to know," was my answer.

"There is one thing we can do," she said quietly; and we bowed ourselves in prayer, and "spread the letter before the Lord." and asked for wisdom to guide us in this important matter which had so suddenly come upon us, and which, if carried out, would completely change all the plans and purposes which we, the young married couple, in all the joyousness of our honeymoon, had just been marking out. We earnestly prayed for Divine light and guidance to be so clearly revealed that we could not be mistaken as to our duty.

As we arose from our knees, I quietly said to Mrs. Young, "Have you any impression on your mind as to our duty in this matter?"

Her eyes were filled with tears, but the voice, though low, was firm, as she replied, "The call has

Ever Yrs.
lovingly,
Elizabeth Young.

come very unexpectedly, but I think it is from God, and we will go."

My church and its kind officials strongly opposed my leaving them, especially at such a time as this, when, they said, so many new converts, through my instrumentality, had been brought into the church.

I consulted my beloved ministerial brethren in the city, and with but one exception the reply was, "Remain at your present station, where God has so abundantly blessed your labors." The answer of the one brother who did not join in with the others has never been forgotten. As it may do good, I will put it on record. When I showed him the letter, and asked what I should do in reference to it, he, much to my surprise, became deeply agitated, and wept like a child. When he could control his emotions, he said, "For my answer let me give you a little of my history.

"Years ago, I was very happily situated in the ministry in the Old Land. I loved my work, my home, and my wife passionately. I had the confidence and esteem of my people, and thought I was as happy as I could be this side of heaven. One day there came a letter from the Wesleyan Mission Rooms in London, asking if I would go out as a missionary to the West Indies. Without consideration, and without making it a matter of prayer, I at once sent back a positive refusal.

"From that day," he continued, "everything went wrong with me. Heaven's smile seemed to have left me. I lost my grip upon my people. My influence for good over them left me, I could not tell how. My once happy home was blasted, and in all my trouble I got no sympathy from my church or in the community. I had to resign my position, and leave the place. I fell into darkness, and lost my hold upon God. A few years ago I came out to this country. God has restored me to the light of His countenance. The Church has been very sympathetic and indulgent. For years I have been permitted to labor in her fold, and for this I rejoice. But," he added, with emphasis, "I long ago came to the resolve that if ever the Church asked me to go to the West Indies, or to any other mission field, I would be careful about sending back an abrupt refusal."

I pondered over his words and his experience, and talked about them with my good wife, and we decided to go. Our loving friends were startled at our resolve, but soon gave us their benedictions, united to tangible evidences of their regard. A blessed peace filled our souls, and we longed to be away and at work in the new field which had so suddenly opened before us.

> "Yes, we will go. We may no longer doubt
> To give up friends, and home, and every tie,
> That binds our heart to thee, our country.
> Henceforth, then
> It matters not if storms or sunshine be
> Our earthly lot, bitter or sweet our cup.
> We only pray, God fit us for the work,
> God make us holy, and our spirits nerve
> For the stern hour of strife. Let us but know
> There is an Arm unseen that holds us up,
> An Eye that kindly watches all our path,
> Till we our weary pilgrimage have done.
> Let us but know we have a Friend that waits
> To welcome us to glory, and we joy
> To tread that drear and northern wilderness."

The grand valedictory services were held in the old Richmond Street Church, Toronto, Thursday, May 7th, 1868. The church was crowded, and the enthusiasm was very great. The honored President of the Conference for that year, the Rev. James Elliott, who presided, was the one who had ordained me a few months before. Many were the speakers. Among them was the Rev. George McDougall, who already had a varied experience of missionary life. He had something to talk about, to which it was worth listening. The Rev. George Young, also, had much that was interesting to say, as he was there bidding farewell to his own church and to the people, of whom he had long been the beloved pastor. Dr. Punshon, who had just arrived from England, was present, and gave one of his inimitable magnetic addresses. The memory of his loving, cheering words abode with us for many a day.

It was also a great joy to us that my honored

Rev. William Young

father, the Rev. William Young, was with us on the platform at this impressive farewell service. For many years he had been one of that heroic band of pioneer ministers in Canada who had laid so grandly and well the foundations of the church which, with others, had contributed so much to the spiritual development of the country. His benediction and blessing were among the prized favors in these eventful hours in our new career.

My father had been intimately acquainted with William Case and James Evans, and at times had been partially associated with them in Indian evangelization. He had faith in the power of the gospel to save Indians, and now rejoiced that he had a son and daughter who had consecrated themselves to this work.

As a long journey of many hundreds of miles would have to be made by us after getting beyond cars or steamboats in the western States, it was decided that we should take our own horses and canvas covered wagons from Ontario with us. We arranged to make Hamilton our starting point; and on Monday, the 11th of May, 1868, our little company filed out of that city towards St. Catharine's, where we were to take passage in a boat for Milwaukee. Thus our adventurous journey was begun.

The following was our party. First, the Rev. George McDougall, who for years had been successfully doing the work of a faithful missionary among the Indians in the distant Saskatchewan country, a thousand miles north west of the Red River country. He had come down to Canada for reinforcements for the work, and had not failed in his efforts to secure them. As he was an old, experienced western traveller, he was the guide of the party.

Next was the Rev. George Young, with his wife and son. Dr. Young had consented to go and begin the work in the Red River Settlement, a place where Methodism had never before had a footing. Grandly and well did he succeed in his efforts.

Next came the genial Rev. Peter Campbell, who, with his brave wife and two little girls, relinquished a pleasant circuit to go to the distant mission field among the Indians of the north west prairies. We had also with us two Messrs. Snyders, brothers of Mrs. Campbell, who had consecrated themselves to the work as teachers among the distant Indian tribes. Several other young men were in our party, and in Dakota we were joined by "Joe" and "Job," a couple of young Indians.

These, with the writer and his wife, constituted our party of fifteen or twenty. At St. Catharine's on the Welland Canal we shipped our outfit, and took passage on board the steamer *Empire* for Milwaukee.

The vessel was very much crowded, and there was a good deal of discomfort. In passing through Lake Michigan we encountered rough weather, and, as a natural result, sea sickness assailed the great majority of our party.

We reached Milwaukee on Sabbath, the 17th of May. We found it then a lively, wide awake Americo-German city. There did not seem to be, on the part of the multitudes whom we met, much respect for the Sabbath. Business was in full blast in many of the streets, and there were but few evidences that it was the day of rest. Doubtless there were many who had not defiled their garments and had not profaned the day, but we weary travellers had not then time to find them.

Although we had taken the precaution to bond everything through to the north west, and had the American Consular certificate to the effect that every regulation had been complied with, we were subjected to many vexatious delays and expenses by the custom house officials. So delayed were we that we had to telegraph to headquarters at Washington about the matter; and soon there came the orders to the over-officious officials to at once allow us to proceed.

Two valuable days, however, had been lost by their obstructiveness. Why cannot Canada and the United States, lying side by side, from the Atlantic to the Pacific, devise some mutually advantageous scheme of reciprocity, by which the vexatious delays and annoyances and expense of these custom houses can be done away with?

We left Milwaukee for La Crosse on the Mississippi on Tuesday evening at eight o'clock. At La Crosse we embarked on the steamer *Milwaukee* for St. Paul. These large flat bottomed steamers are quite an institution on these western rivers. Drawing but a few inches of water, they glide over sandbars where the water is very shallow, and, swinging in against the shore, land and receive passengers and freight where wharves are unknown, or where, if they existed, they would be liable to be swept away in the great spring floods.

The scenery in many places along the upper Mississippi is very fine. High bold bluffs rise up in wondrous variety and picturesque beauty. In some places they are composed of naked rock. Others are covered to their very summit with the richest green. Here a few years ago, the chants of the Indians sounded, and the buffalo swarmed around these buttes, and quenched their thirst in these waters. Now the shrill whistle of the steamer disturbs the solitudes, and echoes and re-echoes with wondrous distinctness among the high bluffs and fertile vales.

We arrived at St. Paul on Thursday forenoon, and found it to be a stirring city, beautifully situated on the eastern side of the Mississippi. We had several hours of good hard work in getting our caravan in order, purchasing supplies, and making all final arrangements for the long journey that was before us.

For beyond this the iron horse had not yet penetrated, and the great surging waves of immigration, which soon after rolled over into those fertile territories, had as yet been only little ripples.

Our splendid horses, which had been cooped up in the holds of vessels, or cramped up in uncomfortable freight cars, were now to have an opportunity for exercising their limbs, and showing of what mettle they were made. At 4 p.m. we filed out of the city. The recollection of that first ride on the prairie will live on as long as memory holds her throne. The day was one of those gloriously perfect ones that are but rarely given us, as if to show what earth must have been before the Fall. The sky, the air, the landscape — everything seemed in such harmony and so perfect, that involuntarily I exclaimed, "If God's footstool is so glorious, what will the throne be?"

We journeyed a few miles, then camped for the night. We were all in the best of spirits, and seemed to rejoice that we were getting away from civilization, and more and more out into the wilderness, although for days we were in the vicinity of frontier villages and settlements, which, however, as we journeyed on, were rapidly diminishing in number.

After several days travelling we camped on the western side of the Mississippi, near where the thriving town of Clear Water now stands. As some of our carts and travelling equipment had begun to show signs of weakness, it was thought prudent to give everything a thorough overhauling before we pushed out from this point, as beyond this there was no place where assistance could be obtained. We had in our camp eight tents, fourteen horses, and from fifteen to twenty persons, counting big and little, whites and Indians. Whenever we camped our horses were turned loose in the luxuriant prairie grass, the only precaution taken being to "hobble" them, as the work of tying their forefeet together is called. It seemed a little cruel at first, and some of our spirited horses resented it, and struggled a good deal against it as an infringement on their liberties. But they soon became used to it, and it served the good purpose we had in view namely, that of keeping them from straying far away from the camp during the night.

A Prairie Scene

At one place, where we were obliged to stop for a few days to repair broken axle trees, I passed through an adventure that will not soon be forgotten. Some friendly settlers came to our camp, and gave us the unpleasant information, that a number of notorious horse thieves were prowling around, and it would be advisable for us to keep a sharp lookout on our splendid Canadian horses. As there was an isolated barn about half a mile or so from the camp, that had been put up by a settler who would not require it until harvest, we obtained permission to use it as a place in which to keep our horses during the nights while we were detained in the settlement. Two of our party were detailed each night to act as a guard. One evening, as Dr. Young's son, George, and I, who had been selected for this duty, were starting from the camp for our post, I overheard our old veteran guide, the Rev. George McDougall, say, in a bantering sort of way, "Pretty guards they are! Why, some Indian boys could go and steal every horse from them without the slightest trouble."

Stung to the quick by the remark, I replied, "Mr. McDougall, I think I have the best horse in the company; but if you or any of your Indians can steal him out of that barn between sundown and sunrise, you may keep him!"

We tethered the horses in a line, and fastened securely all the doors but the large front one. We arranged our seats where we were partially concealed, but where we could see our horses, and could command every door with our rifles. In quiet tones we chatted about various things, until about one o'clock, when all became hushed and still. The novelty of the situation impressed me, and, sitting there in the darkness, I could not help contrasting my present position with the one I had occupied a few weeks before. Then the pastor of a city church, in the midst of a blessed revival, surrounded by all the comforts of civilization; now out here in Minnesota, in this barn, sitting on a bundle of prairie grass through the long hours of night with a breech-loading rifle in hand, guarding a number of horses from a band of horse thieves.

"Hush! what is that?"

A hand is surely on the door feeling for the wooden latch. We mentally say, "You have made too much noise, Mr. Thief, for your purpose, and you are discovered." Soon the door opened a little. As it was a beautiful starlit night, the form of a tall man was plainly visible in the opening. Covering him with my rifle, and about to fire, quick as a flash came the thought, "Better be sure that that man is a horse thief, or one intent on evil, before you fire; for it is at any time a serious thing to send a soul so suddenly into eternity." So keeping my rifle to my shoulder, I shouted out, "Who's there?"

"Why, it's only your friend Matthew," said our tall friend, as he came stumbling along in the darkness; "Queer if you don't know me by this time."

As the thought came to me of how near I had been to sending him into the other world, a strange feeling of faintness came over me, and, flinging my rifle from me, I sank back trembling like a leaf.

Meanwhile the good natured fellow, little knowing the risk he had run, and not seeing the effect his thoughtless action had produced on me, talked on, saying that as it was so hot and close over at the tents that he could not sleep there, he thought he would come over and stop with us in the barn.

There was considerable excitement, and some strong words were uttered at the camp next morning at his breach of orders and narrow escape, since instructions had been given to all that none should, under any consideration, go near the barn while it was being guarded.

At another place in Minnesota we came across a party who were restoring their homes, and "building up their waste places" desolated by the terrible Sioux wars of but a short time before. As they had nearly all suffered by that fearful struggle, they were very bitter in their feelings towards the Indians, completely ignoring the fact that the whites were to blame for that last outbreak, in which nine hundred lives were lost, and a section of country larger than some of the New England States was laid desolate. It is now an undisputed fact that the greed and dishonesty of the Indian agents of the United States caused that terrible war of 1863. The principal agent received $600,000 in gold from the government, which belonged to the Indians, and was to be paid to Little Crow and the other chiefs and members of the tribe. The agent took advantage of the premium on gold, which in those days was very high, and exchanged the gold for greenbacks, and with these paid the Indians, putting the enormous difference in his own pocket. When the payments began, Little Crow, who knew what he had a right to according to the Treaty, said, "Gold dollars worth more than paper dollars. You pay us gold." The agent refused, and the war followed. This is only one instance out of scores, in which the greed and selfishness of a few have plunged the country into war, causing the loss of hundreds of lives and millions in property.

In addition to this, these same unprincipled agents, with their hired accomplices and subsidized press, in order to hide the enormity of their crimes, and to divert attention from themselves and their crookedness, systematically and incessantly misrepresent and vilify the Indian character.

"Stay and be our minister," said some of these settlers to me in one place. "We'll secure for you a good location, and will help you get in some crops, and will do the best we can to make you comfortable."

When they saw we were all proof against their appeals, they changed their tactics, and one exclaimed, "You'll never get through the Indian country north with those fine horses and all that fine truck you have."

"O yes, we will," said Mr. McDougall; "We have a little flag that will carry us in safety through any Indian tribe in America."

They doubted the assertion very much, but we found it to be literally true, at all events as regarded the Sioux; for when, a few days later, we met them, our Union Jack fluttering from the whipstalk caused them to fling their guns in the grass, and come crowding round us with extended hands, saying, through those who understood their language, that they were glad to see and shake hands with the subjects of the "Great Mother" across the waters.

When we, in our journey north, reached their country, and saw them coming down upon us, at Mr. McDougall's orders we stowed away our rifles and revolvers inside of our wagons, and met them as friends, unarmed and fearless. They smoked the pipe of peace with those of our party who could use the weed, and others drank tea with the rest of us. As we were in profound ignorance of their language, and they of ours, some of us had not much conversation with them beyond what could be carried on by a few signs. But, through Mr. McDougall and our own Indians, they assured us of their friendship.

We pitched our tents, hobbled our horses and turned them loose, as usual. We cooked our evening meals, said our prayers, unrolled our camp beds, and lay down to rest without earthly sentinels or guards around us, although the camp fires of these so-called "treacherous and bloodthirsty" Sioux could be seen in the distance, and we knew their sharp eyes were upon us. Yet we lay down and slept in peace, and arose in safety. Nothing was disturbed or stolen.

So much for a clean record of honorable dealing with a people who, while quick to resent when provoked, are mindful of kindnesses received, and are as faithful to their promises and treaty obligations, as are any other of the races of the world.

We were thirty days in making the trip from St. Paul to the Red River settlement. We had to ford a large number of bridgeless streams. Some of them took us three or four days to get our whole party across. We not infrequently had some of our wagons stuck in the quicksand, or so sunk in the quagmires that the combined strength of all the men of our party was required to get them out. Often the ladies of our company, with shoes and stockings off, would be seen bravely wading across wide streams, where now in luxurious comfort, in parlour cars, travellers are whirled along at the rate of forty miles an hour. They were a cheerful, brave band of pioneers.

The weather, on the whole, was pleasant, but we had some drenching rainstorms; and then the spirits of some of the party went down, and they wondered whatever possessed them to leave their happy homes for such exile and wretchedness as this. There was one fearful, tornado-like storm that assailed us when we were camped for the night on the western bank of Red River. Tents were instantly blown down. Heavy wagons were driven before it, and for a time confusion reigned supreme. Fortunately nobody was hurt, and most of the things blown away were recovered the next day.

Our Sabbaths were days of quiet rest and delightful communion with God. Together we worshipped Him who dwells not in temples made with hands. Many were the precious communions we had with Him who had been our Comforter and our Refuge under other circumstances, and who, having now called us to this new work and novel life, was sweetly fulfilling in us the blessed promise: "Lo, I am with you alway, even unto the end of the world."

CHAPTER IV

Still on the route — Fort Garry — Breaking up of our party of missionaries — Lower Fort — Hospitable Hudson's Bay officials — Peculiarities — Fourteen days in a little open boat on stormy Lake Winnipeg — Strange experiences — Happy Christian Indian boatmen — "In peril by water."

At Fort Garry in the Red River settlement, now the flourishing city of Winnipeg, our party, which had so long travelled together, broke up with mutual regrets. The Rev. George Young and his family remained to commence the first Methodist Mission in that place. Many were his discouragements and difficulties, but glorious have been his successes. More to him than to any other man is due the prominent position which the Methodist Church now occupies in the North-West. His station was one calling for rare tact and ability. The Riel Rebellion, and the disaffection of the Metis population, made his position at times one of danger and insecurity; but he proved himself to be equal to every emergency. In addition to the many duties devolving upon him in the establishment of the Church amidst so many discordant elements, a great many extra cares were imposed upon him by the isolated missionaries in the interior, who looked to him for the purchasing and sending out to them, as best he could, of their much needed supplies. His kindly laborious efforts for their comfort can never be forgotten.

The Rev. George McDougall and Peter Campbell, with the teachers and other members of the party, pushed on, with their horses, wagons, and carts, for the still farther north west, the great North Saskatchewan River, twelve hundred miles farther into the interior.

During the first part of their journey over the fertile but then unbroken prairies, the only inhabitants they met were the roving Indians and Metis, whose wigwams and noisy carts have long since disappeared, and have been replaced by the comfortable habitations of energetic settlers, and the swiftly moving trains of the railroads.

From Fort Garry Mrs. Young and myself performed the rest of our journey by water, going down the Red River to its mouth, and then along the whole length of the stormy Lake Winnipeg, and beyond, to our own far off northern home. The trip was made in what is called "the Hudson's Bay inland boat." These boats were constructed like large skiffs, only each end is sharp. They have neither deck nor cabin. They are furnished with a mast and a large square sail, both of which are stowed away when the wind is not favorable for sailing. They are manned by six or eight oarsmen, and are supposed to carry about four tons of merchandise. They can stand a rough sea, and weather very severe gales, as we found out during our years of adventurous trips in them. When there is no favorable wind for sailing, the stalwart boatmen push out their heavy oars, and, bending their sturdy backs to the work, and keeping the most perfect time, are often able to make their sixty miles a day. But this toiling at the oar is slavish work, and the favoring gale, even if it develops into a fierce storm, is always preferable to a dead calm. These northern Indians make capital sailors, and in the sudden squalls and fierce gales to which these great lakes are subject, they display much courage and judgment.

Our place in the boat was in the hind part near the steersman, a pure Indian, whose name was Thomas Mamanowatum, familiarly known as "Big Tom," on account of his almost gigantic size. He was one of nature's noblemen, a grand, true man, and of him we shall have more to say hereafter. Honored indeed was the missionary who led such a man to Christ.

We journeyed on pleasantly for twenty miles down the Red River to Lower Fort Garry, where we found

Roving Indians and Metis

that we should have to wait for several days before the outfit for the boats would be ready. We were, however, very courteously entertained by the Hudson's Bay officials, who showed us no little kindness.

This Lower Fort Garry, or "the Stone Fort," as it is called in the country, is an extensive affair, having a massive stone wall all around it, with the Company's buildings in the center. It was built in stormy times, when rival trading parties existed, and hostile bands were ever on the war path. It is capable of resisting almost any force that could be brought against it, unaided by artillery. We were a little amused and very much pleased with the old time and almost courtly etiquette which abounded at this and the other establishments of this flourishing Company. In those days the law of precedents was in full force. When the bell rang, no clerk of fourteen years standing would think of entering before one who had been fifteen years in the service or of sitting above him at the table. Such a thing would have brought down upon him the severe reproof of the senior officer in charge. Irksome and even frivolous as some of these laws seemed, doubtless they served a good purpose, and prevented many misunderstandings which might have occurred.

Another singular custom, which we did not like, was the fact that there were two dining rooms in these establishments, one for the ladies, and the other for the gentlemen of the service. It appeared to us very odd to see the gentlemen with the greatest politeness escort the ladies into the hall which ran between the two dining rooms, and then gravely turn to the left, while the ladies all filed off into the room on the right. As the arrangement was so contrary to all our ideas and education on the subject, we presumed to question it; but the only satisfaction we could get in reference to it was, that it was one of their old customs, and had worked well. One old crusty bachelor official said, "We do not want the women around us when we are discussing our business matters, which we wish to keep to ourselves. If they were present, all our schemes and plans would soon be known to all, and our trade might be much injured."

Throughout this vast country, until very lately, the adventurous traveller, whose courage or curiosity was sufficient to enable him to brave the hardships or run the risks of exploring these enormous territories, was entirely dependent upon the goodwill and hospitality of the officials of the Hudson's Bay Company. They were uniformly treated with courtesy and hospitably entertained.

Very isolated are some of these inland posts, and quite isolated are the inmates for years at a time. These lonely establishments are to be found scattered all over the upper half of this great American Continent. They have each a population of from five to sixty human beings. These are, if possible, placed in favorable localities for fish or game, but often from one to five hundred miles apart. The only object of their erection and occupancy is to exchange the products of civilization for the rich and valuable furs which are to be obtained here as nowhere else in the world. In many instances the inmates hear from the outside world but twice, and at times but once, in twelve months. Then the arrival of the packet is the great event of the year.

We spent a very pleasant Sabbath at Lower Fort Garry, and I preached in the largest dining room to a very attentive congregation, composed of the officials and servants of the Company, with several visitors, and also some Metis and Indians who happened to be at the fort at that time.

The next day two boats were ready, and we embarked on our adventurous journey for our far off isolated home beyond the northern end of Lake Winnipeg. The trip down Red River was very pleasant. We passed through the flourishing Indian settlement, where the Church of England has a successful Mission among the Indians. We admired their substantial church and comfortable homes, and saw in them, and in the farms, tangible evidence of the power of Christian Missions to elevate and bless those who come under their ennobling influences. The cosy residence of the Venerable Archdeacon Cowley was pointed out to us, beautifully embowered among the trees. He was a man beloved of all; a life long friend of the Indians, and one who was as an angel of mercy to us in after years, when our Nellie died, while Mrs. Young was making an adventurous journey in an open boat on the stormy, treacherous Lake Winnipeg.

This sad event occurred when, after five years residence among the Crees at Norway House, we had instructions from our missionary authorities to go and open up a new Indian Mission among the Saulteaux. I had orders to remain at Norway House until my successor arrived; and as but one opportunity was offered for Mrs. Young and the children to travel in those days of limited opportunities, they started on several weeks ahead in an open skiff manned by a few Indians, leaving me to follow in a birch canoe. So terrible was the heat that hot July, in that open boat with no deck or awning, that the beautiful child sickened and died of brain fever. Mrs. Young found herself with her dying child on the banks of the Red River, all alone among her sorrowing Indian boatmen, "a stranger in a strange land;" no home to which to go; no friends to sympathize with her. Fortunately for her, the Hudson's Bay officials at Lower Fort Garry were made aware of her sorrows, and received her into one of their homes before the child died. The Rev. Mr. Cowley also came and prayed for her, and sympathized with her on the loss of her beautiful child.

As I was far away when Nellie died, Mrs. Young knew not what to do with our precious dead. A temporary grave was made, and in it the body was laid until I could be communicated with, and arrangements could be made for its permanent interment. I wrote at once by an Indian to the Venerable Archdeacon Cowley, asking permission to bury our dead in his graveyard; and there came promptly back, by the canoe, a very brotherly, sympathetic letter, ending up with, "Our graveyards are open before you; in the choicest of our sepulchers bury thy dead." A few weeks after, when I had handed over my mission to Brother Ruttan, I hurried on to the settlement, and with a few sympathizing friends, mostly Indians, we took up the little body from its temporary resting place, and buried it in the St. Peter's Church graveyard, the dear archdeacon himself being present, and reading the beautiful Burial Service of his Church. That land to us has been doubly precious since it has become the repository of our darling child.

As we floated down the current, or were propelled along by the oars of our Indian boatmen, on that first journey, little did we imagine that this sad episode in our lives would happen in that very spot a few years after. When we were near the end of the Indian Settlement, as it is called, we saw several Indians on the bank, holding on to a couple of oxen. Our boats were immediately turned in to the shore near them, and, to our great astonishment, we found out that each boat was to have an addition to its passenger list in the shape of one of these big fellows. The getting of these animals shipped was no easy matter, as there was no wharf or gangway; but after a good deal of pulling and pushing, and lifting up of one leg, and then another, the patient brutes were embarked on the frail crafts, to be our companions during the voyage to Norway House. The position assigned to the one in our boat was just in front of us, broadside on, as the sailors would say; his head often hanging over one side of the boat, and his tail over the other side. The only partition there was between him and us was a single board a few inches wide. Such close proximity to this animal for fourteen days was not very agreeable; but as it could not be helped, it had to be endured.

At times, during the first few days, the ox made some desperate efforts to break loose; and it seemed as though he would either smash our boat to pieces or upset it; but, finding his efforts unsuccessful, he gratefully accepted the situation, and behaved himself admirably. When storms arose he quietly lay down, and served as so much ballast to steady the boat. "Tom," the guide, kept him well supplied with food from the rich nutritious grasses which grew abundantly along the shore at our different camping places.

Lake Winnipeg is considered one of the stormiest lakes on the American continent. It is about three hundred miles long, and varies from eighty to but a few miles in width. It is indented with innumerable bays, and is dangerous to navigators, on account of its many shoals and hidden rocks. Winnipeg, or Wenipak, as some Indians pronounce it, means "the sea," and Keche Wenipak means "the ocean."

The trip across Lake Winnipeg was one that at the present day would be considered a great hardship, taking into consideration the style of the boat and the way we travelled.

Our method of procedure was about as follows. We were aroused very early in the morning by the guide's cry of Koos koos kwa! "Wake up!" Everybody was expected to obey promptly, as there was always a good deal of rivalry between the boats as to which could get away first. A hasty breakfast was prepared on the rocks; after which a morning hymn was sung, and an earnest prayer was offered up to Him Who holds the winds and waves under His control.

Then, "All aboard" was the cry, and soon tents, kettles, axes, and all the other things were hurriedly gathered up and placed on board. If the wind was favorable, the mast was put up, the sail hoisted, and we were soon rapidly speeding on our way. If the oars had to be used, there was not half the alacrity displayed by the poor fellows, who well knew how wearisome their task would be. When we had a favorable wind, we generally dined as well as we could in the boat, to save time, as the rowers well knew how much more pleasant it was to glide along with the favoring breeze than to be obliged to work at the heavy oars. Often during whole nights we sailed on, although at considerable risks in that treacherous lake, rather than lose the fair wind. For, if there ever was, in this world of uncertainties, one route of more uncertainty than another, the palm must be conceded to the voyages on Lake Winnipeg in those Hudson's Bay Company's inland boats. You might make the trip in four days, or even a few hours less; and you might be thirty days, and a few hours over.

Once, in after years, I was detained for six days on a little rocky islet by a fierce northern gale, which at times blew with such force that we could not keep up a tent or even stand upright against its fury; and as there was not sufficient soil in which to drive a tent pin, we, with all our bedding and supplies, were drenched by the pitiless sleet and rain. Often in these later years, when I have heard people, sitting in the comfortable waiting room of a railway station, bitterly complaining because a train was an hour or two late, memory has carried me back to some of those long detentions amid the most disagreeable surroundings, and I have wondered at the trifles which can upset the equanimity of some or cause them to show such fretfulness.

When the weather was fine, the camping on the shore was very enjoyable. Our tent was quickly erected by willing hands; the camp fire was kindled, and glowed with increasing brightness as the shadows of night fell around us. The evening meal was soon prepared, and an hour or two would sometimes be spent in pleasant conversation with our Native friends, who were most delightful travelling companions. Our days always began and closed with a religious service. All of our Indian companions in the two boats on this first trip were Christians, in the best and truest sense of the word. They were the converts of the earlier missionaries of our Church. At first they were a little reserved, and acted as though they imagined we expected them to be very sedate and dignified For, like some white folks, they imagined the "black coat" and his wife did not believe in laughter or pleasantry. However, we soon relieved their minds of those erroneous ideas, and before we reached Norway House we were on the best of terms with each other. We knew but little of their language, but some of them had a good idea of English, and, using these as our interpreters, we got along well.

They were well furnished with Testaments and hymn books, printed in the beautiful syllabic characters; and they used them well. This worshipping with a people who used to us an unknown tongue was at first rather novel; but it attracted and charmed us at once. We were forcibly struck with the reverential manner in which they conducted their devotions. No levity or indifference marred the solemnity of their religious services. They listened very attentively while one of their number read to them from the sacred Word, and gave the closest attention to what I had to say, through an interpreter.

Very sweetly and soothingly sounded the hymns of praise and adoration that welled up from their musical voices. Though we understood them not, yet in their earnest prayers there seemed to be so much that was real and genuine, as in pathetic tones they offered up their petitions. We felt it to be a great privilege and a source of much blessing, when with them we bowed at the mercy seat of our great loving Father, to whom all languages of earth are known, and before whom all hearts are open.

Very helpful at times to devout worship were our

surroundings. As in the ancient days, when the vast multitudes gathered around Him on the seaside and were comforted and cheered by His presence, so we felt on these quiet shores of the lake that we were worshipping Him who is always the same. At times delightful and suggestive were our environments. With Lake Winnipeg's sunlit waves before us, the blue sky above us, the dark, deep, primeval forest as our background, and the massive granite rocks beneath us, we often felt a nearness of access to Him, the Sovereign of the universe, Who "dwells not in temples made with hands," but "Who covers Himself with light as with a garment; Who stretches out the heavens like a curtain; Who lays the beams of His chambers in the waters; Who makes the clouds His chariot; Who walks upon the wings of the wind; Who laid the foundations of the earth, that it should not be removed forever."

Our Sabbaths were days of rest. The Christian Indians had been taught by their faithful missionaries the fourth commandment, and they kept it well. Although far from their homes and their beloved sanctuary, they respected the day. When they camped on Saturday night, all the necessary preparations were made for a quiet, restful Sabbath. All the wood that would be needed to cook the day's supplies was secured, and the food that required cooking was prepared. Guns were stowed away, and although sometimes ducks or other game would come near, they were not disturbed. Generally two religious services were held and enjoyed. The Testaments and hymn books were well used throughout the day, and an atmosphere of "Paradise Regained" seemed to pervade the place.

At first, long years ago, the Hudson's Bay Company's officials bitterly opposed the observance of the Sabbath by their boatmen and tripmen; but the missionaries were true and firm, and although persecution for a time abounded, eventually right and truth prevailed, and the Christian Indians were left to

An Indian Canoe Brigade

keep the day without molestation. And, as has always been found to be the case in such instances, there was no loss, but rather gain. The Christian Indians, who rested the Sabbath day, were never behind. On the long trips into the interior or down to York Factory or Hudson Bay, these Indian canoe brigades used to make better time, have better health, and bring up their boats and cargoes in better shape, than the unbelieving, Metis, or Indians, who pushed on without any day of rest. Years of studying this question, judging from the standpoint of the work accomplished and its effects on men's physical constitution, apart altogether from its moral and religious aspect, most conclusively taught me that the institution of the one day in seven as a day of rest is for man's highest good.

Thus we journeyed on, meeting with various adventures by the way. One evening, rather than lose the advantage of a good wind, our party resolved to sail on throughout the night. We had no compass or chart, no moon or fickle Auroras lit up the watery waste. Clouds, dark and heavy, flitted by, obscuring the dim starlight, and adding to the risk and danger of our proceeding. On account of the gloom, part of the crew were kept on the watch continually. The bowsman, with a long pole in his hands, sat in the prow of the boat, alert and watchful. For a long time I sat with the steersman in the stern of our little craft, enjoying this weird way of travelling. Out of the darkness behind us into the vague blackness before us we plunged. Sometimes through the darkness came the sullen roar and dash of waves against the rocky isles or dangerous shore near at hand, reminding us of the risks we were running, and what need there was of the greatest care.

Our camp bed had been spread on some boards in the rear of our little boat; and here Mrs. Young, who for a time had enjoyed the exciting voyage, was now fast asleep. I remained up with "Big Tom" until after midnight; and then, having exhausted my stock of

Indian words in conversation with him, and becoming weary, I wrapped a blanket around myself and lay down to rest. Hardly had I reached the land of dreams, when I was suddenly awakened by being most unceremoniously thrown, with wife, bedding, bales, boxes, and some drowsy Indians, on one side of the boat. We scrambled up as well as we could and endeavoured to take in our situation. The darkness was intense, but we could easily make out the fact that our boat was stuck fast. The wind whistled around us, and bore with such power upon our big sail that the wonder was that it did not snap the mast or ropes. The sail was quickly lowered, a lantern was lit, but its flickering light showed no land in view.

We had run upon a submerged rock, and there we were held fast. In vain the Indians, using their big oars as poles, endeavoured to push the boat back into deep water. Finding this impossible, some of them sprang out into the water which threatened to engulf them; but, with the precarious footing the submerged rock gave them, they pushed and shouted, when, being aided by a giant wave, the boat at last was pushed over into the deep water beyond. At considerable risk and thoroughly drenched, the brave fellows scrambled on board; the sail was again hoisted, and away we sped through the gloom and darkness.

CHAPTER V.

Arrival at Norway House — Our new home — Rev. Charles Stringfellow — Thunderstorm — Rev. James Evans — Syllabic characters invented — Difficulties overcome — Help from English Wesleyan Missionary Society and from British and Foreign Bible Society —Extensive use of the syllabic characters — The people, Christian and otherwise — Learning lessons by dear experience — The hungry woman — The man with the two ducks — Our first Sabbath in our new field — Sunday school and Sabbath service — Family altars.

We reached Norway House on the afternoon of the 29th of July, 1868, and received a very cordial welcome from James Stewart, Esq., the gentleman in charge of this Hudson's Bay post. This is one of the most important establishments of this wealthy fur-trading company. For many years it was the capital, at which the different officers and other officials from the different districts of this vast country were in the habit of meeting annually for the purpose of arranging the various matters in connection with their prosecution of the fur trade. Here Sir George Simpson, for many years the energetic and despotic governor, used to come to meet these officials, travelling by birch canoe, manned by his matchless crew of Iroquois Indians, all the way from Montreal, a distance of several thousand miles. Here immense quantities of furs were collected from the different trading posts, and then shipped to England by way of Hudson's Bay.

The sight of this well kept establishment, and the courtesy and cordial welcome extended to us, were very pleasing after our long toilsome voyage up Lake Winnipeg. But still we were two miles and a half from our Indian Mission, and so were full of anxiety to reach the end of our journey. Mr. Stewart, however, insisted on our remaining to tea with him, and then took us over to the Indian village in his own row boat, manned by four sturdy Highlanders. Before we reached the shore, sweet sounds of melody fell upon our ears. The Wednesday evening service was being held, and songs of praise were being sung by the Indian congregation, the notes of which reached us as we neared the shore and landed upon the rocky beach. We welcomed this as a pleasing omen, and rejoiced at it as one of the grand evidences of the Gospel's power to change. Not many years ago the yells of the conjurer, and the whoops of the Indians, were here the only familiar sounds. Now the sweet songs of Zion are heard, and God's praises are sung by a people whose lives attest the genuineness of the work accomplished.

We were cordially welcomed by Mrs. Stringfellow in the Mission house, and were soon afterwards joined by her husband, who had been conducting the religious services in the church. Very thankful were we that after our long and adventurous journey for two months and eighteen days, by land and water, through the good providence of God we had reached our field of toil among the Cree Indians, where for years we were to be permitted to labor.

Mr. and Mrs. Stringfellow remained with us for a few days before they set out on their return trip to the province of Ontario. We took sweet counsel together, and I received a great deal of valuable information in reference to the work among these natives. For eleven years the missionary and his wife had toiled and suffered in this northern land. A good degree of success had attended their efforts, and we were much pleased with the state in which we found everything connected with the Mission.

While we were at family prayers the first evening after our arrival, there came up one of the most terrific thunderstorms we ever experienced. The heavy Mission house, although built of logs, and well mudded and clap-boarded, shook so much while we were on our knees that several large pictures fell from the walls; one of which, tumbling on Brother Stringfellow's head, put a very sudden termination to his evening devotions.

Rossville Mission, Norway House, was commenced by the Rev. James Evans in the year 1840. It has been, and still is, one of the most successful Indian Missions in America. Here Mr. Evans invented the syllabic characters, by which an intelligent person can learn to read the Word of God in ten days or two weeks. Earnestly desirous to devise some method by which the Indians could acquire the art of reading in an easier manner than by the use of the English alphabet, he invented these characters, each of which stands for a syllable. He carved his first type with his pocket knife, and procured the lead for the purpose from the tea chests of the Hudson's Bay Company's post. His first ink he made out of soot from the chimney, and his first paper was birch bark. Great was the excitement among the Indians when he had perfected his invention, and had begun printing in their own language. The conjurers, and other Indians, were very much alarmed, when, as they expressed it, they found the "bark of the tree was beginning to talk."

The English Wesleyan Mission Society was impressed with the advantage of this wonderful invention, and the great help it would be in carrying on the blessed work. At great expense they sent out a printing press, with a large quantity of type, which they had had especially cast. Abundance of paper, and everything else essential, were furnished. For years portions of the Word of God, and a goodly number of hymns translated into the Cree language, were printed, and incalculable good resulted.

Other missionary organizations at work in the country quickly saw the advantage of using these syllabic characters, and were not slow to avail themselves of them. While all lovers of missions rejoice at this, it is to be regretted that some, from whom better things might have been expected, were anxious to take the credit of the invention, instead of giving it to its rightful owner, the Rev. James Evans. It is a remarkable fact, that so perfectly did Mr. Evans do his work, that no improvement has been made as regards the use of these characters among the Cree Indians.

Other missionaries have introduced them among other tribes, with additions to meet the sounds used in those tribes which are not found among the Crees. They have been successfully utilized by the Moravians among the Eskimos.

On our arrival at Rossville the Indians crowded in to see the new missionary and his wife, and were very cordial in their greetings. Even some unsaved Indians, dressed up in their picturesque costumes, came to see us, and were very friendly.

As quickly as possible we settled down to our work, and tried to grasp its possibilities. We saw many pleasing evidences of what had been accomplished by faithful predecessors, and were soon convinced of the greatness of the work yet to be done. For, while from our church, and the houses of our Christian people, the songs of Zion were heard, our ears were saluted by the shouts and yells of old Indian conjurers and medicine men, added to the monotonous sounds of their drums, which came to us nightly from almost every point in the compass, from islands and headlands not far away.

Our first Sabbath was naturally a very interesting day. Our own curiosity to see our people was doubtless equalled by that of the people to see their new missionary. Unbelievers flocked in with Christians, until the church was crowded. We were very much pleased with their respectful demeanor in the house of God. There was no laughing or frivolity in the sanctuary. With their moccasined feet and cat like tread, several hundred Indians did not make one quarter the noise often heard in Christian lands, made by audiences one-tenth the size. We were much delighted with their singing. There is a peculiar plaintive sweetness about Indian singing that has for me a special attractiveness. Scores of them brought their Bibles to the church. When I announced the lessons for the day, the quickness with which they found the places showed their familiarity with the sacred volume. During prayers they were old fashioned Methodist enough to kneel down while the Sovereign of the universe was being addressed. They sincerely and literally entered into the spirit of the Psalmist when he said: "O come, let us worship and bow down: let us kneel before the Lord our maker."

I was fortunate in securing for my interpreter a thoroughly good Indian by the name of Timothy Bear. He was of an emotional nature, and rendered good service to the cause of Christ. Sometimes, when interpreting for me the blessed truths of the gospel, his heart would get fired up, and he would become so absorbed in the theme that he would in a most eloquent way beseech and plead with the people to accept this wonderful salvation.

As the days rolled by, and we went in and out among them, and contrasted the lost with the Christian Indian, we saw many evidences that the gospel is still the power of God unto salvation, and that, whenever accepted in its fullness, it brings not only peace and joy to the heart, but is attended by the secondary blessings of civilization. The Christian Indians could easily be picked out by the improved appearance of their homes, as well as by the marvelous change in their lives and actions.

We found out, before we had been there many days, that we had much to learn about Indian customs and habits and modes of thought. For example: the day after Mr. and Mrs. Stringfellow had left us, a poor woman came in, and by sign language let Mrs. Young know that she was very hungry. On the table were a large loaf of bread, a large piece of corned beef, and a dish of vegetables, left over from our boat supplies. My good wife's sympathies were aroused at the poor woman's story, and, cutting off a generous supply of meat and bread, and adding thereto a large quantity of the vegetables and a quart of tea, she seated the woman at the table before the hearty meal. Without any trouble the guest disposed of the whole, and then to our amazement, began pulling up the skirt of her dress at the side till she had formed a capacious pocket. Reaching over, she seized the meat, and put it in this large receptacle, the loaf of bread quickly followed, and lastly, the dish of vegetables. Then, getting up from her chair, she turned towards us, saying, "Na-nas-koo-moo-wi-nah," which is the Cree for thanksgiving. She gracefully backed out of the dining room, holding carefully on to her supplies. Mrs. Young and I looked in astonishment, but said nothing till she had gone out. We could not help laughing at the queer

Fat ducks

sight, although the food which had disappeared in this unexpected way was what was to have been our principal support for two or three days, until our supplies should have arrived. Afterwards, when expressing our astonishment at what looked like the greediness of this woman, we learned that she had only complied with the strict etiquette of her tribe. It seems it is their habit, when they make a feast for anybody, or give them a dinner, if fortunate enough to have abundance of food, to put a large quantity before them. The invited guest is expected to eat all he can, and then to carry the rest away. This was exactly what the poor woman did. From this lesson of experience we learnt just to place before them what we felt our limited supplies enabled us to give at the time.

One day a fine looking Indian came in with a couple of fat ducks. As our supplies were low, we were glad to see them; and in taking them I asked him what I should give him for them. His answer was, "O, nothing; they are a present for the missionary and his wife." Of course I was delighted at this exhibition of generosity on the part of this entire stranger to us so soon after our arrival in this wild land. The Indian at once made himself at home with us, and kept us busy answering questions and explaining to him everything that excited his curiosity. Mrs. Young had to leave her work to play for his edification on the little melodeon. He remained to dinner, and ate one of the ducks, while Mrs. Young and I had the other. He hung around all the afternoon, and did ample justice to a supper out of our supplies. He tarried with us until near the hour for retiring, when I gently hinted to him that I thought it was about time he went to see if his wigwam was where he left it.

"Oh," he exclaimed, "I am only waiting."

"Waiting?" I said; "for what are you waiting?"

"I am waiting for the present you are going to give me for the present I gave you."

I at once took in the situation, and went off and got him something worth half a dozen times as much as his ducks, and he went off very happy.

When he was gone, my good wife and I sat down, and we said, "Here is lesson number two. Perhaps, after we have been here a while, we shall know something about the Indians."

After that we accepted no presents from them, but insisted on paying a reasonable price for everything we needed which they had to sell.

Our Sunday's work began with the Sunday school at nine o'clock. All the boys and girls attended, and often there were present many of the adults. The children were attentive and respectful, and many of them were able to repeat large portions of Scripture from memory. A goodly number studied the catechism translated into their own language. They sang the hymns sweetly, and joined with us in repeating the Lord's Prayer.

The public service followed at half past ten o'clock. The morning service was always in English, although the hymns, lessons, and text would be announced in the two languages. The Hudson's Bay officials who might be at the Fort two miles away, and all their employees, regularly attended this morning service. Then, as many of the Indians understood English, and our object was ever to get them all to know more and more about it, this service usually was largely attended by the people. The great Indian service was held in the afternoon. It was all their own, and was very much prized by them. At the morning service they were very dignified and reserved; at the afternoon they sang with an enthusiasm that was delightful, and were not afraid, if their hearts prompted them, to come out with a glad "Amen!"

They bring with them to the sanctuary their Bibles, and very sweet to my ears was the rustle of many pages as they rapidly turned to the lessons of the day in the

Old or New Testament. Sermons were never considered too long. Very quietly and reverently did the people come into the house of God, and with equal respect for the place, and for Him whom there they had worshipped, did they depart. Dr. Taylor, one of our missionary secretaries, when visiting us, said at the close of one of these hallowed afternoon services, "Mr. Young, if the good people who help us to support missions and missionaries could see what my eyes have beheld today, they would most cheerfully and gladly give us ten thousand dollars a year more for our Indian missions."

Every Sunday evening I went over to the Fort, by canoe in summer, and dog train in winter, and held a service there. A little chapel had been specially fitted up for these evening services. Another service was also held in the church at the Mission by Indians themselves. There were among them several who could preach very acceptable sermons, and others who, with a burning eloquence, could tell, like Paul, the story of their own conversion, and beseech others to be likewise reconciled to God.

We were surprised at times by seeing companies of unbelieving Indians stalk into the church during the services, not always acting in a way becoming to the house or day. At first it was a matter of surprise to me that the Christian Indians put up with these irregularities. I was very much astounded one day by the entrance of an old Indian called Tapastanum, who, rattling his ornaments, and crying, "Ho! Ho!" came into the church in a sort of trot, and gravely kissed several of the men and women. As the Christian Indians seemed to stand the interruption, I felt that I could. Soon he sat down, at the invitation of Big Tom, and listened to me. He was grotesquely dressed, and had a good sized looking glass hanging on his breast, kept in its place by a string hung around his neck. To aid himself in listening, he lit his big pipe and smoked through the rest of the service. When I spoke to the people afterwards about the conduct of this man, so opposite to their quiet, respectful demeanor in the house of God, their expressive, charitable answer was: "Such were we once, as ignorant as Tapastanum is now. Let us have patience with him, and perhaps he, too, will soon decide to give his heart to God. Let him come; he will get quiet when he gets the light."

The week evenings were nearly all filled up with services of one kind or another, and were well attended, or otherwise, according as the Indians might be present at the village, or away hunting, or fishing, or "tripping" for the Hudson's Bay Company. What pleased us very much was the fact that in the homes of the people there were so many family altars. It was very delightful to take a quiet walk in the evening through the village, and hear from so many little homes the voice of the head of the family reading the precious Word, or the sound of prayer and praise. Those were times when in every professed Christian home in the village there was a family altar.

CHAPTER VI

Constant progress — Woman's sad condition without Christ — Illustrations — Wondrous changes produced by Christianity — Illustrations — New Year's Day Christian festival — The aged and feeble ones first remembered — Closing thanksgiving services.

We found ourselves in a Christian village surrounded by traditional religion. The contrast between the two classes was very evident.

The Christians, as fast as they were able to build, were living in comfortable houses, and earnestly endeavouring to lift themselves up in the social circle. Their personal appearance was better, and cleanliness was accepted as next to godliness. On the Sabbaths they were well dressed, and presented such a respectable and devout appearance in the sanctuary as to win the admiration of all who visited us. The great majority of those who made a profession of faith lived honest, sober, and consistent lives, and thus showed the genuineness of the change wrought in them by the glorious gospel of the Son of God.

One of the most delightful and tangible evidences of the thoroughness and genuineness of the change was seen in the improvement in the family life. Such a thing as genuine home life, with mutual love and sympathy existing among the different members of the family, was unknown in their lost state. The men, and even boys, considered it a sign of courage and manliness to despise and shamefully treat their mothers, wives, or sisters. Christianity changed all this; and we were constant witnesses of the genuineness of the change wrought in the hearts and lives of this people by the preaching of the gospel, by seeing how woman was uplifted from her degraded position to her true place in the household.

My heart was often pained at what I saw among some of the wild bands around us. When, by canoe in summer, or dog train in winter, I have visited these wild men, I have seen the proud, lazy hunter come stalking into the camp with his gun on his shoulder, and in loud, imperative tones shout out to his poor wife, who was busily engaged in cutting wood, "Get up there, you dog, my old woman, and go back on my tracks in the woods, and bring in the deer I have shot; and hurry, for I want my food!" To quicken her steps, although she was hurrying as rapidly as possible, a stick was thrown at her, which fortunately she was able to dodge.

Seizing the long carrying strap, which is a piece of leather several feet in length, and wide at the middle, where it rests against the forehead when in use, she rapidly glides away on the trail made by her husband's snow shoes, it may be for miles, to the spot where lies the deer he has shot. Fastening one end of the strap to the haunches of the deer, and the other around its neck, after a good deal of effort and ingenuity, she succeeds at length in getting the animal, which may weigh from a hundred and fifty to two hundred pounds, on her back, supported by the strap across her forehead. Panting with fatigue, she comes in with her heavy burden, and as she throws it down she is met with a sharp stern command from the lips of her husband, who has thought it beneath his dignity to carry in the deer himself, but who imagines it to be a sign of his being a great brave thus to treat his wife. The gun was enough for him to carry. Without giving the poor tired creature a moment's rest, he shouts out again for her to hurry and be quick; he is hungry, and wants his dinner.

The poor woman, although almost exhausted, knows full well, by the bitter experience of the past, that to delay an instant would bring upon herself severe punishment, and so she quickly seizes the scalping knife and deftly skins the animal, and fills a pot with the savory venison, which is soon boiled and placed before his highness. While he, and the men and boys whom he may choose to invite to eat with him, are rapidly devouring the venison, the poor woman has her first moments of rest. She goes and seats herself down where women, girls and dogs are congregated, and there women and dogs struggle for the half picked bones which the men, with derisive laughter, throw among them!

This was one of the sad aspects of the unbelieving Indians which I often had to witness as I travelled among those bands that had not, up to that time, accepted the gospel. When these poor women get old and feeble, very sad and deplorable is their condition. When able to toil and slave, they are tolerated as necessary evils. When aged and weak, they are shamefully neglected, and often, put out of existence.

One of the missionaries, on visiting a certain band, preached from those blessed words of the Savior: "Come unto Me, all ye that labor and are heavy laden, and I will give you rest." In his sermon he spoke about life's toils and burdens, and how all men had to work and labor. The men of the congregation were very angry at him; and at an indignation meeting which they held, they said, "Let him go to the women with that kind of talk. They have to carry all the heavy burdens, and do the hard work. Such stuff as that is not for us men, but for the women." So they were offended by him.

At a small Indian settlement on the north eastern shores of Lake Winnipeg lived a chief by the name of Moo-koo-woo-soo, who deliberately strangled his mother, and then burnt her body to ashes. When questioned about the horrid deed, he coolly and heartlessly said that as she had become too old to snare rabbits or catch fish, he was not going to be bothered with keeping her, and so he deliberately put her to death. Such instances could be multiplied many times. Truly "the tender mercies of the wicked are cruel."

In delightful contrast to these sad sights among the lost natives around us, were the kindly ways and happy homes of the converted Indians. Among them a woman occupied her true position, and was well and lovingly treated. The aged and infirm, who but for the gospel would have been dealt with as Moo-koo-woo-soo dealt with his mother, had the warmest place in the little home and the daintiest morsel on the table. I have seen the sexton of the church throw wide open the door of the sanctuary, that two stalwart young men might easily enter, carrying in their arms their invalid mother, who had expressed a desire to come to the house of God. Tenderly they supported her until the service ended, and then they lovingly carried her home again. But for the gospel's blessed influences on their natures they would have died before doing such a thing for a woman, even though she was their own mother.

Life for the women was not now all slavery. They had their happy hours, and knew well how to enjoy them. Nothing, however, seemed so to delight the women as much as to be gliding about in the glorious summer time in their light canoes. And sometimes, combining pleasure with profit, many a duck was shot by these young Indian maidens.

This changed feeling towards the aged and afflicted ones we have seen manifested in a very expressive and blessed way at the great annual New Year's Feast. It was customary for the Indians, long before they became Christians, to have a great feast at the beginning of the New Year. In the old times, the principal article of food at these feasts was dogs, the eating of which was accompanied by many other ceremonies. The missionaries, instead of abolishing the feast, turned it into a religious festival. I carried out the methods of my worthy predecessors at Norway House, and so we had a feast every New Year's Day.

The Crees call this day "Ooche-me-gou Kesigow," which literally means "the kissing day," as on this day men claim the right to kiss every woman they meet; and strange to say, every woman expects to be kissed. It used to amuse me very much to see thirty or forty Indians, dressed up in their finest apparel, come quietly marching into the Mission house, and gravely kiss Mrs. Young on her cheek. When I used to tease her over this strange phase of unexpected missionary experience, she would laughingly retort, "O, you need not laugh at me. See that crowd of women out there in the yard, expecting you to go out and kiss them!" It was surprising how much work that day kept me shut in my study; or if that would not avail, I used to select a dear old sweet faced, white haired grandma, the mother of the chief, and say, "Now I am going to kiss grandma; and as I kiss her you must all consider yourselves kissed." This institution is more ancient among them than shaking hands, about which they knew nothing until it was introduced by the whites.

For weeks before New Year's Day great preparations were made for the feast. A council would be called, and the men would have recorded what they were willing to give towards it. Some, who were good deer hunters, promised venison. Others promised so many beavers. Perhaps there were those who knew where bears had made their winter dens, and they agreed to go and kill them for the feast. Others, who were good fur hunters, stated their willingness to exchange some of the furs they would catch for flour and tea and sugar at the trading post.

Thus the business went on, until enough was promised, with the liberal supplies given by the Hudson's Bay Company officials and the missionary, to make the affair a great success. An out building of the Mission, called "the fish house," was the place where all these various things, as they were obtained, were stored. Months were sometimes consumed in collecting the meat. But Jack Frost is a good preservative, and so nothing spoiled. A few days before the feast, Mrs. Young would select several of the Indian women, and under her superintendency the various

"Many a duck was shot by these young Indian Maidens"

supplies would be cooked. Very clever were these willing helpers; and in a short time a quantity of food would be piled up, sufficient for all, although it is well known that Indians have good appetites.

When the great day arrived, the men quickly removed the seats out of the church, and there put up long tables. Great boilers of tea were made ready, and every preparation was completed for a good time. But, before a mouthful was eaten by any of the eight hundred or thousand persons present, the chief used to ask me for a pencil and a piece of writing paper; and then, standing on a box or bench, he would shout out, "How many of our people are aged, or sick, or afflicted, and cannot be with us today?" As one name after another was mentioned, he rapidly wrote them down. Then he read over the list, and said, "Let us not forget any one." Somebody shouted out, "There is an old woman ten miles up the river towards the old Fort." Somebody else said, "Have you the name of that boy who was accidentally shot in the leg?" Their names were both put down. Then somebody said, "There are two or three left behind in the tent of the unbelievers, while the rest have come to the feast." "Let us feed those who have come, and send something with our kind greetings to the others," is the unanimous response.

When it was certain that none had been overlooked, a request was made to me for all the old newspapers and packing paper I could give them, and soon loving hands were busily engaged in cutting off large pieces of different kinds of meat and arranging them with the large flat cakes in generous bundles. To these were added little packages of tea and sugar. In this way as many large bundles each containing an assortment of everything at the feast would be made up as there were names on the paper. Then the chief would call in, from where the young men were busily engaged in playing football, as many of the fleet runners as there were bundles, and giving each his load, would indicate the person to whom he was to give it, and also would add, "Give them our New Year's greetings and sympathy, and tell them we are sorry they cannot be with us today."

Very delightful were these sights to us. Such things paid us a thousand fold for our hardships and sufferings. Here, before a mouthful was eaten by the healthy and vigorous ones, large generous bundles, that would last for days, were sent off to the aged and infirm or wounded ones, who in all probability, but for the blessed influences of the gospel, if not quickly and cruelly put out of existence, would have been allowed to linger on in neglect and wretchedness.

Even the young runners seemed to consider that it was an honor to be permitted to carry these bundles, with the loving messages, to the distant homes or wigwams where the afflicted ones were. It was quite amusing to watch them tighten up their belts and dash off like deer. Some of them had several miles to go; but what cared they on this glad day?

According to seniority the tables were filled, and the feast began as soon as the "Grace before meat" had been sung. Mrs. Young had her own long table, and to it she invited not only the Hudson's Bay Company's people, but as many of the aged and worthy from among the Indians as we wished specially to honor. Sometimes we filled one table with ones who had come in from some distant forest home, attracted by the reports of the coming great feast. Through their stomachs we sometimes reached their hearts, and won them to Christ.

Thus for hours the feast continued, until all had been supplied. None were neglected, and everybody was happy. Then with a glad heart they sang:

"Praise God, from whom all blessings flow."

When all the guests were satisfied, what was left was carried off by the needy ones, among whom it was generously divided; the tables were quickly taken down by the men, and the church was speedily swept clean by some active women. The seats and pews were replaced, and every arrangement was made for the great annual New Year's meeting. The church was lit up; and when the audience had gathered, a chairman was appointed, and after singing and prayer, speeches were made by several of the Indians.

Many pleasant and many sensible things were said. Some of the sober minded ones reviewed the year just gone, with all its blessings and mercies, and expressed the hope that the one on which they had entered would be crowned with blessings. Some of the speeches referred to Treaty matters with the government, and others were in reference to their hunting and fishing. Some were bright and witty, and were received with laughter and applause. Others were of a serious, religious character, and were equally welcome, and touched responsive hearts. With pleasure I noticed that in them all the most frequent word was "Na-nas-koomoo-win-ah," which means "thanksgiving," and for this my heart rejoiced. Thus ended, with the Doxology and benediction, these happy days, in which we saw so many evidences that the preaching of the gospel had not been in vain.

CHAPTER VII

Oxford House Mission — Visited by canoe — Description of the useful craft — Indian skill — Oxford Lake — Dr. Taylor — Edward Papanekis — Still on the trail by birch canoe — Narrow escape from being crushed by the ice — On stormy Lake Winnipeg — Pioneering farther north — Successes —"Show us the Father, and it sufficeth us" — Christ accepted in the place of idols.

I had received instructions from the Missionary Secretaries to visit Oxford Mission as soon as possible, and to do all I could for its upbuilding. This Mission had had a good measure of success in years gone by. A church and Mission house had been built at Jackson's Bay, and many of the Indians had been converted. But the village was too far from the Hudson's Bay Company's Post, where the Indians traded, and where naturally they gathered. For several years the work had been left in charge of a Native teacher. Making all the arrangements I could for the successful prosecution of the work in my absence, I left Norway House in a small canoe, manned by two Christian Indians, one of whom was my interpreter. With this wonderful little boat I was now to make my first intimate acquaintance. For this wild land of broad lakes, rapid rivers and winding creeks, the birch bark canoe is the boat of all others most admirably fitted. It is to the Indian here what the horse is to his brother on the great prairies, or what the camel is to those who live and wander in Arabian deserts. The canoe is absolutely essential to these natives in this land, where there are no other roads than the intricate devious water routes. It is the frailest of all boats, yet it can be loaded down to the water's edge, and, under the skilful guidance of these Indians, who are unquestionably the finest canoe men in the world, it can be made to respond to the with life and reason. What they can do in it, and with it, appeared to me at times perfectly marvelous. Yet when we remember that for about five months of every year some of the hunters almost live in it, this may not seem so very wonderful. It carries them by day, and in it, or under it, they often sleep by night. At the many portages which have to be made in this land, where the rivers are so full of falls and rapids, one man can easily carry it on his head to the smooth water beyond. In it we have travelled thousands of miles, while going from place to place with the blessed tidings of salvation to these wandering bands scattered over my immense circuit. Down the wild rapids we have rushed for miles together, and then out into great Lake Winnipeg, or other lakes, so far from shore that the distant headlands were scarcely visible. Foam-crested waves have often seemed as though about to overwhelm us, and treacherous gales to swamp us, yet the faithful, well trained canoe men were always equal to every emergency, and by the accuracy of their judgment, and the quickness of their movements, appeared ever to do exactly the right thing at the right moment. As a result, I came at length to feel as much at home in a canoe as anywhere else, and with God's blessing was permitted to make many long trips to those who could not be reached in any other way, except by dog-trains in winter.

Good canoe makers are not many, and so really good canoes are always in demand.

Frail and light as this Indian craft may be, there is a great deal of skill and ingenuity required in its construction.

Great care is needed in taking the bark from the tree. A long incision is first made up and down in the bark of the tree. Then, from this cut, the Indian begins, and with his keen knife gradually peels off the whole of the bark, as high up as his incision went, in one large piece or sheet. And even now that he has

Taking the bark from the trees for canoe making

safely got it off the tree, the greatest care is necessary in handling it, as it will split or crack very easily. Cedar is preferred for the woodwork, and when it can possibly be obtained, is always used. But in the section of the country where I lived, as we were north of the cedar limit, the canoe makers used pieces of the spruce tree, split very thin, as the best substitute for cedar that our country afforded.

All the sewing of the pieces of birch bark together, and the fastening of the whole to the outer frame, is done with the long slender roots of the balsam or larch trees, which are soaked and rubbed until they are as flexible as narrow strips of leather. When all the sewing is done, the many narrow limber pieces of spruce are crowded into their places, giving the whole canoe its necessary proportions and strength. Then the seams and weak spots are well covered over with melted pitch, which the Indians obtain from the spruce and balsam trees.

Great care is taken to make the canoe water tight. To accomplish this, the boat is often swung between trees and filled with water. Every place where the slightest leak is discovered is marked, and, when the canoe is emptied, is carefully attended to.

Canoes vary in style and size. Each tribe using them has its own patterns, and it was to me an ever interesting sight, to observe how admirably suited to the character of the lakes and rivers were the canoes of each tribe or district.

The finest and largest canoes were those formerly made by the Lake Superior Indians. Living on the shores of that great inland sea, they required canoes of great size and strength. These "great north canoes," as they were called, could easily carry from a dozen to a score of paddlers, with a cargo of a couple of tons of goods. In the old days of the rival fur traders, these great canoes played a very prominent part. Before steam or even large sailing vessels had penetrated into those northern lakes, these canoes were extensively used. Loaded with the rich furs of those wild forests, they used to come down into the Ottawa River, and thence on down that great stream, often even as far as Montreal.

Sir George Simpson, the energetic but despotic and unprincipled governor of the Hudson's Bay Company for many years, used to travel in one of these birch canoes all the way from Montreal up the Ottawa, on through Lake Nipissing into Georgian Bay; from thence into Lake Superior, and on to Thunder Bay. From this place, with indomitable pluck, he pushed on back into the interior, through the Lake of the Woods, down the tortuous river Winnipeg into the Lake of the same name. Along the whole length of this lake he annually travelled, in spite of its treacherous storms and annoying head winds, to preside over the Council and attend to the business of the wealthiest fur trading company that ever existed, over which he watched with eagle eye, and in every department of which his distinct personality was felt. His famous Iroquois crew are still talked about, and marvelous are the stories in circulation around many a northern camp fire of their endurance and skill.

How rapid the changes which are taking place in this world of ours! It seems almost incredible, in these days of mighty steamships going almost everywhere on our great waters, to think that there are hundreds of people still living who distinctly remember when the annual trips of a great governor were made from Montreal to Winnipeg in a birch bark canoe, manned by Indians.

Of this light Indian craft Longfellow wrote:

> "Give me of your bark, O Birch tree!
> Of your yellow bark, O Birch tree!
> Growing by the rushing river,
> Tall and stately in the valley!
> I a light canoe will build me,
> Build a swift canoe for sailing.

* *

> "Thus the Birch canoe was builded
> In the valley, by the river,
> In the bosom of the forest;
> All its mystery and its magic,
> All the brightness of the birch tree,
> All the toughness of the cedar,
> All the larch tree's supple sinews;
> And it floated on the river
> Like a yellow leaf in autumn,
> Like a yellow water-lily."

We left for Oxford Mission on the 8th of September. The distance is over two hundred miles, through the wildest country imaginable. We did not see a house with the exception of those built by the beavers from the time we left our Mission home until we reached our destination. We paddled through a bewildering variety of picturesque lakes, rivers, and creeks. When no storms or fierce head winds impeded us, we were able to make fifty or sixty miles a day. When night overtook us, we camped on the shore. Sometimes it was very pleasant and romantic. At other times, when storms raged and we were drenched with the rain so thoroughly that for days we had not a dry stitch upon us, it was not quite so agreeable.

We generally began our day's journey very early in the morning, if the weather was at all favorable, and paddled on as rapidly as possible, since we knew not when head winds might arise and stop our progress. The Oxford route is a very diversified one. There are lakes, large and small, across which we had to paddle. In some of them, when the wind was favorable, the Indians improvised a sail out of one of our blankets. Lashing it to a couple of oars, they lifted it up on the favoring wind, and thus very rapidly did we speed on our way.

At times we were in broad beautiful rivers, and then paddling along in little narrow creeks amid reeds and rushes. We passed over, or as they say in that country, "made" nine portages around picturesque falls or rapids. In these portages one of the Indians carried the canoe on his head. The other made a great load of the bedding and provisions, all of which he carried on his back. My load consisted of the two guns, ammunition, two kettles, the bag containing my changes of clothes, and a package of books for the Indians we were to visit. How the Indians could run so quickly through the portages was to me a marvel. Often the path was but a narrow ledge of rock against the side of the great granite cliff. At other times it was through quaking bog or treacherous muskeg. To them it seemed to make no difference. On they went with their heavy loads at that swinging Indian stride which soon left me far behind. On some of my canoe trips the portages were several miles long, and through regions so wild that there was nothing to indicate to me the right direction. When we were making them, I used to follow on as long as I knew I was in the right way. When I lost the trail, I at once stopped and patiently waited until one of those faithful men, having carried his load safely to the end, would come back for me. Quickly picking up my load, he would hurry off, and even then, unencumbered as I was, it was often as much as I could do to keep up with him.

Oxford Lake is one of the most beautiful and picturesque lakes I ever saw. It is between twenty and thirty miles long and several miles wide. It is studded with islands of every imaginable variety. Its waters are almost as transparent as the clear, fresh air above it. When no breath ripples its surface, one can look down into its crystal depths and see, many feet below, the great fish quietly moving about.

To visit the Indians who fish in its waters, and hunt upon its shores, I once brought one of our Missionary Secretaries, the eloquent Rev. Lachlin Taylor, D.D. The trip down had not been one of the most pleasant. The rains had drenched him, and the mosquitoes had plagued him with such persistency, that he loudly bemoaned his lot in being found in a country that was cursed with such abominable insects.

One night I heard him muttering between his efforts to get them out of his tent, where he declared they were attacking him in battalions:

> "They throng the air, and darken heaven,
> and curse this Western land."

However, when we reached Oxford Lake, the mosquitoes left us for a time. The sun came out in splendor, and we had some days of rarest beauty. The good doctor regained his spirits, and laughed when I teased him on some of his strong expressions about the country, and told him that I hoped, as the result of his experience, he, as all Missionary Secretaries ought, would have a good deal of sympathy for the missionaries who live in such regions for years together.

We camped for the night on one of the most picturesque points. We had two canoes, and to man them four Indians from our Norway House Mission. As the doctor was an enthusiastic fisherman, he decided that we must stop during the forenoon, while he tried his hand. His first haul was a splendid pike over two feet long. Great was his excitement as his success was assured. Eloquence poured from him; we were flooded with it. The Indians looked on in amazement while he talked of the beauties of the lake and islands, of the water and the sky.

"Wait a moment, doctor," I said. "I can add to the wild beauty of the place something that will please your artistic eye."

I requested two fine looking Indians to launch one of the canoes, and to quietly paddle out to the edge of an island which abruptly rose from the deep, clear waters before us, the top of which had in it a number of splendid spruce and balsams, massed together in natural beauty. I directed the men to drop over the side of the canoe a long fishing line, and then, posing them in striking attitudes in harmony with the place, I asked them to keep perfectly still until every ripple made by their canoe had died away.

I confess I was entranced by the loveliness of the sight. The reflections of the canoe and men, and of the islands and rocks, were as vivid as the actual realities. So clear and transparent was the water, that where it and the air met there seemed but a narrow thread between the two elements. Not a breath of air stirred, not a ripple moved. It was one of those sights which come to us but seldom in a lifetime, where everything is in perfect unison, and God gives us glimpses of what this world, His footstool, must have been before sin entered.

"As the Doctor was an enthusiastic fisherman..."

"Doctor," I said quietly, for my heart was full of the Doxology, "tell me what you think of that vision."

Standing up, with a great rock beneath his feet, in a voice of suppressed emotion he began. Quietly at first he spoke, but soon he was carried away with his own eloquence:

"I know well the lochs of my own beloved Scotland, for in many of them I have rowed and fished. I have visited all the famed lakes of Ireland, and have rowed on those in the Lake counties of England. I have travelled far and often on our great American lakes, and have seen Tahoe, in all its crystal beauty. I have rowed on the Bosphorus, and travelled on the Nile. I have lingered in the gondola on the canals of Venice, and have traced Rob Roy's canoe in the Sea of Galilee, and on the old historic Jordan. I have seen, in my wandering in many lands, places of rarest beauty, but the equal of this mine eyes have never gazed upon."

Never after did I see the lake as we saw it that day.

On it we have had to battle against fierce storms, where the angry waves seemed determined to engulf us. Once, in speeding along as well as we could from island to island, keeping in the lee as much as possible, we ran upon a sharp rock and punctured our canoe. We had to use our paddles desperately to reach the shore, and when we had done so, we found our canoe half full of water, in which our bedding and food were soaked. We hurriedly built a fire, melted some pitch, and mended our canoe, and hurried on.

On this lake, which can give us such pictures of wondrous beauty, I have encountered some of the greatest gales and tempests against which I have ever had to contend, even in this land of storms and blizzards. Then in winter, upon its frozen surface it used to seem to me that the Frost King held high carnival. Terrible were the suffering of both dogs and men on some of those trips. One winter, in spite of all the wraps I could put around me, making it possible for me to run for riding was out of the question, so intense was the cold every part of my face exposed to the pitiless blast was frozen. My nose, cheeks, eyebrows, and even lips, were badly frozen, and for days after I suffered. Cuffy, the best of my Newfoundland dogs, had all of her feet frozen, and even Jack's were sore for many a day after. My loyal Indian friends suffered also, and we all declared Oxford Lake to be a cold place in winter, and its storms worse than the summer mosquitoes.

The Indians of Oxford Lake were among the finest in all the great northwest. It was ever a joy to meet them as I used to do once in summer by canoe trip, and then again in winter by dog train. God blessed my visits to them. The old members were cheered and comforted as the gospel was preached to them, and the sacraments administered. Some who followed the old ways were induced to renounce their old lives, and the cause of religion was more and more established. The Rev. Mr. Brooking, and later, the studious and devoted Rev. Orrin German, did blessed service in that lonely Mission. At the present time the Rev. Edward Papanekis is the missionary there.

Long years ago I found Edward, a careless, sinful young man. Once he rushed into the Mission house under the influence of liquor, and threatened to strike me. But the blessed truth reached his heart, and it was my joy to see him a humble suppliant at the Cross. His heart's desire was realized. God has blessedly led him on, and now he is faithfully preaching that same blessed gospel to his countrymen at Oxford Mission.

In responding to the many Macedonian cries, my circuit kept so enlarging that I had to be in journeying often. My canoes were sometimes launched in spring, before the great floating ice fields had disappeared, and through tortuous open channels we carefully paddled our way, often exposed to great danger.

On one of these early trips we came to a place where for many miles the moving ice fields stretched out before us. One narrow channel of open water only was before us. Anxious to get on, we dashed into it, and rapidly paddled ourselves along. I had two experienced Indians, and so had no fear, but expected some novel adventures and had them with interest.

Our hopes were that the wind would widen the channel, and thus let us into open water. But, to our disappointment, when we had got along a mile or so in this narrow open space, we found the ice was quietly but surely closing in upon us. As it was from four to six feet thick, and of vast extent, there was power enough in it to crush a good sized ship; so it seemed that our frail birch bark canoe would have but a poor chance.

I saw there was a reasonable possibility that when the crash came we could spring on to the floating ice. But what should we do then? was the question, with canoe destroyed and us on floating ice far from land.

However, as the Indians kept perfectly cool, I said nothing, but paddled away and watched for the development of events. Nearer and nearer came the ice; soon our channel was not fifty feet wide. Already behind us the floes had met and we could hear the ice grinding and breaking as the enormous masses met in opposite directions. Now it was only about twenty feet from side to side. Still the men paddled on, and I kept paddling in unison with them. When the ice was so close that we could easily touch it on either side with our paddles, one of the Indians quietly said, "Missionary, will you please give me your paddle?" I quickly handed it to him, when he immediately thrust it with his own into the water, holding down the ends of them so low horizontally under the canoe that the blade end was out of water on the other side of the boat. The other Indian held his paddle in the same position, although from the other side of the canoe. Almost immediately after that, the ice crowded in upon us. But as the points of the paddles were higher than the ice, of course they rested upon it for an instant. This was what these coolheaded, clever men wanted. They had a fulcrum for their paddles, and so they pulled carefully on the handle ends of them, and, the canoe sliding up as the ice closed in and met with a crash under us, we found ourselves seated in it on the top of the ice. The craft, although only a frail birch bark canoe, was not in the least injured.

As we quickly sprang out of our canoe, we carried it away from where the ice had met and was being ground into pieces by the momentum with which it met. I could not but express my admiration to the men at this clever feat.

After some exciting work we reached the shore, and there patiently waited until the wind and sun cleared away the ice, and we could venture on. My plan was to spend at least a week in each Indian village or encampment, preaching three times a day, and either holding school with the children, or by personal entreaty beseeching men and women to be reconciled to God. When returning from the visit, which was a very successful one, we had to experience some of the inconveniences of travelling in such a frail bark as a birch canoe on such a stormy lake as Winnipeg.

The weather had been very unsettled, and so we had cautiously paddled from point to point. We had dinner at what the Indians call Montreal Point, and then started for the long crossing to Old Norway House Point, as it was then called. It is a very long, open traverse, and as lowering clouds threatened us we pulled on as rapidly as our three paddles could propel us. When out a few miles from land the storm broke upon us, the wind rose rapidly, and soon we were riding over great white crested billows. My companions were very skillful, and we had no fear; but the most skillful management was necessary to safely ride the waves, which soon in size were rivalling those of the ocean. A canoe is a peculiar craft, and requires an experienced hand in these great storms.

We were getting on all right, and were successfully climbing the big waves in quick succession, alert and watchful that no sudden erratic move should catch us off our guard and overturn us. At length we met a wave of unusual height, and succeeded in climbing up into its foaming crest all right. Then down its side our little craft shot with the apparent velocity of a sled down a toboggan slide. When we reached the bottom of this trough of the sea, our canoe slapped so violently upon the water that the birch bark on the bottom split from side to side. Of course the water rushed in upon us with uncomfortable rapidity. The more we paddled the worse the water entered, as the exertion strained the boat and opened the rent. Quickly folding up a blanket, I carefully placed it over the long rent, and kneeled down upon it to keep it in place. The man in the front of the canoe put down his paddle, and taking up the kettle, baled as rapidly as he could, while the Indian in the stern, and myself in the middle, plied our paddles for dear life. We turned towards the Spider Islands, which were over a mile away, and by vigorous work succeeded in reaching one of them, although our canoe was half full of water. Then could we enter into David's words, as for life we struggled, and our little craft was tossed on the cross sea in our efforts to reach a place of safety: "They reel to and fro, and stagger like a drunken man, and are at their wit's end. Then they cry unto the Lord in their trouble, and He bringeth them out of their distresses."

We paddled up as far as we could on a smooth granite rock that came out gradually in the water. Then out we sprang, and strong hands dragged our little canoe up beyond the reach of the waves. We hastily pulled out our dripping blankets, soaked food and other things, and then, overturning the canoe, emptied it of water; and as we saw the large break in the bottom, we realized as we had not before the danger we had been in, and the providential escape which had been ours. So, with glad hearts, we said, "We do praise the Lord for His goodness, and for His wonderful works to the children of men."

We quickly built a fire, and melted some pitch, a quantity of which is always carried ready for such emergencies. The long rent was covered over with a piece of cloth well saturated in the boiling pitch, a quantity more was poured over, and the whole was carefully smoothed out over the weak place. Soon it cooled and hardened, and the work was done. We ate a little food, and then launched our frail craft and pushed on. No serious accidents again troubled us, and we ended this long canoe trip, as we had done many others, thankful that we had such blessed opportunities to go to the remote places as heralds of the Cross, and doubly thankful when we were safe at home again.

On one of my canoe trips, when visiting unbelieving bands in the remote Nelson River District, I had some singular experiences, and learned some important lessons about the craving of the lost heart after God.

We had been journeying on for ten or twelve days when one night we camped on the shore of a lake-like river. While my guides were busily employed in gathering wood and cooking the supper, I wandered off and ascended to the top of a well wooded hill which I saw in the distance. Very great indeed was my surprise, when I reached the top, to find myself in the presence of the most startling evidences of idolatry.

The hill had once been densely covered with trees, but about every third one had been cut down, and the stumps, which had been left from four to ten feet high, had been carved into rude representations of the human form. Scattered around were the dog ovens, which were nothing but holes dug in the ground and lined with stones, in which at certain seasons, as part of their religious ceremonies, some of their favorite dogs, white ones were always preferred, were roasted, and then devoured by the excited crowd. Here and there were the tents of the old conjurers and medicine men, who, combining some knowledge of disease and medicine with a great deal of spirit worship, held despotic sway over the people. The power of these old conjurers over the Indians was very great. They were generally lazy old fellows, but succeeded nevertheless in getting the best that was going, as they held other Indians in such terror of their power, that gifts in the shape of fish and game were constantly flowing in upon them. They have the secret art among themselves of concocting some poisons so deadly that a little put in the food of a person who has excited their displeasure will cause death almost as soon as a dose of strychnine. They have other poisons which, while not immediately causing death to the unfortunate victims, yet so affect and disfigure them that, until death releases them, their suffering is intense and their appearance frightful.

Here on this hill top were all these sad evidences of the lost condition of the people. I wandered around and examined the idols, most of which had in front of them, and in some instances on their flat heads, offerings of tobacco, food, red cotton, and other things. My heart was sad at these evidences of such idolatry, and I was deeply impressed with my need of wisdom and aid from on high, so that when I met the people who here worshipped these idols I might so preach Christ and Him crucified that they would be constrained to accept Him as their all sufficient Savior.

While I lingered, and mused, and prayed, the shadows of the night fell on me, and I was shrouded in gloom. Then the full moon rose up in the east, and as her silvery beams shone through the trees and lit up these grotesque idols, the scene presented a strange weird appearance. My faithful guides, becoming alarmed at my long absence for the country was infested by wild animals were on the search for me when I returned to the camp fire. We ate our evening meal, sang a hymn, and bowed in prayer. Then we wrapped ourselves up in our blankets, and lay down on the granite rocks to rest. Although our bed was hard and there was no roof above us, we slept sweetly, for the day had been one of hard work and strange adventure.

After paddling about forty miles the next day we reached the Indians of that section of the country, and remained several weeks among them. With the exception of the old conjurers, they all received me very cordially. These old conjurers had the same feelings toward me as those who made silver shrines for Diana of Ephesus had toward the first preachers of Christianity in their city. They trembled for their occupation. They well knew that if I succeeded in inducing the people to become Christians their occupation would be gone, and they would have to settle down to work for their own living, like other people, or starve. I visited them as I did the rest of the encampment, but they had enmity in their hearts toward me. Of all their efforts to injure or destroy me of course I knew not. That their threats were many I well understood; but He who had said, "Lo, I am with you alway," mercifully watched over me and shielded me from their evil deeds. My two Indian friends also watched as well as prayed, with a vigilance that seemed untiring. Very pleasant, indeed, are my memories of my faithful Indian comrades on those long journeys. Their loyalty and devotion could not be excelled. Everything that they could do for my safety and happiness was cheerfully done.

We held three religious services every day, and between these services taught the people to read in the syllabic characters. One day, in conversing with a fine old Indian, I said to him, "What is your religion? If you have any clear idea of a religion, tell me in what you believe."

His answer was: "We believe in a good Spirit and in a bad spirit."

"Why, then," I said, "do you not worship the good Spirit? I came through your sacred grounds, and I saw where you had cut down some trees. Part you had used as fuel with which to cook your bear or deer meat; out of the rest you had made an idol, which you worship. How is one part more sacred than the other? Why do you make and worship idols?"

I can never forget his answer, or the impressive and almost passionate way in which the old man replied:

"Missionary, the Indian's mind is dark, and he cannot grasp the unseen. He hears the great Spirit's voice in the thunder and storms. He sees the evidences of His existence all around, but neither he nor his fathers have ever seen the great Spirit, or any one who has; and so he does not know what He looks like. But man is the highest creature that he knows of, and so he makes his idols like a man, and calls it his 'Manito.' We only worship them because we do not know what the great Spirit looks like, but these we can understand."

Suddenly there flashed into my mind the request of Philip to the Lord Jesus: "Show us the Father, and it suffices us;" and the wonderful answer: "Have I been so long time with you, and yet hast thou not known Me, Philip? He that hath seen Me hath seen the Father; and how sayest thou then, Show us the Father?"

I opened my Cree Bible at that wonderful chapter of disinterested love, the fourteenth of John, and preached unto them Jesus, in His two natures, Divine and human. While emphasizing the redemptive work of the Son of God, I referred to His various offices and purposes of love and compassion, His willingness to meet us and to save us from perplexity and doubt, as well as from sin. I spoke about Him as our elder brother, so intimately allied to us, and still retaining His human form as He pleads for us at the throne of God. I dwelt upon these delightful truths, and showed how Christ's love had so brought Him to us, that with the eye of faith we could see Him, and in Him all of God for which our hearts craved. "Whom having not seen, we love; in whom, though now we see Him not, yet believing, we rejoice with joy unspeakable and full of glory."

For many days I needed no other themes. They listened attentively, and the Holy Spirit applied these truths to their hearts and consciences so effectively that they gladly received them. A few more visits effectually settled them in the truth. They have cut down their idols, filled in the dog ovens, torn away the conjurers' tents, cleared the forest, and banished every vestige of the old life. And there, at what is called "the Meeting of the Three Rivers," on that very spot where idols were worshipped amidst horrid orgies, and where the yells, rattles, and drums of the old conjurers and medicine men were heard continuously for days and nights, there is now a little church, where these same Indians, transformed by the glorious gospel of the Son of God, are "clothed and in their right mind, sitting at the feet of Jesus."

My visits to Nelson River so impressed me with the fact of the necessity of some zealous missionary going down there and living among the people, that in response to appeals made, the Rev. John Semmens, whose heart God had filled with missionary zeal, and who had come out to assist me at Norway House, nobly resolved to undertake the work. He was admirably fitted for the arduous and responsible task. But no language of mine can describe what he had to suffer. His record is on high. The Master has it all, and He will reward. Great were his successes, and his triumphs.

At that place, where I found the stumps carved into idols, which Brother Semmens has so graphically described, the church, mainly through his instrumentality and personal efforts, has been erected. In the last letter which I have received from that land, the writer says: "The Indians now all profess themselves to be Christians. Scores of them by their lives and testimonies assure us of the blessed consciousness that the Lord Jesus is indeed their own loving Savior. Every conjuring drum has ceased. All vestiges of the old life are gone, we believe for ever."

"The wilderness and the solitary place shall be glad for them, and the desert shall rejoice and blossom as the rose."

Grandly has this prophecy been fulfilled, and dwarfs into insignificance all the suffering and hardship endured in the pioneer work which I had in beginning this Mission. With a glad heart I rejoice that "unto me, who am less than the least of all saints, is this grace given, that I should preach among the Gentiles the unsearchable riches of Christ."

CHAPTER VIII

The wild north land — The two methods of travel, by canoe and dog train — The native dogs — St. Bernard and Newfoundland dogs — The dog sleds — The guide — The dog drivers — The long journeys — Night traveling — Wondrous visions of the night.

So destitute are these wild northlands of roads that there are really no distinct words in the languages of these northern tribes to represent land vehicles. In translating such words as "wagon" or "chariot" into the Cree language, a word similar to that for "dog sled" had to be used.

No surveyor, up to the years about which I am writing, had visited these regions, and there were literally no roads as understood in civilized lands.

So numerous are the lakes and rivers that roads are unnecessary to the Indian in the summer time. With his light birch canoe he can go almost everywhere he desires. If obstructions block his passage, all he has to do is put his little canoe on his head, and a short run will take him across the portage, or around the cataracts or falls, or over the height of land to some other lake or stream, where he quickly embarks and continues his journey.

All summer travelling is done along the water routes. Naturally the various trading posts and Indian villages or encampments are located on the edges of the lakes or rivers, or very near them, so as to be most conveniently reached in this way. So short are the summers that there are only about five months of open water to be depended upon in these high latitudes. During the other seven months the dog sled is the only conveyance for purposes of travelling. So rough and wild is the country that we know of no vehicle that could take its place, and no animals that could do the work of the dogs.

As the years of toil rolled on, my mission field or circuit so enlarged that it extended irregularly north and south over five hundred miles, with a width in some places of over three hundred. In summer I travelled over it in a birch canoe, and in winter with my dog-trains.

At first it seemed very novel, and almost like child's play, to be dragged along by dogs, and there was almost a feeling of rebellion against what seemed such frivolous work.

The dogs generally used are the Eskimo breed, although in many places they have become so mixed with other varieties as to be almost unrecognizable. The pure Eskimo sled dogs are well built, compact animals, weighing from eighty to a hundred and twenty pounds. They are of various colors, and have a close, warm, furry coat of hair. They have sharp pointed ears and very bushy, curly tails. They are the most notorious thieves. I never could completely break an Eskimo dog of this habit. It seemed ingrained in their very natures. I have purchased young puppies of this breed from the natives, have fed them well, and have faithfully endeavoured to bring them up in the way in which they ought to go, but I never could get them to stay there. Steal they would, and did, whenever they had an opportunity.

This serious defect may have been the result of the constant and unremitting neglect with which Indians generally treat their dogs. They are fond of them in a way, and are unwilling to part with them, except at a good price, yet, except when working them, they very seldom feed them. The dogs are generally left to steal their living, and some of them become very clever at it, as more than once I found to my sorrow. When the fishing is successful, or many deer have been killed, the dogs, like their owners, are fat and flourishing. When food is scarce, the dogs' allowance is the first cut off. We could always tell at a glance, when a band of Indians came in to visit our village from their distant hunting

"With his light canoe he can go almost anywhere"

grounds, how they had prospered. If they and their dogs were fat and good natured, they had had abundance of food. If, while the people looked fairly well, the dogs were thin and wolfish, we knew they had fared but moderately. If the dogs were all gone and the people looked gaunt and famine stricken, we knew they had had hard times, and, as a last resort, had eaten their poor dogs to keep themselves alive.

Some of the Indians who feed their dogs in winter, never think of doing so in summer. The result is that, as they have to steal, hunt, or starve, they become adept in one or the other. Everything that is edible, and many things apparently unedible, are devoured by them. They fairly howled with delight when they found such things as old leather moccasins, dog harness, whips, fur caps, mitts, and similar things. They greedily devoured all they could, and then most cunningly buried the rest. Many of them go off in summer time on long fishing excursions. I once, when away on a canoe trip, met a pack of them up a great river over a hundred miles from their home. When we first saw them at a long distance, we mistook them for wolves, and began to prepare for battle. The quick eyes of my Indian canoe men soon saw what they were, and putting down our guns, we spent a little time in watching them. To my great surprise I found out that they were fishing on their own account. This was something new to me, and so I watched them with much interest.

On the side of the river on which they were was a shallow, reedy marsh, where the water was from a few inches to a foot in depth. In these shallow waters, at certain seasons of the year, different varieties of fish are to be found. The principal is the jackfish, or pike, some of which are over three feet long. As they crowd along in these shallows, often with their back fins out of the water, they are observed by the dogs, who quietly wade out, often to a distance of many yards, and seize them with such a grip that, in spite of their struggles, they are carried in triumph to the shore, and there speedily devoured. Sometimes the dogs will remain away for weeks together on these fishing excursions, and will return in much better condition than when they left.

During the winter of the first Riel Rebellion, when all our supplies had been cut off, my good wife and I got tired of dining twenty one times a week on fish, varied only by a pot of boiled muskrats, or a roast hind quarter of a wild cat. To improve our bill of fare, the next summer, when I went into the Red River Settlement, I bought a sheep, which I carefully took out with me in a little open boat. I succeeded in getting it safely home, and put it in a yard that had a heavy stockade fence twelve feet high around it. In some way the dogs got in and devoured my sheep.

The next summer, I took out a couple of pigs, and put them into a little log stable with a two inch spruce plank door. To my great disgust, one night the dogs ate a hole through the door and devoured my pigs.

There seemed to be a good deal of the wolf in their nature. Many of them never manifested much affection for their masters, and never could be fully depended upon. Still I always found that even with Eskimo dogs patience and kindness went farther than anything else in teaching them to know what was required of them, and in inducing them to accept the situation. Some of them are naturally lazy, and some of them are incorrigible shirks; and so there is in dog driving a capital opportunity for the exercise of the cardinal virtue of patience.

As my Mission increased in size, and new appointments were taken up, I found I would have to be on the move nearly all the winter if those who longed for the Word of Life were to be visited. Do the best I could, there were some bands so remote that I could only visit them twice a year. In summer I went by canoe, and in winter by dog-train. After a few wretched experiences with native dogs, where I suffered most intensely, as much on account of their inferior powers as anything else, I began to think of the many splendid St. Bernard and Newfoundland dogs I had seen in civilized lands, doing nothing in return for the care and affection lavished upon them. These thoughts, which came to me while far from home, were promptly followed by action as soon as that terrible trip was ended, in which every part of my face exposed to the intense cold had been frozen, even to my eyebrows and lips.

Missionary Secretaries were amused at the requisition for dogs, and had their laughs at what they called "my unique request," and wrote me to that effect. Thanks, however, to the kindness of such men as the Hon. Mr. Sanford, of Hamilton, the Hon. Mr. Ferrier, of Montreal, and other friends, I had in my possession some splendid dogs before the next season opened, and then the work went on with increasing interest and satisfaction. With splendid, well trained dogs, I could so shorten the time of the three hundred mile trip, that, instead of shivering seven or eight nights in a hole dug in the snow, we could reduce the number to four or five.

Those who have experienced the suffering and hardship of camping out in the forest with the temperature ranging from thirty to sixty degrees below zero, will agree that to escape two or three nights of it meant a good deal.

I found by years of experience that the St. Bernard and Newfoundland dogs had all the good qualities, and none of the defects, of the Eskimo dog. By kindness and firmness they were easily broken in, and then a whip was only an ornamental appendage of the driver's picturesque costume. Of these splendid dogs I often had in my possession, counting old and young, as many as twenty at a time. The largest and best of them all was Jack, a noble St. Bernard. He was black as jet, and stood over thirty-three inches high at his fore shoulder. When in good working trim, he weighed about a hundred and sixty pounds. He had no equal in all that northern land. Several times he saved my life, as we shall see further on. No whip ever ruffled his glossy coat; no danger ever deterred him from his work, when he with his marvelous intelligence once got to know what was expected of him. No blizzard, no matter how fickle and changeful, could lead him off from the desired camping place, even if the courage of other dogs failed them, and even though the guides gave up in despair.

The distance we could travel with dogs depended, of course, very much on the character of the trail or route. On the frozen surface of Lake Winnipeg, when no blinding gales opposed us, and our dogs were good and loads not too heavy, we have made from seventy to ninety miles a day. One winter I accomplished a journey from Fort Garry to Norway House in five days and a half a distance of nearly four hundred miles. When we were toiling along in the dense forests, where the snow lay deep and the obstructions were many, and the country was broken with hills and ravines, we often did not make more than a third of that distance, and then suffered much more than when we had made much greater journeys under more favorable conditions.

The dog sleds are made of two oak or birch boards, about twelve feet long, eight or nine inches wide, and from half an inch to an inch thick. These two boards are fastened securely together, edge to edge, by crossbars. Then one of the ends is planed down thin, and so thoroughly steamed or soaked in hot water that it can easily be bent or curved up to form what is called the head of the sled. It is then planed smooth, and fitted out with side loops. The front bars are those to which the traces of the dogs are attached, and the others along the sides are used to fasten the load securely. When finished, allowing two or three feet for the curled up head, a good dog sled is nine or ten feet long, and from sixteen to eighteen inches wide.

Sometimes they are fitted with canvas sides and a comfortable back. Then they are called carioles. When the dogs were strong enough, or the trail was a well beaten one, or we were travelling on the great frozen lakes, I was able to ride the greater part of the time. Then it was not unpleasant or toilsome work. But many of my winter trails led me through the primeval forests, where the snow was often very deep, the hills were steep, the fallen trees many, and the standing ones thickly clustered together. On such journeys there was but little riding. One had to strap on his snowshoes, and help the faithful Indians to tramp down the deep snow in the trail, so the poor dogs could drag the heavily loaded sleds along.

Four dogs constitute a train. They are harnessed in tandem style, as all this vast country north of the fertile prairies is a region of forests. The Eskimo style of giving each dog a separate trace, thus letting them spread out in a fan like form, would never do in this land of trees and dense under brush.

The harness, which is made of moose skin, is often decorated with ribbons and little musical bells. Strange as it may appear, the dogs were very fond of the bells, and always seemed to travel better and be in greater spirits when they could dash along in unison with their tinkling. Some dogs could not be more severely punished than by taking the bells off their harness.

The head dog of the train is called "the leader." Upon him depends a great deal of the comfort and success, and at times the safety, of the whole party. A really good leader is a very valuable animal. Some of them are so intelligent that they do not require a guide to run ahead of them, except in the most dense and unbeaten forest trails. I had a long legged white dog, of mixed breed, that always seemed to consider a guide a nuisance, when once he had got into his big head an idea of what I wanted him to do. Outside of his harness, Old Voyager, as we called him, was a morose, sullen, unsociable brute. So hard to approach was he that generally a rope about sixty feet long, with one end fastened around his neck, trailed out behind him. When we wanted to catch him, we generally had to start off in the opposite direction from him, for he was as cunning as a fox, and ever objected to being caught. In zigzag way we moved about until he was thrown off his guard, and then by and by it was possible to come near enough to get hold of the long rope and haul him in. When once the collar was on his neck, and he had taken his place at the head of the party, he was the unrivalled leader. No matter how many trains might happen to be travelling together, no one thought of taking first place while Old Voyager was at hand.

Lake Winnipeg is very much indented with deep, wide bays. The headlands are from five to thirty miles apart. When dog travelling on that great lake in winter, the general plan is to travel from headland to headland. When leaving one where perhaps we had slept or dined, all we had to do was to turn Old Voyager's head in the right direction, and show him the distant point to which we wished to go; and although it might be many miles away, a surveyor's line could not be much straighter than the trail our sleds would make under his unerring guidance.

I have gone into these details about this mode of travelling, because there is so little known about it in the outside world. Doubtless it will soon become a thing of the past, as the Indians are settling down in their reservations, and, each tribe or band having a resident missionary, these long, toilsome journeys will not be essential.

The companions of my long trips were the famed Indian runners of the north. The principal one of our party was called "the guide." To him was committed the responsibility of leading us by the quickest and safest route to the band of Indians we wished to visit with the good news of a Savior's love. His place was in front of the dogs, unless the way happened to lead us for a time over frozen lakes or well beaten trails, where the dogs were able to go on alone, cheered by the voice of their drivers behind. When the trail was of this description, the guide generally strode along in company with one of the drivers.

As the greater part of my work was in the forest regions, there were many trips when the guide was always at the front. Marvelously gifted were some of these men. The reader must bear in mind the fact that there were no roads or vestiges of a path. Often the whole distance we wished to go was through the dense unbroken forest. The snow, some winters, was from two to four feet deep. Often the trees were clustered so closely together that it was at times difficult to find them standing far enough apart to get our sleds, narrow as they were, between them. In many places the under brush was so dense that it was laborious work to force our way through it. Yet the guide on his large snowshoes was expected to push on through all obstructions, and open the way where it was possible for the dog sleds to follow. His chief work was to mark out the trail, along which the rest of us travelled as rapidly as our loaded sleds, or wearied limbs, and often bleeding feet, would allow.

Wonderfully clever and active were these guides in this difficult and trying work. To them it made but little difference whether the sun shone brightly, or clouds obscured the sky. On and on they pushed without hesitancy or delay. There were times when the sun's rays were reflected with such splendor from the snowy wastes, that our eyes became so affected by the glare, that it was impossible to travel by sunlight. The black eyes of the Indians seemed very susceptible to this disease, which they call "snow blindness." It is very painful, as I know by sad experience. The sensation is like that of having red hot sand thrown on the eyeballs. Often the faithful dog drivers used to suffer so from it that, stoical as they naturally are, I have known them to groan and almost cry out like children in the camp.

Once, in travelling near Oxford Lake, we came across a couple of Indians who were stone blind from this disease. Fortunately they had been able to reach the woods and make a camp and get some food ready before total blindness came upon them. We went out of our way to guide them to their friends.

To guard against the attack of this disease, which seldom occurs except in the months of March and April, when the increasing brightness of the sun, in those lengthening days, makes its rays so powerful, we often travelled only during the night time, and rested in the sheltered camps during the hours of sunshine. On some of our long trips we have travelled eight nights continuously in this way. We generally left our camp about sundown. At midnight we groped about as well as we could, aided by the light of the stars or the brilliant auroras, and found some dry wood and birch bark, with which we made a fire and cooked a midnight dinner. Then on we went until the morning light came. Then a regular camp was prepared, and breakfast cooked and eaten, and the dogs were fed, instead of at night. Prayers said, and ourselves wrapped up in our blankets and robes, we slept until the hours of brilliant sunshine were over, then on we went.

It always seemed to me that the work of the guide would be much more difficult at night than during the daytime. They, however, did not think so. With unerring accuracy they pushed on. It made no matter to them whether the stars shone out in all the beauty and brilliancy of the Arctic sky, or whether clouds arose and obscured them all. On the guide pushed through tangled underwood or dense gloomy forest, where there were not to be seen, for days, or rather nights, together, any other tracks than those made by the wild beasts of the forest.

Sometimes the wondrous auroras blazed out, flashing and scintillating with a splendor indescribable. At times the whole heavens seemed aglow with their fickle, inconstant beauty, and then various portions of the sky were illumined in succession by their ever changing bars, or columns of colored light. Man's mightiest fireworks display, dwarfed into insignificance in the presence of these celestial visions. For hours at a time have I been entranced amid their glories. So bewildering were they at times to me that I have lost all ideas of location, and knew not which was north or south.

But to the experienced guide, although, like many of the Indians, he had a keen appreciation of the beauties of nature, so intent was he on his duties that these changing auroras made no difference, and caused him no bewilderment in his work. This, to me, was often a matter of surprise. They are very susceptible in their natures, and their souls are full of poetry, as many of their expressive and beautiful names indicate. To them, in their lost state, those scintillating bars of colored light were the spirits of their forefathers, rank after rank, rushing out to battle. Yet, while on our long trips I have had Indians as guides who became intensely interested in these wondrous visions of the night, I never knew them to lose the trail or become confused as to the proper route.

Very pleasant are my memories of different guides and dog drivers. With very few exceptions they served me loyally and well. Most of them were devoted Christian men. With me they rejoiced to go on these long journeys to their countrymen who were still groping in the darkness, but most of them longing for the light. Many of them were capable of giving exhortations or addresses; and if not able to do this, they could, Paul-like, tell the story of their conversion, and how they had found the Savior.

My heart warms to those faithful men, my companions in many a storm, my bed-fellows in many a cold wintry camp. Memory brings up many incidents where they risked their lives for me, and where, when food was about exhausted, and the possibilities of obtaining additional supplies for days were very poor, they quietly and unostentatiously put themselves on quarter rations, for days together, that their beloved missionary might not starve.

Some of them have finished their course. Up the shining trail, following the unerring Guide, they have gone beyond the auroras and beyond the stars right to the throne of God.

CHAPTER IX

On the trail with the dogs, to fields ripe for the reaper — The place — The trip — The winter camp — The bitter cold — Enduring hardness — Death shaking hands with us — Many days on the trail.

In January, 1869, I started on my first winter trip to Nelson River, to visit a band of Indians there, who had never yet seen a missionary or heard the glad tidings of salvation. Their principal gatherings were at the little trading post on the Burntwood River. Their hunting grounds extended so very far north that they bordered on those of the Eskimo, with whom, however, the Indians have no dealings. Between these two races, the Indian and the Eskimo, there is no affinity whatever. They differ very materially in appearance, language, customs, and beliefs. Though they will seldom engage in open hostilities, they are very rarely at peace with each other, and generally strive to keep as far apart as possible.

The weather was bitterly cold, as the temperature ranged from thirty-five to fifty-five below zero. Our course was due north all the way. The road we made, for there was none ahead of the snow shoe tracks of our guide, was a rugged, unbroken forest path. As the country through which we passed is rich in fur bearing animals, we saw many evidences of their presence, and occasionally crossed a hunter's trail. We passed over twenty little lakes, averaging from one to thirty miles in diameter. Over these our dogs drew us very fast, and we could indulge in the luxury of a ride; but in the portages and wood roads our progress was very slow, and generally all of us, with our snowshoes on, and at times with axes in hand, had to tramp on ahead and pack the deep snow down, and occasionally cut out an obstructing log, that our dogs might be able to drag our heavily laden sleds along. Sometimes the trees were so thickly clustered together that it was almost impossible to get our sleds through them. At times we were testing our agility by climbing over fallen trees, and then on our hands and knees had to crawl under reclining ones. Our faces were often bleeding, and our feet bruised. There were times when the strap of my snowshoes so frayed and lacerated my feet that the blood soaked through the moccasins and webbing of the snowshoes, and occasionally the trail was marked with blood. We always travelled in single file. At the head, ran or walked the guide, as the roads would permit. On these trips, when I got to understand dog driving, I generally followed next; and behind me were three other dog trains, each with an Indian driver.

Sometimes the snow was so deep that the four dog drivers went ahead of the dogs, immediately behind the guide, and, keeping in line with him, industriously packed down the snow, that the dogs might the more easily drag the heavy sleds along. The reason why our loads were so heavy was this. We were not in a country where, when night overtook us, we could find some hospitable home to welcome us. Neither were we where there were hotels or houses in which for money we could secure lodgings. We were in one of the most desolate and thinly inhabited parts of the world, where those who travel long distances see no human beings, except the Indian hunters, and these but rarely. Hence, in spite of all our efforts to make our loads as light as possible, they would be heavy, although we were only carrying what was considered absolutely essential. We had to take our provisions, fish for our dogs, kettles, tin dishes, axes, bedding, guns, extra clothing, and various other things, to meet emergencies that might arise.

The heaviest item on our sleds was the fish for the dogs. Each dog was fed once a day, and then received two good whitefish, each weighing from four to six pounds. So that if the daily allowance for each dog averaged five pounds, the fish alone on each sled would weigh one hundred and twenty pounds, when we began a trip of a week's duration. Then the bitter cold and the vigorous exercise gave both the drivers and the missionary good appetites, and so the food provided for them was of significant weight.

We generally stopped about half an hour before sundown in order to have time, before darkness enshrouded us, to prepare our camp. As we journeyed on we had observed that the guide who had been running along in front had been, for the last half hour or so, carefully scanning the forest to the right and left. At length he stopped, and as we came up to him we said, "Well, Tom, what is the matter?"

His answer was, "Here is a good place for our camp."

"Why do you think so?" we asked.

He replied, "Do you see those balsams? They will furnish us with a bed, and this cluster of dry, dead small trees will give us the wood we need for our fire." So we quickly set to work to prepare for our all night stay in the woods.

The dogs were soon unharnessed, and seemed thankful to get their heads out of their collars. They were never tied up, neither did they ever desert us, or take the back track for home. Some of the younger ones often organized a rabbit hunt on their own responsibility, and had some sport. The older and wiser ones looked around for the most cosy and sheltered spots, and there began to prepare their resting places for the night. They would carefully scrape away the snow until they came to the ground, and there, with teeth and paws, would make the spot as smooth and even as possible. They would then curl themselves up, and patiently wait until they were called to supper. After unharnessing our dogs, our next work was with our axes, and there was a good sharp one for the missionary, to cut down some of the green balsams and dry, dead trees. Then using our snowshoes as shovels, from the place selected for our camp we soon scraped away the snow, piling it up as well as we could to the right, left, and in rear of where we were to sleep. On the ground thus cleared of snow we spread out a layer of the balsam boughs, and in front, where the wind would blow the smoke from us, we made up a large fire with the small dry trees which we had cut down.

On this blazing log fire we put our two kettles, which we had filled with snow. When it melted down, we refilled the kettles, until enough water was secured. In the large kettle we boiled a piece of fat meat, of goodly size, and in the other we made our tea.

On my first trip I carried with me a tin basin, a towel, and a cake of soap. At our first campfire, when the snow had been melted in our kettle, I asked the guide to give me a little of the water in my basin. Suspecting the purpose for which I wanted it, he said, "What are you going to do with it?"

"Wash my face and hands," I replied.

Very earnestly he answered, "Please, Missionary, do not do so."

I was longing for a good wash, for I felt like a chimney sweep. We had been travelling for hours through a region of country where, in the previous summer, great forest fires had raged, leaving many of the trunks of the trees charred and black. Against some of them we had often rubbed, and to some of them, or their branches, we had to cling as we went dashing down some of the ravines. The result of these weary hours of toil amid charred trunks was very visible, and I rejoiced that an opportunity had arrived when I could wash off the sooty stuff. Great indeed was my surprise to hear this strong protest on the part of my guide against my doing anything of the kind.

"Why should I not wash?" I said, holding up my blackened hands.

"You must not let water touch you out in the open air, when it is so very cold as it is today," was his answer.

I was very inexperienced then, and not willing to lose my wash, which I so much needed; I did not heed the warning. Having a blazing fire before me and a good dry towel, I ventured to take the wash, and for a minute or two after felt much better. Soon, however, there were strange prickling sensations on the tops of my hands, and then they began to chap and bleed, and they became very sore, and did not get well for weeks. The one experiment of washing in the open air with the temperature in the fifties below zero was quite enough. In the following years I left the soap at home and only carried the towel. When very much in need of a wash, I had to be content with a dry rub with the towel. Mrs. Young used to say, when I returned from some of these trips, that I looked like old mahogany. The bath was then considered a much needed luxury.

For our food, when travelling in such cold weather, we preferred the fattest meat we could obtain. From personal experience I can endorse the statements of Arctic explorers about the value of fat or oil and blubber as articles of food, and the natural craving of the system for them. Nothing else seemed to supply the same amount of internal heat. As the result of experience, we carried the fattest kind of meat.

As soon as the snow was melted down in the larger of our kettles, meat sufficient for our party was soon put on and boiled. While it was cooking, we thawed out the frozen fish for our dogs. Such is the effect of the frost that they were as hard as stone, and it would have been cruel to have given them in that state to the noble animals that served us so well. Our plan was to put down a small log in front of the fire, so close to it that when the fish were placed against it, the intensity of the heat would soon thaw them out. The hungry dogs were ever sharp enough to know when their supper was being prepared; and as it was the only meal of the day for them, they crowded around us and were impatient at times, and had to be restrained.

Sometimes, in their eagerness and anxiety for their food, for it often required a long time for the fire to thaw the fish sufficiently for us to bend them, the dogs in crowding one before the other would get into a fight, and then there would be trouble. Two dogs of the same train very seldom fought with each other. Yoke fellows in toil, they were too wise to try to injure each other in needless conflict. So, when a battle began, the dogs quickly ranged themselves on the sides of their own comrades, and soon it was a conflict of train against train. At first I thought it cruel not to feed them more frequently, but I found as all experienced dog drivers had told me, that one good meal a day was the best for them. So great were my sympathies for them that sometimes I would give them a good breakfast in the morning; but it did not turn out to be of any real benefit. The additional meal made them sluggish and short winded, and they did not seem to thrive so well. Good whitefish was the best food we could give them, and on this diet they could thrive and work as on no other.

A goodly number of dog shoes were very necessary on these rough trips. Dogs' feet are tender, and are liable to injury from various causes. On the smooth glare ice the pads of the feet would sometimes wear so thin that they bled a good deal. Then on the rough roads there was always the danger of their breaking off a claw or running a sliver through the webbing between the toes. Many of the wise old dogs that had become accustomed to these shoes, and thus knew their value, would suddenly stop the whole train, and by holding up an injured foot very eloquently, if mutely, tell the reason why they had done so.

The dog shoes are like heavy woolen mitts without the thumbs, made in different sizes. When a foot is injured, the mitt is drawn on and securely tied with a piece of soft deerskin. Then the grateful dog, which perhaps had refused to move before, springs to his work, often giving out his joyous barks of gratitude. So fond do some of the dogs become of these warm woolen shoes that instances are known where they have come into the camp from their cold resting places in the snow, and would not be content until the men got up and put shoes on all of their feet. Then, with every demonstration of gratitude, they have gone back to their holes in the snow.

Our dogs having been fed, we next make our simple arrangements for our own supper.

A number of balsam boughs are spread over the spot near the fires, from which the snow has been scraped away by our snowshoes. On these is laid our table cloth, which was generally an empty flour bag, cut down the side. Our dishes, all of tin, are placed in order, and around we gather with vigorous appetites. It is fortunate that they are so good, as otherwise our homely fare would not be much prized. The large piece of fat meat is served up in a tin pan, and our pint cups are filled up with hot tea. If we are fortunate enough to have some bread which was far from being always the case, we thaw it out and eat it with our meat. Vegetables were unknown on these trips. Our great staple was fat meat, and the fatter the better; morning, noon, and night, and often between times did we stop and eat fat meat. If we did vary the menu, it would be by making a raid on the dogs' supply, and in the evening camp cooking ourselves a good kettle of fish.

As we dared not wash our hands or faces, of course such a thing as washing dishes was unknown. When supper was in progress, Jack Frost made us busy in keeping ourselves and provisions warm. I have seen the large piece of meat put back into the pot three times during the one meal, to warm it up. I have seen the ice gather on the top of the cup of tea that a few minutes before was boiling vigorously in the kettle.

After supper wood was cut, to be in readiness for the morning's fire; and every break in clothes or harness was repaired, that there might be no delay in making a good start. Then the guide, who always had charge of all these things, when satisfied that all was arranged, would say, "Missionary, we are ready for prayers." The Bible and hymn book were brought out, and the Indians gathered round me, and there together we offered up our evening devotions. Would that our readers could have seen us! The background is of dense balsam trees, whose great drooping branches, partially covered with snow, sweep the ground. Above us are the bright stars, and, it may be, the flashing auroras. In front of us is the blazing fire, and scattered around us, in picturesque confusion, are our dogsleds, snowshoes, harness, and the other essentials of our outfit. A few of the dogs generally insisted on remaining up until their masters had retired, and they were now to be seen in various postures around us. With uncovered heads, no matter how intense the cold, Christian Indians listened reverently, while in their own language I read from the precious volume which they have learned to love so well. Then together we sang a hymn. Frequently it would be the Evening Hymn, the verse of which in their beautiful Cree language is as follows:

> "Ne mahmechemou ne muntome
> Kahke wastanahmahweyan,
> Kah nah way yemin Kechahyah
> Ah kwah-nahtahtah-kwahnaoon."

After singing we bow in prayer. There is there, as there should be everywhere, a consciousness of our dependence upon the great Helper for protection and support, and so the prayer we sang,

> "Keep me, O keep me, King of Kings,
> Beneath Thine own Almighty wings,"

is indeed our heart's desire.

Sometimes we are a hundred and fifty miles from the nearest human habitation. We are camping out in the woods in a hole dug in the snow. We have no walls around us but the snow thrown out of the place in which we are huddled, with perhaps the addition of some balsam boughs. We have no roof above us but the stars. There in that place we are going to lie down and try to sleep during that bitter cold night. The light fire will soon go out. A foot of snow may fall upon us, and its coming will be welcomed, as its warmth will lessen our shivering. Prowling grey wolves may come near us, but the terrible Frost King is more to be feared then they.

Does anybody, who knows the efficacy of prayer, wonder that, as we draw near to God, "by prayer and supplication, with thanksgiving," we crave the assurance of His favor and smile, and that He, who never slumbers or sleeps, will be our Guardian and our Friend?

After prayers we soon retire to rest. The guide's familiar words soon after prayers used to be, "Now, Missionary, I will make your bed." This was his work, and he was adept at it. He first spread out a layer of evergreen boughs, and then on these he laid a large buffalo robe, and upon this a heavy blanket. Then, placing my pillow so that my head would be farthest away from the fire, he would say to me, "Now, if you will get into bed, I will cover you up and tuck you in."

Such a thing as disrobing out there in a wintry camp is unknown, unless, as the result of the violent exercise of running all day, a person's underclothing has become very damp by perspiration, and it is not safe to sleep in it in that condition.

Some travellers sleep in a fur bag, in which they manage to insert themselves, and then have it tightened around their necks. Then a large fur hood over the usual head gear completes their sleeping apparel. I used to wrap myself up in a heavy overcoat over my usual apparel, and then putting on long buffalo skin boots, fur mitts, cap, cape, and big scarves, considered myself rigged up for retiring. When thus wrapped, I used to have some difficulty in getting down into the bed, although it was only on the ground. When in position, the guide would throw over me another heavy blanket and fur robe. Then very skillfully, and in a way most motherly, he would begin at my feet and carefully tuck me in. Rapidly and deftly did he proceed with his work, and almost before I was aware of what he was doing, he had reached my head, which he began to cover completely up with the heavy robe which he seemed to be crowding down under my back and shoulders.

The first time he packed me in in this manner I was only able to stand it for a minute or two, as I thought I should be smothered. So I very suddenly threw up my arms and sent the whole upper covering off in a hurry.

"Do you wish to smother me, man?" I said. "I cannot live with my head covered up like that!"

Without any annoyance at my having so quickly undone his work, he replied very kindly, "I know it must be hard work for you white people to sleep with your heads completely covered up, but you will have to do it here, or you will freeze to death. You must be very careful, for this seems to be a very cold night indeed." Then he called my attention to the distant thunder-like sounds which we had been hearing occasionally during the evening. That, he told me, was the ice, from four to six feet thick, on the great lake, cracking in the bitter cold. "Look at the smoke," he added. "See how it keeps very near the ground. It does that in the bitter cold nights."

From the trees around us we heard occasionally a sharp pistol like report, loud enough at times to make a nervous person fancy that lurking enemies were firing at us.

The observant Indians say these loud reports are burstings in the trees caused by the freezing of the sap.

Admiring his cleverness and kindness, I told him that I had been taught that every person requires so many cubic feet of fresh air; and, cold or no cold, how did he think I could get my share with my head covered up as he desired? "You must do with less out here," he said, as he proceeded to cover me up again, while I tried to arrange myself so that I could at least have a small portion of air. Kindly and patiently he humored me, and then, when he had finished tucking me in, he said, "Now, Missionary, good night; but don't stir. If you do, you may disarrange your coverings while you sleep, and you may freeze to death without waking up."

"Don't stir!" What a command, I thought, to give a tired traveller whose bones ache from his long snow shoe tramping in the woods, whose nerves and muscles are unstrung, and who, like others when thus fatigued, has even found it helpful to his rest and comfort to turn occasionally and stretch his limbs!

In this frame of mind, and under this order, which, after all, I felt must be obeyed for fear of the dire results that might follow, I at length managed to fall asleep, for I was very weary. After a while I woke up to a state of semi-consciousness, and found myself tugging and pulling at what I thought in my dreamy condition was the end of an axe handle. The vague impression on my mind was, that some careless Indian had left his axe just behind my head, and in the night the handle had fallen across my face, and I had now got hold of the end of it. Fortunately for me, I very quickly after this woke fully up, and then found out that what I had imagined to be the end of an axe handle was my own nose; and a badly frozen one it was, and both of my ears were about in the same condition.

With the guide's last orders in my ears, I think I must have gone to sleep all right, but I suppose, from the unusual smothering sensation, unconsciously I must have pushed down the robes from my face, and uncovered my head and my hand, and then gradually returned to consciousness with the above results. However, after a few nights of this severe kind of discipline, I at length became as able to sleep with my head covered up as an Indian.

When a foot or eighteen inches of snow fell upon us, we rejoiced, for it added to our comfort, and caused us to sleep the better. Under this additional covering we generally rested a couple of hours longer than usual, often to make up for the loss of sleep of the previous nights, when we had found it impossible, or had considered it dangerous, to go to sleep.

The hardest work and the most disagreeable is the getting up from such a bed in such a place. Often, in spite of the intense cold, we are in a kind of a clammy perspiration, on account of the many wraps and coverings about us. As we throw off these outer garments, and spring up in our camp, Jack Frost instantly assails us in a way that makes us shiver, and often some are almost compelled to cry out in bitter anguish.

Fortunately the wood is always prepared the night before, and so, as quickly as possible, a great roaring fire is built up, and our breakfast of strong tea and fat meat is prepared and eaten with all speed.

There were times when the morning outlook was gloomy indeed, and our position was not an enviable one. On one of my trips, of only a hundred and eighty miles, in order to save expense, I only took with me one companion, and he was a young Indian lad of about sixteen years of age. We each had our own train of dogs, and as Old Voyager was leader we guided him by voice alone, and he did not disappoint us. One morning, when we sprang up from our wintry camp bed, we found that several inches of snow had fallen upon us during the night. As soon as possible we arranged our wood in order and endeavoured to kindle our fire. We had been late the previous evening in reaching this camping place, and so had to grope around in the rapidly increasing darkness for our wood. It was of very inferior quality, but as we had succeeded in cooking our suppers with part of it, we had not anticipated any trouble with the rest. The snow which had fallen upon it had not improved it, and so, as we lighted match after match, we were at first disgusted, and then alarmed, at finding that the poor stuff persistently refused to ignite. Of course we had to take our hands out of our big fur mitts when trying to light the matches. Before we had succeeded in our attempts to start the fire our hands began to chill, and soon they were so powerless that we were not able to hold a match in our fingers. Very naturally we became alarmed, but we persevered as long as possible. I remember that, taking one of the matches between my teeth and holding up an axe before me, I tried to jerk my head quick enough to light it in that way, but the experiment was not a success.

Suddenly there came the consciousness that we were not far from perishing if we could not make a fire. I quickly turned to my young comrade, and saw by the look in his face that he also grasped the situation, and was terrified at the outlook.

"Alec," I said, "this is a serious thing for us."

"Yes, Missionary," said he. "I am afraid we die here. If we can make no fire and have no breakfast, I am afraid we will freeze to death."

"Not so bad as that yet, Alec," I said. "God is our refuge and help. He has given us other ways by which we can get warm. As quickly as possible get on your snowshoes, and up with your hood and on with your mitts, and I will do likewise, and now see if you can catch me.

In much less time than I have taken to describe it, we were rigged up for rapid snowshoe running, and were off. Away I rushed through the woods as rapidly as I could on my snowshoes. The lad followed me, and thus we ran chasing and catching each other alternately as though we were a couple of boisterous school boys instead of a missionary and his Indian companion striving to save themselves from freezing to death.

After about half an hour of this most vigorous exercise, we felt the warmth coming back to our bodies, and then the hot blood began working its way out to our benumbed hands, and by and by we could bend our fingers again. When we felt the comfortable glow of warmth over our whole bodies, we rushed back again to the camp, and, gathering a quantity of birch bark which we found loosely hanging from the trees, and which is very flammable, we soon had a good fire and then our hot breakfast. At our morning devotions which followed there was a good deal of thanksgiving, and the grateful spirit continued in our hearts as we packed up our loads, harnessed up our dogs, and sped on our way. It was a very narrow escape. The King of Terrors looked us both in the face that cold morning, and very nearly chilled us into death by the icy fingers of the Frost King.

As the hours of daylight in the winter months in these high latitudes are so few, we generally roused ourselves up several hours before daylight. Often my kindhearted men endeavoured to get up first, and have a rousing fire made and breakfast cooked, before I would awake. This, however, did not occur very often, as such a bed was not conducive to sleep; so, generally, after about four or five hours in such a state of suffocation, I was thankful to get up the instant I heard anyone stirring. I would rather freeze to death than be suffocated.

There were times, not a few, when I was the first to get up, and kindle the fire and cook the breakfast before I called my faithful wearied companions, who, long accustomed to such hardships, could sleep on soundly, where for me it was an absolute impossibility. Sometimes my men, when thus aroused, would look up at the stars and say "Assam weputch," i.e., "Very early." All I had to do was to look gravely at my watch, and this satisfied them that it was all right. The breakfast was quickly eaten, our prayers were said, our sleds loaded, dogs captured and harnessed (with the Eskimo ones this was not always an easy task) and we were ready to start.

Before starting we generally threw the evergreen brush on which we had slept on the fire, and by its ruddy, cheerful light began our day's journey. When some mornings we made from twenty-five to forty miles before sunrise, the Indians began to think the stars were about right after all, and the missionary's

"Here the black bears are very numerous"

watch very fast. However, they were just as willing to get on rapidly as I was, and so did not find fault with the way in which I endeavoured to hurry our party along. I paid them extra whenever the record of a trip was broken, and we could lessen the number of nights in those open air camps in the snow.

We were six days in making our first winter trip to Nelson River. In after years we reduced it to four days. The trail is through one of the finest fur producing regions of the northwest. Here the wandering Indian hunters make their living by trapping such animals as the black and silver foxes, as well as the more common varieties of that animal. Here are to be found otter, mink, marten, beaver, ermine, bear, wolf, and many other kinds of the fur bearing animals. Here the black bear are very numerous. On one canoe trip one summer we saw no less than seven of them, one of which we shot and lived on for several days.

The adventurous fur traders come to purchase these valuable skins, and great fortunes have been made in the business. If, merely to make money and get rich, men are willing to come and put up with the hardships and privations of the country, what a disgrace to us if, for their souls' sake, we are afraid to follow in these hunters' trail, or, if need be, show them the way, that we may go with the glad story of the Savior's love!

CHAPTER X

Nelson River — A demonstrative welcome — First religious service — A four hour sermon — The Chief's eloquent reply — The old man with grandchildren in his wigwam — "Our Father" — "Then we are brothers" — "Yes" — "Then why is the white brother so long time in coming with the Gospel to his Indian brother?" — Glorious successes.

It was at my second visit to Nelson River that the work really commenced. Through some unforseen difficulty at the first visit, many of the natives were away. Hunting is even at the best a precarious mode of obtaining a livelihood. The movements of the herds of caribou, upon the flesh of which many of these Indians subsist for the greater part of the year, are very erratic. It is often difficult to arrange for a place of meeting, where food can be obtained in sufficient abundance while the religious services are being held.

It used to be very discouraging, after having travelled for several days together, either by canoe in summer, or dog-trains in winter, to reach a certain place which had been arranged for meeting, and find very few present. The deer and other animals on which they had expected to live, had gone in another direction, and the Indians had been obliged to follow them.

Everything, however, favored us on our second visit. We found over fifty families camped at the place of meeting, and full of curiosity to see the missionary. They had all sorts of strange notions in their minds. When Mr. Rundle, of the English Wesleyan Church, first went among some of the tribes of the great Saskatchewan country with his open Bible, preaching the wonderful gospel truths, great was the excitement of the people to know where this strange man had come from. So a great council was summoned, and the conjurers were ordered to find out all about it. After a great deal of drumming and dreaming and conjuring, they gravely reported that this strange man with his wonderful Book had been wrapped up in an envelope, and had come down from the Great Spirit on a rainbow!

The Nelson River Indians welcomed me very cordially, and were much more demonstrative in their greetings than were any of the other tribes I had visited, although I had my share of strange welcomes. Here the custom of handshaking was but little known, but the more ancient one of kissing prevailed. Great indeed was my amazement when I found myself surrounded by two hundred and fifty or three hundred Indians, men, women, and children, whose faces seemed in blissful ignorance of soap and water, but all waiting to kiss me. I felt unable to stand the ordeal, and so I managed to put them off with a shake of the hand, and a kind word or two.

At eight o'clock the next morning we called the Indians together for the first public religious service which most of them had ever attended. They were intensely interested. The Christian Indians from Norway House aided me in the opening services, and, being sweet singers, added very much to the interest. We sang several hymns, read a couple of lessons from the Bible, and engaged in prayer. At about nine o'clock I read as my text those sublime words: "For God so loved the world, that He gave His only begotten Son, that whosoever believeth in Him should not perish, but have everlasting life."

They listened with the most enrapt attention, while for four hours I talked to them of some of the truths of this glorious verse. They had never heard a sermon before, and were ignorant of the simplest truths of our blessed Christianity. I had to make everything plain and clear as I went along. I could not take anything for granted with that audience. I had to take them back to the creation and fall. Then I spoke of God's love in providence and grace; and of His greatest act of love, the gift of His only begotten beloved Son, the Lord Jesus Christ, who died that we might live. I dwelt on the benefits which come to us from the personal acceptance of the Savior. I tried hard to show how we, who had wandered so far away, were invited back to actual adoption into God's great family, as a conscious reality. I spoke of the universality and impartiality of God's love; of His willingness to receive all, to fill our hearts with joy and peace, to comfort us all through life, to sustain us in death, and then to take us to everlasting life in a world of light and glory.

The ever blessed Spirit most graciously applied the truth, as I tried, in the simplest and plainest way, to bring it down to their comprehension. The attention they gave showed that my words were being understood. Their bright eyes glistened and at times were filled with tears, and as I closed, the long pent-up silence gave place to loud exclamations of delight.

Then we translated into their language and sang part of the good old hymn:

> "O for a thousand tongues to sing
> My great Redeemer's praise,
> The glories of my God and King,
> The triumphs of His grace!"

Again we bowed in prayer, and, at my request, they repeated after me all the petitions which in short easy sentences we offered up to Him who is the hearer and answerer of prayer. A spirit of awe and solemnity seemed to rest upon us. It was the first time the great majority had ever attempted to pray in the Name of Jesus, and I felt a sweet assurance that those simple petitions, from the hearts and lips of those poor people, were not despised by Him whose great heart of love beats so true to all. After prayer I requested them all to again seat themselves on the ground, as I wished to hear from them about these great truths which I had come so far to tell them of. I wanted to know what were their wishes and determinations about becoming Christians. When I had finished, every eye turned towards the principal chief, as these Indians, like the other tribes, have their unwritten laws of precedence. He rose up from his place among his people, and, coming near me on my right hand, he made one of the most thrilling addresses I ever heard. Years have passed away since that hour, and yet the memory of that tall, straight, impassioned Indian is as vivid as ever. His actions were many, but all were graceful. His voice was particularly fine and full of pathos, for he spoke from his heart. Here is the bare outline of his speech, as, with my interpreter to aid me, I shortly afterwards wrote it down.

"Missionary, I have long lost faith in our old way of worship." Then pointing down to the outer edge of the audience, where some old conjurers and medicine men were seated, he said, "They know I have not cared for our old religion. I have neglected it. And I will tell you, Missionary, why I have not believed in our old religion for a long time. I hear God in the thunder, in the tempest, and in the storm. I see His power in the lightning that shivers the tree into kindling wood. I see His goodness in giving us the moose, caribou, beaver, and the bear. I see His lovingkindness in giving us, when the south winds blow, the ducks and geese; and when the snow and ice melt away, and our lakes and rivers are open again, I see how He fills them with fish. I have watched these things for years, and I see how during every moon of the year He gives us something; and so He has arranged it, that if we are only industrious and careful, we can always have something to eat. So thinking about these things which I had observed, I made up my mind years ago, that this Great Spirit, so kind and so watchful and so loving, did not care for the beating of the conjurer's drum, or the shaking of the rattle of the medicine man. So I for years have had no religion."

Then turning towards me and looking me in the face, he said, in tones that thrilled me, "Missionary, what you have said today fills up my heart and satisfies all its longings. It is just what I have been expecting to hear about the Great Spirit. I am so glad you have come with this wonderful story. Stay as long as you can; and when you have to go away, do not forget us, but come again as soon as you can."

Loud expressions of approval greeted these words of the chief. When he had finished, I said, "I want to hear from others, and I want your own views on these important things. Many responded to my request, and, with the exception of an old conjurer or two, who feared for their occupation, all spoke in the same strain as did the head chief. The last to speak was an old man with grizzly hair, and wild, excited movements. He was a queer, savage looking man, and came from the rear of the company to the front with strange springy movements. His hair was braided, and reached to his knees. Threading his way through the audience, he came up close to me, and then, pushing his fingers into his hair as far as its braided condition would allow, he exclaimed in a tone full of earnestness, "Missionary, once my hair was as black as a crow's wing, now it is getting white. Grey hairs here, and grandchildren in the wigwam, tell me that I am getting to be an old man; and yet I never before heard such things as you have told us today. I am so glad I did not die before I heard this wonderful story. Yet I am getting old. Grey hairs here, and grandchildren yonder, tell the story. Stay as long as you can, Missionary, tell us much of these things, and when you have to go away, come back soon, for I have grandchildren, and I have grey hairs, and may not live many winters more. Do come back soon."

He turned as though he would go back to his place and sit down; but he only went a step or two before he turned round and faced me, and said, "Missionary, may I say more?"

"Talk on," I said, "I am here now to listen."

"You said just now, 'Notawenan'." ("Our Father.")

"Yes," I said, "I did say, 'Our Father'."

"That is very new and sweet to us," he said, "We never thought of the Great Spirit as Father. We heard Him in the thunder, and saw Him in the lightning, and tempest, and blizzard, and we were afraid. So, when you tell us of the Great Spirit as Father, that is very beautiful to us."

Hesitating a moment, he stood there, a wild, picturesque Indian, yet my heart had strangely gone out in loving interest and sympathy to him.

Lifting up his eyes to mine, again he said, "May I say more?"

"Yes," I answered, "say on."

"You say, 'Notawenan' (Our Father). He is your Father?"

"Yes, He is my Father."

Then he said, while his eyes and voice yearned for the answer, "Does it mean He is my Father—poor Indian's Father?"

"Yes, O yes!" I exclaimed. "He is your Father too."

"Your Father—missionary's Father, and Indian's Father, too?" he repeated.

"Yes, that is true," I answered.

"Then we are brothers?" he almost shouted out.

"Yes, we are brothers," I replied. The excitement in the audience had become something wonderful. When our conversation with the old man had reached this point, and in such an unexpected, and yet dramatic manner, had so clearly brought out, not only the Fatherhood of God, but the oneness of the human family, the people could hardly restrain their expressions of delight. The old man, however, had not yet finished, and so, quietly restraining the most demonstrative ones, he again turned to me, and said—

"May I say more?"

"Yes, say on; say all that is in your heart."

Never can I forget his answer.

"Well, I do not want to be rude, but it does seem to me that you, my white brother, have been a long time in coming with that great Book and its wonderful story, to tell it to your Indian brothers in the woods."

This question thrilled me, and I found it hard to answer. This is the question that millions of weary, longing, waiting souls, dissatisfied with their false religions, and craving for that soul rest which only can be found in the hearty acceptance of the glorious gospel of the Son of God, are asking. I tried to apologize for the slowness of the advancement of the Redeemer's kingdom, and the apathy of those who, while acknowledging the brotherhood of humanity, so often forget that they are their brother's keeper.

We closed the service for a brief period, and then, as soon as a hurried dinner had been eaten, we all assembled again for the afternoon service. This second service lasted for five hours. After singing and prayer, I read the beautiful story of the Ethiopian eunuch, and the baptismal service. I endeavoured to explain what we meant by becoming Christians, and stated that I was willing to baptize all who would renounce the old way, with its polygamy, conjuring, gambling, and other vices, and from that time begin to worship the true God. Polygamy was the greatest stumbling block among them, as some of them had three or four wives. Intemperance here is but little known, on account perhaps of the great difficulty of importing liquor into a region so remote from civilization.

After I had spent a long time in making clear the doctrines of the blessed Book, and had answered many questions, I invited all who were willing to comply with these conditions, and desired baptism, to come to the front of the audience, where I was standing.

About forty men and women immediately responded, and came forward and seated themselves at my feet. Some were trembling, others were weeping; all seemed moved. Then I read the beautiful Scripture lessons in connection with the baptismal service for children, and dwelt upon the love of Jesus for children, and His willingness to receive them. I invited the parents to consecrate their children to God, even if they themselves were as yet undecided. We had a solemn and impressive time.

All desired new names, and for the great majority I had to make the selection. While baptizing them and selecting Christian names as additions to their generally poetic and expressive Indian names, my constant prayer was, that they might "see His face, and His name" be written "in their foreheads."

Still there was some opposition. Satan would not thus easily be dispossessed or driven out. Old conjurers and medicine men, faithful followers of the enemy, quickly began their opposition. Their selfish natures were aroused. They were shrewd enough to see that if I succeeded, as I was likely to do, they, like Demetrius, the shrine maker of Diana, would soon be without an occupation. So at this afternoon gathering they were there to oppose. But they were in such a helpless minority that they dared do no worse than storm and threaten. One savage old conjurer rushed up to me, just as I was about to baptize his wife, who, with many others, had come for this sign and seal of her acceptance of Christ. Before I had perceived his purpose, or had power to stop him, he seized and shook her roughly, and, looking at me, in his impotent wrath, said in an insulting manner,

"Call her Atim (dog)."

"No," I said, looking kindly at the poor trembling

woman, "I will do nothing of the kind; but I will give her the sweetest name ever borne by woman, for it was the name of the mother of Jesus."

So I baptized her, "Mary".

We spent several days in giving lessons in the syllabic characters between the religious services, three of which we endeavoured to hold each day. Sometimes we assembled all the people together, and, with these characters marked on the side of a rock with a burnt stick, we taught them as best we could. At other times we went from tent to tent, and gave them lessons, and had religious conversation and prayer.

It was on one of these rounds of wigwam visitations that I came across Pe-pe-qua-na-pua, or Sandy Harte, the story of whose life and conversion has been so widely circulated. Several acquired such a knowledge of these characters that, by persevering for a few weeks, they were able to read very nicely in the blessed Book.

I left with them several dozen copies of the New Testament, hymn books, and catechisms in their own language.

So great was their anxiety for religious instruction, that many of them remained for three days after they had eaten all of their provisions. When I first heard this, I could hardly credit it, but found out by personal investigation that it was the actual fact. With tears in their eyes they bade me farewell, and said, that on account of their famishing children they must start off for their fishing and hunting grounds. But they added, "What we have heard from you will make us glad and thankful all the time."

With my faithful travelling companions, I made a trip out from Nelson River to another small band about thirty miles away. We spent the Sabbath in a miserable wigwam, where the snow and sleet dashed in upon us, making us shiver in spite of all we could do. Still, as the poor people were anxious to hear the gospel, we soon forgot our physical discomforts in the joy of preaching this great salvation. Nineteen of them accepted Christ as their Savior, and were baptized. We held a meeting for the purpose of hearing them tell of their wishes as to this blessed religion. Many very interesting things were said. We here record only one.

A fine looking man said, "What has fully decided me to endeavor to be a good Christian all my days is this. The missionary has told us many reasons, all sufficient to decide us; but the one that came very near to my heart was, that all the little children who have died have been taken to that better land, and there they are with the loving Savior in heaven. My little ones have passed away, leaving my heart sore and bleeding. I yearn after them; I long to meet them again. So I want so to live that when I die Jesus will permit me to embrace them, and never be separated from them again."

On this trip, we found at another small camp a young girl, about twelve years of age, dying of tuberculosis. I talked to her of Jesus and heaven, and prayed with her several times. When the closing scene drew near, she said to her sorrowing mother, "I am glad the praying man has told me such words of comfort. I have lost that dread of death I had. I believe that dear Jesus will take me to that better land; but, mother, when you come, will you look for me until you find me: for I do wish to see you again."

Is it any wonder that I became deeply attached to these Nelson River Indians? I visited them twice a year, and by pen and voice pleaded for them until my heart's desire was obtained, and a beloved brother volunteered to go and live among them. Of him with joy I write.

CHAPTER XI

A welcome accession — The Rev. John Semmens — A devoted young missionary — First to reside at Nelson River — In labor and in peril often — In journeys often by dog-trains together — The centenarian Christian — William Papanekis — His godly life and wondrous translation.

One cold wintry morning we were gladdened by the arrival of a dear brother and colleague in the work, the Rev. John Semmens, who had left a comfortable charge in Ontario, and had come out to help me in the blessed work. Brother Semmens had to taste, early in his missionary work among the Indians, some of the dangers incident to such a life. He came to us at Norway House in the depth of the winter, and suffered much from the intense cold and blizzards. One night, while trying to rest in the camp in the woods on his way out, a fierce storm blew down a large tree, which fell very close to him. Providentially no one was hurt.

He soon became very popular among the Indians, for whom he subsequently gave many years of successful, self-denying toil. His presence with us in our home was a great joy. None but those who have been deprived of the pleasure of the society and fellowship of kindred spirits can realize what a benediction this sweet spirited and devoted young brother was in our home. With one great object before us, that of doing the greatest possible good we could to the Indians among whom we were called to labor, and fortunately seeing "eye to eye" as to the methods of our work, we spent some months and different years in harmony in doing what we could.

Brother Semmens' name will ever be associated with the Nelson River Mission, as he was the first missionary to go and live in that region of the country and among those wandering aborigines, who had received me with such expressions of joy when on my visits, so few, alas! and far between. Very many indeed were Mr. Semmens' hardships. Their wandering life made his work slow and at times discouraging. He had not at first a knowledge of their language, and could not always get an interpreter. However, as the love of Christ was the constraining motive, he persevered, and great indeed was his success among them.

We will not here insert any of the many thrilling incidents of his romantic pioneer work among them. We hope that from his fluent pen will come his own record, which will be a very valuable addition to missionary literature. Often did we, like the early ones sent out by the Master in pairs, go together on some long and difficult exploring tours. At many a camp fire and in many a wigwam have we talked and pleaded with the wandering Indians, and have besought them to be reconciled to God. Hundreds of miles have we tramped on together, until our limbs were cramped and our feet were bleeding; and then, in the cold camp after supper and prayers, have we crowded in close together under the same robes and tried to sleep. Will either of us ever forget the trip in to District Meeting at Winnipeg, where on the great Lake we got separated from the rest of our party, but by rapid travelling reached the comfortable home and cordial welcome of our beloved Chairman, the Rev. George Young, thus escaping the terrible blizzard in which so many suffered? Then the return trip was equally exciting and perilous. We left Winnipeg on the Saturday afternoon with our heavily loaded dog sleds. At Mr. Sifton's, near Selkirk, we were cordially welcomed, and here we remained in quiet rest and joyous worship during the Sabbath day. When the clock struck the hour of midnight, we exchanged our black clothes for our leather suits. We harnessed up our dogs, and then, after eating a midnight meal, we bade our host and hostess farewell, and pushed out under the stars on our long journey to the far North. Mr. Semmens'

"We exchanged our black clothes for our leather suits."

journey would not be finished until he was six or seven hundred miles nearer the North Pole.

Mr. Sifton told me in after years, that they could only sit there and weep as they thought of our starting off in the bitter cold and gloom of that midnight hour on such a journey. Missionary work to them from that hour took on itself additional interest, and ever after much greater, if possible, was their love for those who for His sake were willing to endure hardness in extending the knowledge of His Name.

Before the sun rose, we were near the Willow Islands, and there we had our breakfast. It was getting late in the winter season, and so the reflection of the brilliant rays of the sun on the dazzlingly white snowy waste of Lake Winnipeg gave us both a touch of snow blindness. Still, as we could see a little, we only stopped when it was necessary, and rapidly hurried on. When about twenty miles from Beren's River night came down upon us, but I could not bear the idea of having again to sleep in a miserable camp when home was so near, for at this time I was in charge of the new work among the Saulteaux. So I said to Brother Semmens, and to our two well disciplined dog drivers, "Courage, men, a little longer; let us not stop here in the bitter cold when our homes are so near." The Indians responded with a will, and rejoiced that we were to go on. But my beloved Brother Semmens was completely tired out, and my heart was filled with sorrow as I saw how utterly exhausted he was. Throwing himself down on the cold, icy surface of the lake, he said, "Throw me out a blanket and a piece of pemmican, and leave me here. I cannot go a step further. The rest of you have wives and children to lure you on to your homes; I have none. I can go no farther. My feet are bleeding from the straps of my snow shoes. I will stay here. Never mind me."

Thus the dear fellow talked, for he was exhausted and discouraged. I did not feel much better, but I tried to put a bold face on the matter, and I said, "No, indeed, we will not leave you here. We are going on, and we are going to take you with us; and a good supper under a roof, and then a warm bed, are to be yours before morning comes."

One of my dogs, called Muff, a magnificent but over ambitious St. Bernard, the gift of Mrs. Andrew Allen, of Montreal, had broken her collar bone during this trip. The plan generally adopted, when such an accident happens to one of the dogs, was to kill it at once, and then push on with the diminished train. However, as Muff was such a valuable dog, and there was a possibility of her recovering, I decided to carry her home, although we were a long distance from it. I so arranged my sled that she could ride upon it, and she soon became quite reconciled to her place. But it meant a good deal of hard running for me. Before the accident occurred, I could ride a great part of the time, although we had over six hundred pounds weight upon the sled. However, as Jack was one of the train, I was able to ride when the ice was good. Now, however, with one dog less in the train, and that one as so much additional weight on the sled, it meant the end of my riding for that trip.

Very quickly did I decide how to act in order to help my dear companion in tribulation. With our axes my companions and I chopped a hole in the solidly packed snow and ice near the shore of the lake. In this we spread out a buffalo robe, and on it we placed the injured dog. Then around her we placed the greater part of the load of the dog sled, and then covered all up as well as we could with the large deer skin sleigh wrapper. Giving the dog orders to guard well the supplies from prowling wild animals, and making a large number of tracks as an additional precaution, we left Muff there with her goods.

Then we drove the dogs over to the spot where Mr. Semmens lay, and, wrapping him well up in robes and putting a little pillow under his head, we tied him on the sled, and started off on the last stage of our journey. We were all so weary that we made but slow progress, and it was after midnight before the welcome Mission house was reached, and we were within the walls of home.

Mr. Semmens had fortunately slept most of the way. A good supper, after a warm bath, and then a long, sweet, dreamless sleep, that lasted until nearly noon of the next day, wonderfully refreshed his spirits, and as he came down and greeted us, his first words were, "O Egerton, I am so glad you did not leave me there to perish on the ice!"

Still in his prime, with a noble wife and precious children around him, he is in that land doing good service for the Master. From him we yet expect to hear good tidings, for in physical strength and mental equipment and thorough consecration to his work he is the peer of any who there toil.

The Centenarian

One of the first Indians to attract our attention at Norway House was a venerable looking old man of more than usual height. His appearance was quite patriarchal. His welcome had been most cordial, and his words seemed to us like a loving benediction. He called us his children, and welcomed us to our home and work in the name of the Lord Jesus.

As he was very aged, and had to come a long distance from his home to the Sunday morning service, we invited him, on the first Sunday after our arrival at the Mission, to dine with us. He was very grateful, and said this would enable him to remain for the afternoon native service, which he dearly prized. He was not only a blessed Christian, but a natural gentleman. We were so drawn towards him that we invited him to dine with us, and then rest awhile, each Sabbath between the services.

Like all the old Indians, his age was unknown, but

it must have been over a century, as men above fifty said he was called an old man when they were boys. The fact that his name had been on the Hudson's Bay Company's book for eighty years, as a skilful hunter, makes it quite safe to class him as a centenarian.

His testimony to the blessedness of the gospel was very clear and delightful. He "knew whom he had believed," and ever rejoiced in the blessed assurance that he would have grace given to keep him to the end. He was one of the first converts of the early missionaries, and had remained true and steadfast. He had been a successful Class Leader for many years, and faithfully and well did he attend to his duties. If any of his members were not at the meeting, he knew the reason why before the next evening, if they were within five or six miles of his home.

As he lived a couple of years after we reached the Mission, we got to be very well acquainted, and it was ever a blessing to talk to him of spiritual things. I had a very convincing evidence one day of the thoroughness with which he had renounced his old way of life and its sinful practices. We had been talking on various subjects, and the matter of different kinds of beliefs came up. As he had a very retentive memory, and I had been told that he was the best authority on old Indian religions and ways, I took out of my pocket a note book and pencil, and said, "Mismis (Grandfather), I want you to tell me some things about your old conjurings and religions. I may want to write a book some time, and put some of these things in it."

The dear old man's face became clouded, and he shook his head and remained silent.

I urged my request, saying I felt certain he, from his great age, must have much to talk about. For his answer, he sat down in his chair, and, putting his elbows on his knees, buried his face in his hands, and seemed lost in a kind of reverie.

I waited for a few minutes, for all was hushed and still. His family had heard my question, and they had become intensely interested. The silence became almost painful, and so I said in a cheery strain, "Come, grandfather, I am waiting to write down what you have to say."

Suddenly he sprang up in a way that startled us all, and, stretching out his hand like an orator, he began:

"Missionary! the old wicked life is like a nightmare, like a bad dream, like a terrible sickness that made us cry out with pain. I am trying to banish it, to forget it, to wipe it out of my memory. Please do not ask me to talk about it, or to bring it up. I could not sleep; I would be miserable."

Of course I put away my book and pencil, and did not further trouble the dear old man, who seemed so loath to talk about his old belief.

The next Sunday after this interview we had a Fellowship Meeting in the church. One of the first to speak was this venerable grandfather. He said, "The missionary wanted me to talk to him about my old religion. I could not do it. It was my enemy. It only made me miserable. The more I followed it, the more unhappy I was. So I have cast it out of my life, and from my heart. Would that I could wash it out of my memory!" Then he added, "But perhaps the memory of it helps to make me love my Savior better, as I can remember from what He has saved me. I was so far from him, and so dark and sinful. He reached down His strong arm and lifted me out of the dark place, and put me into the light. O, I am so thankful Jesus saved me, and I love to talk about it."

And he did talk about it, and our hearts rejoiced with him.

Of him it could be truthfully said, "What he once loved he now hates, and does it so thoroughly that he does not even wish to talk about it."

While writing these pleasant memories, perhaps I cannot do better than here record the remarkable closing scenes of the life of this venerable old man, the patriarch of the village. His family was a large one. He had several sons. Worthy, excellent men they were. About some of them we shall have interesting things to say. The youngest, Edward, it was my joy to lead into the sweet assurance that his sins were all forgiven. In July, 1889, he was ordained, in Winnipeg, to the office and work of the Christian ministry.

Martin, another of his sons, was one of my most loved and trusted guides, and my companion, for thousands of miles, in birch canoe by summer, and dog trains by winter. We have looked death in the face together many times, but I never knew him to flinch or play a coward's part. Supplies might fail, and storms and head winds delay us, until starvation stared us in the face, and even the missionary himself began to question the wisdom of taking these journeys where the chances were largely against our return, when from Martin, or one of the others, would come the apt quotation from the sacred Word, or from their musical voices the cheering hymn which said,

> "Give to the winds thy fears;
> Hope, and be undismayed:
> God hears thy sighs, and counts thy tears,
> God shall lift up thy head.
>
> "Through waves and clouds and storms
> He gently clears thy way:
> Wait thou His time, so shall this night
> Soon end in joyous day."

Very precious and very real were many of the blessed promises, and their fulfillment, to us in those times of

"We have looked death in the face together many times."

peril and danger, when death seemed to be so near, and we so helpless and dependent upon the Almighty arm.

Another son of this old saint was Samuel, the courageous guide and modest, unassuming Christian. He was the one who guided his well loaded brigade up the mighty Saskatchewan River to the rescue of the whites there, and having safely and grandly done his work, "holding on to God," went up the shining way so triumphantly that there lingered behind on his once pallid face some radiance of the glory like that into which he had entered; and some seeing it were smitten with a longing to have it as their portion, and so, then and there, they gave themselves to God. Of him we shall hear more farther on.

One day when the venerable father met his class, he told his members that his work was nearly done, and very soon indeed he expected to pass over to the better land. Although as well as he had been for months, yet he had a premonition that the end of his life was near. Very lovingly and faithfully did he talk to them, and exhorted them to be faithful to the end.

The next day he sent for me, and requested me to appoint one of his sons as leader of his class, if I thought him worthy of the place.

I said, "We do not want to lose you. Your class members all love you. Why resign your position?"

A strange look in his face told me that he had set his heart on joining another company, and that it seemed as though he was only postponing his departure until his little affairs on earth were set in order.

"I am going very soon now, and I want to have everything settled before I go; and I shall be so glad to see my son William leader of my class, if you think it best."

As the son was a most excellent man the appointment was made, much to the aged father's delight.

The next day he had assembled all the old members who had renounced their old ways and become Christians at the same time he did over thirty years before. There were enough of them to fill his house, and all came who possibly could. They sang and prayed together, and then he stood up before them and addressed them in loving and affectionate words.

As I sat there and looked upon the scene, while, for about an hour, he was reviewing the past, and talking of God's goodness in bringing them out of darkness, and conferring so many blessings upon them, I thought of Joshua's memorable gathering of the elder people at Shechem to hear his dying charge. At his request I administered to them all, and those of his many relations who were worthy, the sacrament of the Lord's Supper. It was a most impressive time. He whose dying we celebrated seemed in Spirit very blessedly near.

Then perhaps another hour was spent, at his desire, in singing his favorite hymns and in prayer. He entered with great spirit into the devotions, and many said afterwards, "Heaven seemed very near." I shook hands with him and said, "Good bye," and returned to my home. With the exception of a little weariness on account of the exciting services through which he had passed, I saw no change in him. His voice was just as cheery, his eye as bright, his grip as firm as usual, and I saw no reason why he should not live a good while yet.

About an hour after, while talking the matter over with Mrs. Young, and giving her some of the specially interesting incidents of the memorable services with our dear old friend, there was a sudden call for me by an Indian, who, rushing in without any ceremony, exclaimed, "Come quickly; grandfather is dead!" I hurriedly returned with him, and found that the aged patriarch had indeed passed away.

They told me that after I had left them he continued for a time to speak loving words of counsel and advice to them. Then, as had been his habit, he lay down on his bed, and drew his blanket around him, as though prepared for rest. As they knew he must be weary, they kept very still, so as not to disturb him. Not hearing him breathe, one of them touched him, and found that he had fallen into that sleep which here knows no waking. He was not, for God has taken him.

It was a remarkable death. The great difficulty among us seemed to be, to realize the presence of death at all. He suffered from no disease, and never complained of pain. His mind was unclouded till the last. In his humble position he had done his work, and done it well; and so now, with all the confidence of a loving child resting in the arms of a mother, he laid his head down on the bosom of his Lord.

With rejoicing, rather than weeping, we laid in the little graveyard all that was mortal of William Papanekis. We missed him very much, for his presence was like the sunshine, and his prayers were benedictions upon us all.

CHAPTER XII

Rev. James Evans, the peerless missionary — His journeys by canoe and dog-train — The Cree syllabic characters, his invention — Lord Dufferin's words concerning him — His successes — His trials — Accidental shooting of his interpreter — Surrendering himself to the avengers — Adopted into a Chipewyan family — Visit to England — Sudden death.

Without any question, the Rev. James Evans was the grandest and most successful of all our Indian missionaries. Of him it can be said most emphatically, while others have done well, he excelled them all.

In burning zeal, in heroic efforts, in journeys often, in tact that never failed in many a trying hour, in success most marvelous, in a vivacity and sprightliness that never succumbed to discouragement, in a faith that never faltered, and in a zeal for the spread of our blessed Christianity that never grew less, James Evans stands among us without a peer.

If full accounts of his long journeys in the wilds of the great north west could be written, they would equal in thrilling interest anything of the kind known in modern missionary annals. There is hardly an Indian Mission of any prominence today in the whole of the vast north-west, whether belonging to the Church of England, the Roman Catholic, or the Methodist Church, that James Evans did not commence; and the reason why the Methodist Church today does not hold them all is, because the apathetic Church did not respond to his thrilling appeals, and send in men to take possession and hold the fields as fast as they were successfully opened up by him.

From the northern shores of Lake Superior away to the ultima Thule that lies beyond the waters of Athabasca and Slave Lakes, where the aurora borealis holds high carnival; from the beautiful prairies of the

Bow and Saskatchewan Rivers to the muskegs and sterile regions of Hudson Bay; from the fair and fertile domains of Red and Assiniboine Rivers, to the foothills of the Rocky Mountains, enduring footprints of James Evans may still be seen. At many a camp fire, and in many a lonely wigwam, old Indians yet linger, whose eyes brighten and whose tongues wax eloquent as they recall that man whose deeds live on, and whose converts from the old ways are still to be counted by scores. Many a weary hour has been charmed away, as I have listened to Papanekis the elder, Henry Budd, or some other old Indian guide or dog driver, or canoe man, while they rehearsed the thrilling adventures, narrow escapes, wonderful deliverances, and also some of the tragic events, through which they passed in company with the "Nistum Ayumeaookemou," the "first missionary."

The dog drivers loved to talk about Mr. Evans' wonderful train of half dogs, half wolves, with which for years he travelled. With great enthusiasm they would talk of their marvelous speed and endurance, of their fierceness and sagacity; of how, when the nights in the wintry camps were unusually cold say fifty or sixty degrees below zero these fierce animals would crowd into the camp, and lying on their backs, would hold up both their fore and hind feet, and thus mutely beg for someone to have compassion upon them and put on the warm woolen dog shoes.

His canoe trips were often of many weeks duration, and extended for thousands of miles. No river seemed too rapid, and no lake too stormy, to deter him in his untiring zeal to find the Indian in his solitudes, and preach to him the ever blessed gospel. Ever on the lookout for improvements to aid him in more rapid transit through the country, Mr. Evans constructed a canoe out of sheet tin. This the Indians called the "Island of light," on account of its flashing back the sun's rays as it glided along propelled by the strong

"No river seemed too rapid, and no lake too stormy."

paddles in the hands of the well trained crew. With them they carried in this novel craft solder and soldering iron, and when they had the misfortune to run upon a rock they went ashore and quickly repaired the injured place.

Mr. Evans had been for years a minister and missionary in the Canadian Methodist Church. With the Rev. William Case he had been very successfully employed among the Indians in the province of Ontario. When the English Wesleyan Society decided to begin work among the neglected tribes in the Hudson's Bay Territories, the Rev. James Evans was the man appointed to be the leader of the devoted band. In order to reach Norway House, which was to be his first principal Mission, his household effects had to be shipped from Toronto to England, and thence reshipped to York Factory on the Hudson Bay. From this place they had to be taken up by boats to Norway House in the interior, a distance of five hundred miles. Seventy times they had to be lifted out of these inland boats and carried along the portages, around falls and cataracts before they reached their destination.

Mr. Evans himself went by boat from Toronto. The trip from Thunder Bay in Lake Superior to Norway House was performed in a birch bark canoe. Hundreds of Indians listened to his burning messages, and great good was done by him and his faithful companions in arms, among them being the heroic Mr. Barnley, and Mr. Rundle, of the English Wesleyan Church.

The great work of Mr. Evans' life, and that with which his name will be ever associated, was undoubtedly the invention and perfecting of what is now so widely known as the Cree syllabic characters. What first led him to this invention was the difficulty he and others had in teaching the Indians to read in the ordinary way. They are hunters, and so are very much on the move, like the animals they seek. Today their tents are pitched where there is good fishing, and perhaps in two weeks they are far away in the deep forests, where roam the caribou, or on the banks of streams where the beavers build their wonderful dams and curious homes. The main thought in this master missionary's mind was, "Can I possibly devise a plan by which these wandering people can learn to read more easily?"

The principle of the characters which he adopted is phonetic. There are no silent letters. Each character represents a syllable; hence no spelling is required. As soon as the alphabet is mastered, (and a few additional secondary signs, some of which represent consonants, and some aspirates, and some partially change the sound of the main character), the Indian student, be he a man or woman of eighty, or a child of six years, can commence at the first chapter of Genesis and read on, slowly of course at first, but in a few days with surprising ease and accuracy.

Many were Mr. Evans' difficulties in perfecting this invention and putting it in practical use, even after he had got the scheme clear and distinct in his own mind. He was hundreds of miles away from civilization. Very little indeed had he with which to work. Yet with him there was no such word as failure. Obtaining, as a great favor, the thin sheets of lead that were around the tea chest of the fur traders, he melted these down into little bars, and from them cut out his first types. His ink was made out of the soot of the chimneys, and his first paper was birch bark. After a good deal of effort, and the exercise of much ingenuity, he made a press, and then the work began.

Great indeed was the amazement and delight of the Indians. The fact that the bark could "talk" was to them most wonderful. Portions of the Gospels were first printed, and then some of the beautiful hymns. The story of this invention reached the Wesleyan Home Society. Generous help was afforded. A good supply of these types was cast in London, and with a good press and all the essential requisites, including a large quantity of paper, was sent out to that Mission, and for years it was the great point from which considerable portions of the Word of God were scattered among the wandering tribes, conferring unnumbered blessings upon them. In later years the noble British and Foreign Bible Society has taken charge of the work; and now, thanks to their generosity, the Indians have the blessed Word scattered among them, and thousands can read its glorious truths.

All the churches having missions in that great land have availed themselves, more or less, of Mr. Evans' invention. To suit other tribes speaking different languages, the characters have been modified or have had additions to them, to correspond with sounds in those languages which were not in the Cree. Even in Greenland the Moravian missionaries are now using Evans' syllabic characters with great success among the Eskimo.

When Lord Dufferin was Governor General of the Dominion of Canada, hearing that a couple of missionaries from the Indian tribes were in Ottawa, where he resided, he sent a courteous request for us to call upon him. With two or three friends, Mr. Crosby, our successful and energetic missionary from British Columbia, and I, obeyed the summons.

The interview was a very pleasant and profitable one. Lord Dufferin questioned Mr. Crosby about British Columbia and his work, and was pleased to hear of his great success. After a bright and earnest conversation with me in reference to the Indians of the North West Territories, in which his Excellency expressed his solicitude for the welfare and happiness of the aboriginal tribes of forest men, he made some inquiries in reference to missionary work among them, and seemed much pleased with the answers I was able to give. In mentioning the help I had in my work, I showed him my Cree Testament printed in Evans' syllabic characters, and explained the invention to him.

At once his curiosity was excited, and, jumping up, he hurried off for pen and ink, and got me to write out the whole alphabet for him; and then, with that glee and vivacity for which his lordship was so noted, he constituted me his teacher, and commenced at once to master them.

As their simplicity, and yet wonderful adaptation for their designed work, became evident to him for in a short time he was able to read a portion of the Lord's Prayer Lord Dufferin was much excited, and, getting up from his chair and holding up the Testament in his hand, exclaimed, "Why, Mr. Young, what a blessing to humanity the man was who invented that alphabet!"

Then he added, "I profess to be a kind of a literary man myself, and try to keep posted up in my reading of what is going on, but I never heard of this before. The fact is, the nation has given many a man a title, and a pension, and then a resting place and a monument in Westminster Abbey, who never did half so much for his fellow creatures."

Then again he asked, "Who did you say was the author or inventor of these characters?"

"The Rev. James Evans," I replied.

"Well, why is it I never heard of him before, I wonder?"

My reply was, "My lord, perhaps the reason why you never heard of him before was because he was a humble, modest Methodist preacher."

With a laugh he replied, "That may have been it," and then the conversation changed.

Mr. Evans was ever anxious that the Indian converts should at once be made to understand all the duties and responsibilities of the new life on which they were entering. He was a fearless man, and boldly declared unto them the whole counsel of God. Knowing the blighting, destroying influences of the "fire water" upon the Indian race, he made the Church a total abstinence society, and, as all missionaries should, he set them the example of his own life. Then, as regards the keeping of the Sabbath, he took his stand on the Word of God, and preached the absolute necessity of the one day's rest in seven. In later years we saw the good results of the scriptural lessons which he and his worthy successors taught in reference to the holy day.

Many and severe were the trials, and mysterious some of the persecutions, which this glorious man had to bear. Because of his unswerving loyalty to truth, and his conscientious and fearless teaching of all the commandments of God's Word, some in high authority, who at first were supposed to be friendly, turned against him, and became his unprincipled foes. The trouble first seemed to begin when Mr. Evans taught the Indians to "Remember the Sabbath day to keep it holy." At his request, they, when hunting or fishing or tripping in the months of open water, rested on the Lord's day. Short sighted employers, unconscious of the fact, so often demonstrated, that they who rest the one day in seven can do more work in the other six, opposed this teaching, and, when they could not stop it, assailed the missionary in a way that must have caused a jubilee in hell. I shall not go into particulars. Most of the principal actors are now in the presence of the Judge of all the earth. He who suffered for a time the name of this devoted servant of His to be so shamefully clouded has cleared all the mists away; and like the silver refined by the furnace, so has it been in this case.

But persecutions, and even these bitter assaults upon his character, could not turn him from the most intense activity in his blessed life work. Like an Apostle Paul in primitive times, or like a Coke or Asbury in the early years of this century, so travelled James Evans. When we say he travelled thousands of miles each year on his almost semi-continental journeys, we must remember that these were not performed by coach or railroad, or even with horse and carriage, or in the saddle or sailing vessel, but by canoe and dog train. How much of hardship and suffering that means, we are thankful but few of our readers will ever know. There are a few of us who do know something of these things, and this fellowship of his suffering knits our hearts in loving memory to him who excelled us all, and the fragrance of whose name and unselfish devotion to his work met us almost everywhere, although years had passed away since James Evans had entered into his rest. "He being dead yet speaks." To write about him and his work is a labor of love. Would that the pen of some ready writer give us a biography of this missionary of such versatility of gifts, and such marvelous success in his work!

Room only have I here, in addition to what has already been written, to give some account of the sad event of his life, the accidental shooting of his interpreter, Joseph Hasselton, and the after consequences.

Word reached Mr. Evans one year, that the priests were endeavouring to crowd up into the Athabasca and Mackenzie River country, and get a foothold among some very interesting Indians whom Mr. Evans had visited and found very anxious for the truth. Desirous that they should not be led away from the simplicity of the gospel, he felt that the best plan was for him to hurry up by light canoe and get into that country and among the Indians before the priests arrived. They had gone the usual route up the Saskatchewan, and from thence were to go over the height of land, and then by boat down the streams, which from those regions run towards the Arctic Ocean.

Mr. Evans' plan was to take what is called "the back route," that was, to go partly down the Nelson River, and then, turning westward through an almost endless succession of lakes and rivers and portages, arrive before the other parties, although several weeks of severest toil would be passed in making the long journey. With his beloved interpreter, who was one of the most remarkable Indians of his day, a man who could talk almost every Indian language spoken by the natives of the land, and what was better, a devoted Christian, full of zeal and enthusiasm for the work, and with another reliable native from whom I received my information as to what occurred, the long journey was commenced. For several days they made good progress, and were rejoicing at the prospect of success. One morning, very early, while they were paddling along on the great Nelson River, Hasselton, the interpreter, who was in the front of the canoe, said, "I see some ducks in those reeds near the shore. Hand me the gun." In these small canoes the guns are generally kept in the stern with the muzzles pointing back, so as to prevent accidents. The man who was in the stern quickly picked up the gun, and foolishly drew back the hammer. With the muzzle pointing forward he passed the gun to Mr. Evans, who did not turn his head, as he was earnestly looking if he also could see the ducks. As Mr. Evans took the gun he unfortunately let the trigger, which had no guard around it, strike against the thwart of the canoe. Instantly it went off, and the contents were discharged into the head of the poor man in front. He turned his dying eyes upon Mr. Evans, and then fell over, a corpse. It was an awful accident, and doubly painful on account of the unfortunate surroundings. Here the two survivors were, about two hundred miles from any habitation. They could not take the body back with them. For days they would meet none to whom they could tell their story. They went ashore, and when their first paroxysm of grief was over, they had to dig, as best they could, a grave in the wilderness, and there bury their dead.

They turned their faces homeward, and very sorrowful indeed was the journey. Great was the grief at the village, and greater still the consternation when it was discovered what Mr. Evans had resolved to do. His interpreter was the only Christian among his relatives. The rest of them still lived by the old ways. Life for life was their motto, and many had been their deeds of cruelty and bloodshed in seeking that revenge which occupied so large a place in their hearts. They lived several hundred miles away, and Mr. Evans resolved to go and surrender himself to them, tell them what he had done, and take all the consequences. Many friends, knowing how quick those people were to act when aroused by the news of the death of a relative for often before he hears all the circumstances does he strike the fatal blow urged him not to go himself, but to send a mediator. To this suggestion he turned a deaf ear, and having made his will and left all instructions as to the work if he should never return, and bidden farewell to his stricken family, who never expected to see him alive again, he started off on his strange and perilous journey. Reaching the distant village, he walked into the tent of the parents of his interpreter, and told them that his heart was broken, and why. Angry words were uttered, and tomahawks and guns were freely handled, while he described the tragic scene. Feeling so utterly miserable that he little cared whether they killed him or let him live, there he sat down on the ground in their midst, and awaited their decision. Some of the hot headed ones were for killing him at once; but wiser counsels prevailed and it was decided that he must be adopted into the family from which he had shot the son, and be all to them, as far as possible, that their son had been. This had been a good deal. Becoming a Christian had made him kind and loving, and so all that he could spare of his wages, earned while interpreting for Mr. Evans, had been faithfully sent to his parents. Mr. Evans assumed as his Indian name that of this family, and a good son indeed they found in him.

When he left to return to his Mission they kissed him, and acted towards him with as much affection as such people can show. Many were the gifts which were sent to them by their adopted son, who took good care of them as long as he lived.

But while this difficulty was thus tided over, the memory of it never faded away from Mr. Evans. He was never the same man after. Yet he did not allow it to deter him from the most vigorous prosecution of his work. Indeed, it seemed to his people as though he tried to bury his sorrow in incessant toil, and labors so abundant, that but few even of the Indians "in journeys often" could equal him.

To aid the further prosecution of his labors, and to excite greater interest in the well being of the Indians of British North America, Mr. Evans went to England to speak about his work and its needs. His story of marvelous incidents and varied experiences in this land of which so little was known, produced a deep impression, and great crowds came out to hear him, and insisted on his continuing at great length his wonderful description of travelling by canoe and dog-train, and the long desire there was in the hearts of the Indians for the gospel.

On November 23, 1846, after having spoken at Keelby in Lincolnshire, he returned with his wife, who was in every respect a devoted helpmate for such a work, to the home of the gentleman and lady with whom they were stopping. While chatting on various subjects, Mrs. Evans turned to her husband, who was comfortably seated in a large arm chair, and said, "My dear, I have had such a strange presentiment—that we shall never see Norway House and those faithful Indians again." He turned to her and said, with something of his old enthusiasm, "Why should that thought trouble you, my dear? Heaven is just as near from England as from America."

The two ladies said, "Good night!" and retired, leaving Mr. Evans and the gentleman of the house to chat together a little longer. Shortly after, the gentleman said something to Mr. Evans, and, receiving no answer, he turned from the fire and looked at him. At first he thought he had fallen asleep, but this was only for an instant. Springing up and going to him, he found that the immortal spirit had so quietly and gently flitted away, that there had not been the slightest sob or cry. The noble Indian missionary was dead. The eloquent tongue was hushed forever. For his return hundreds of anxious weeping Indians in those northern wilds would long and wait, but wait in vain. He had been conveyed by angel bands to that innumerable company of redeemed, blood washed saints around the throne of God, which even then had received many happy converted Indians, who, brought to God by his instrumentality, had finished their course with joy, and before him had entered through the gates into the city, and were there to welcome him.

INITIALS.	SYLLABLES.				FINALS.	
	ā	e	o	a	·	
a	▽	△	▷	◁	◦	ow
wa	▽·	△·	▷·	◁·	X	Christ
pa	V	∧	>	<	'	p
ta	U	∩	⊃	⊂	'	t
ka	ᑫ	ᑭ	ᑯ	ᑲ	'	k
cha	ᒉ	ᒋ	ᒍ	ᒐ	-	h
ma	ᒣ	ᒥ	ᒧ	ᒪ	c	m
na	ᓀ	ᓂ	ᓄ	ᓇ	ɔ	n
sa	ᓭ	ᓯ	ᓱ	ᓴ	⌒	s
ya	ᔦ	ᔨ	ᔪ	ᔭ	⸮	r
					⸮	l

Cree Syllabic Alphabet

Hundreds, since then, of his spiritual children have had the "abundant entrance ministered unto" them, and they have joined him in that rapidly increasing throng. And although many years have passed away since he preached to them his last sermon, at many a campfire, and in many a wigwam, still linger old men, and women too, whose eyes glisten and then become bedimmed with tears as they think of him who so long ago went on before. But while they weep, they also rejoice that that salvation, which, as the result of his preaching, they accepted, is still their solace and their joy. Clinging to it and its great Author, they shall by and by meet their missionary and loved ones who have finished their course and gained the eternal shores.

On the opposite page are the syllabic characters, as invented by Mr. Evans; and on this we give the Lord's Prayer in Cree, as printed in them.

Perhaps the following explanation will help the student who may have a wish to master this wonderful invention.

In the alphabet the first line of characters, the equilateral triangle in four positions, reads as follows: a, e, oo, ah.

The Lord's Prayer

The addition of the little dot, as seen in the second line, adds to any character after which it is placed the sound of w. So this second line read wa, we, woo, wah.

The following lines read thus: pa, pe, poo, pah; ta, te, too, tah; ka, ke, koo, kah; cha, che, choo, chah; ma, mee, moo, mah; na, ne, noo, nah; sa, se, soo, sah; ya, ye, yoo, yah.

With a little patience the Lord's Prayer can be read even without a teacher.

I have gone to an Indian band far away in the northern wilderness, and after they have become willing to receive the truth, I have commenced to teach them to read the Word of God. Very limited indeed were our appliances, for we were hundreds of miles from the nearest school house. But from the camp fire, where we had cooked our bear's meat or beaver, I would take a burnt stick, and with it make these syllabic characters on the side of a rock, and then patiently repeat them over and over again with my school of often three generations of Indians together, until they had some idea of them. Then I would give them the copies of the Bible I had brought, and at the first verse of Genesis we would begin. It paid for the hardships of the trip a thousand fold to see the looks of joy and delight on their faces as they themselves were able to read that wonderful verse.

CHAPTER XIII

Sowing and reaping — Beautiful incident — "Help me to be a Christian!" — Thirty years between the sowing and the reaping — Sorrowing, yet stubborn, Indians induced to yield by the expression, "I know where your children are!"

While in our everyday missionary life there were dark hours, and times when our faith was severely tried, there was, on the other hand, much to encourage us to persevere in the blessed work among these Cree Indians.

An incident that occurred to us brought up very forcibly to our minds the couplet:

"Whate'er may die
and be forgot,
Work done for God,
it dieth not."

I was sitting, one pleasant day in June, in my study at Norway House, absorbed in my work, when I was startled by a loud "Ahem!" behind me. I quickly sprang up, and turning round, discovered that the man who had thus suddenly interrupted me in my thoughts was a big, stalwart Indian. He had come into the room in that catlike way in which nearly all of the Indians move. Their moccasined feet make no sound, and so it is quite possible for even scores of them to come into the house unheard. Then, as Indians have a great dislike to knocking, they generally omit it altogether, and unceremoniously enter, as this man had done, and as quietly as possible.

My first glance at him told me that he was an entire stranger, although I had by this time become acquainted with some hundreds of the natives. I shook hands with him and said a few commonplace things to him, to which I thought he paid but little heed.

I pointed to a chair, and asked him to be seated, but instead of doing so, he came up close to me and said with great earnestness: "Missionary, will you help me to be a Christian?"

Surprised and pleased by this abrupt question, I replied, "Certainly I will. That is my business here."

"Will you help my wife and children also to become Christians?" he added with equal emphasis.

"Of course I will," I answered again. "It was for just such work as that my good wife and I came from our far away home to live in this land."

Naturally I had already become very much interested in this big, bronzed Indian; and so I said to him, "Tell me who you are, and from what place you have come."

I made him sit down before me, and he told me the following remarkable story. I wish I could put into the narrative his pathos and his dramatic action. He did not keep his seat very long after he began talking, but moved around, and at times was very much excited. He said:

"Many years ago, when I was a little boy, I was kindly cared for by the first missionary, Mr. Evans. I was a poor orphan. My father and mother had died, leaving no one to care for me; so the good missionary took me to his own house and was very kind to me. 'Tis true I had some relatives, but they were not Christians, and so there was not much love in their hearts towards a poor orphan boy. So Mr. Evans took me to his house, and was very kind to me. He gave me clothes, food, and a home. He taught me to read the new letters he had made for our people, and told me much about the Great Spirit and His Son Jesus. He taught me and other children to pray to God, and he often talked to us about Him, and how kind and good He was. He kept me with him two or three years, and I was very well off indeed in having such a home and such a friend, if I had only known it.

"One summer, among the many Indians who came to trade their furs at the Company's store, was one family who lived very far away. They seemed to take a liking to me, and often would talk to me. They had no little boy, they said, in their wigwam, and they told me a lot of foolish stuff about how much happier I would be, if I lived with them, than I was here, where I had to obey the white man. Like the foolish child that I was, I listened to this nonsense, and one night, when they had got everything ready to start, I slipped quietly out of the house and joined them. We paddled hard most of the night, for we felt that we had done wrong, and did not know but we should be followed.

"After travelling many days we reached their hunting grounds and wigwams. I did not find it as pleasant as they had told me it would be. Often they were very cruel to me, and sometimes we did not have much to eat. But I dared not run away, for there was no place to which I could go, except to other wicked Indians; and they would only make things worse. They were all very bad Indians, and very much afraid of the medicine men. All the worship they did was to the bad spirit. They were afraid of him, and so they worshipped him, so that he might not do them much harm. I became as bad as any of them. I tried to forget all that the good missionary had told me. I tried to wipe all his teachings and prayers from my memory. All he had told me about the Good Spirit and His Son, I tried to forget.

"I grew up to be a man. I had become a wicked unbeliever; but I was a good hunter, and one of the men sold me one of his daughters to be my wife. We have quite a family. Because I had seen, when I was a little boy, how Christian Indian men treat the women better than the other Indians treat theirs, I treated my wife and children well. I was never cruel to them. I love my wife and children.

"Last winter, you remember, the snow was very deep. I had taken my family and gone out into the region of deer and other animals, and there had made my hunting lodge for the winter. There we set our traps for the fur bearing animals. We took a good many of the smaller animals that have furs, but the larger ones, that are good for food, were very few. We had a hard time, as food was very scarce. I could not find any deer to shoot, and we had come far from the great lakes and rivers, and so had no fish.

"At length it seemed as though we must starve. I tried hard to get something, but I seemed to fail every time. Sometimes, when I did manage to get within range of the moose or caribou, and I fired, my gun, which is only a flintlock, would only flash the powder in the pan, and so the charge would not go off. The noise, however, had so frightened the animal that he had rushed away before I could get ready to fire again.

"At length it got so bad with us that I became completely discouraged, and I said, 'I will only try once more; and if I do not succeed in shooting a deer,

I will shoot myself.' So I took up my gun and hurried into the forest away from my half starved family. I cautiously tramped along on my snowshoes all the first day, and did not see even a track. I made a little camp and lay down cold and hungry. I hunted all the next day and only got a rabbit. This I ate in the little camp I made the second night in the snow. On the third day I hunted until about noon. Then feeling very weak and hungry, I got so discouraged that I said, as I sat down on a log covered with snow, 'I will die here. I am weak with hunger, I can go no further.' I was cross and angry, and I said, as I talked to myself, 'No use trying any more.' Then I loaded my gun with a heavy charge of powder and two bullets, and drew back the hammer. My plan was to put the muzzle of the gun against the side of my head, and then press on the trigger with my big toe, which you know moves easily in the moccasin. Just as I was getting ready thus to kill myself, something seemed to speak to me, 'William!' I pushed the gun away, for I was frightened. I looked all around, but could not see anybody. Then I found that the voice was in me, and it began to talk to me out of my heart. As I listened it seemed to say, 'William, do you not remember what the missionary told you long ago about the Great Spirit? He said He was kind and forgiving, and that even if we did wander far away from Him, if we became sorry and would come back, He would forgive. Do you not remember, William, he said that if we ever got into great trouble, the Great Spirit was the best friend to whom to go to help us out? You are in great trouble, William. Don't you think you had better come back to Him?'

"But I trembled and hesitated, for I was ashamed to come. I thought over my life, how I had run away from the kind missionary who had taken me, a poor orphan boy, into his home, and fed and clothed me, and taught me so much about the true way. Then I remembered so well how I had tried to wipe out from my memory all I had learned about the Great Spirit and His Son, and the good Book. I had denied to these people that I knew anything about the white man's religion. I had been very bad, and had got very far away. How could I come back? Still all the answer I got was, 'You had better come back.'

"There I sat and trembled, and I felt I was too mean to come back. But all the answer I got was, 'It is meaner to stay away, if what the missionary said is true.' While I was hesitating what to do, and all trembling in the cold, I seemed to hear my wife and children in the wigwam far away crying for food. This decided me. So I turned round and kneeled down in the snow by the log, and began to pray. I hardly know what I said, but I do remember I asked the Great Spirit to forgive this poor Indian who had got so far away from Him, and had been so wicked, and had tried to wipe Him out of his memory. I told Him I was sorry, and wanted to do better; and there in the snow I promised, if He would forgive and help me in my trouble, and give something for my wife and children to eat, I would, just as soon as the snow and ice left the rivers and lakes, go and find the missionary, and ask him to help me to be a Christian.

"While I prayed I felt better. I seemed to feel in my heart that help was coming. I got up from my knees, and it seemed as though that prayer had strengthened me like food. I forgot I was cold and hungry. I took up my gun with a glad heart, and away I started. I had not gone far before a large caribou came dashing along. I fired and killed him. I was very glad. I quickly skinned him, and I soon made a fire and cooked some of the meat. Then I pulled down a small tree, and fastened part of the meat into the top of it, and let it swing up again, so as to keep it from the wolves and wolverines. Then I took the rest on my back and hurried home to my hungry wife and children. Soon after I went back for the rest of the caribou, and found it all right.

"Since that hour we have always had something. I have hunted hard, and have had success. None of us have been hungry since. The Great Spirit has been all that the missionary said He would be to us. He has cared for us, and given us all that we have needed.

"I have not forgotten my promise made while kneeling in the snow beside the log in the woods. The snow has gone, and the ice has left the lakes and rivers. I have launched my canoe, and have come with my wife and children to ask you to help us to be Christians."

We were very much pleased to hear such a wonderful experience, which was thus leading him back to God; and we told him so. When we learned that all this time he had been talking, his wife and children were patiently sitting in the canoe outside at the shore, we hurried out with him and brought them into the Mission house.

Mrs. Young, and one or two others, attracted by William's earnest words, had come into my study, and had heard most of his story, and of course were also deeply interested. Out of our scant supplies we gave the whole family a good hearty meal, and we both did what we could by words and actions to make them feel that we were their friends, and would do all we could to help them to be Christians. We were delighted to find that since that memorable day when at the snow covered log in the forest William had bowed in prayer, he had been diligent in teaching his family all that he could remember of the blessed truths of the gospel. They had gladly received it and were eager for more.

I called together some of the head men of the village, and told them the story of this family, and what William had said about his early life. A few of the older people remembered the circumstance of his adoption by Mr. Evans after the death of his parents, whom they remembered well. Happy Christians themselves, and anxious that others should enjoy the same blessedness, they rejoiced at William's return, and especially with such a desire in his heart. So they at once gave the exile a place among themselves, and some needed help. Thorough and genuine were the changes wrought in the hearts of that family by Divine grace, and they have remained firm and true. In their house was a family altar, and from the church services they were never absent, unless far off in distant hunting grounds.

Various were the arguments which the Good Spirit gave us to use in persuading men and women to be reconciled to God. Here is a beautiful illustration:

"Where Are Our Children?"

On the banks of a wild river, about sixty miles from Beaver Lake, I visited a band of Indians, who seemed determined to resist every appeal or entreaty I could make to induce them to listen to my words. They were so dead and indifferent that I was for a time quite disheartened. The journey to reach them had taken about eight days from home through the dreary wilderness, where we had not met a single human being. My two faithful canoe men and I had suffered much from the character of the route, and the absence of game, which had caused us more than once to wrap ourselves up in our blankets and lie down supperless upon the granite rocks and try to sleep. The rain had fallen upon us so persistently that for days the water had been dripping from us, and we had longed for the sunshine that we might get dry again.

We had met with some strange adventures, and I had had another opportunity for observing the intelligence and shrewdness of my men, and their quickness in arriving at right conclusions from very little data. Many think of the Indians as savages and uncivilized, yet in some respects they are highly educated, and are gifted with a quickness of perception not excelled by any other people in the world. We had the following illustration of it on this trip.

As most of the Indians had gone away in the brigades to York Factory, to carry down the furs and to freight up the goods for the next winter's trade, I could not find any canoe men who were acquainted with the route to the band which I wished to visit. The best I could do was to secure the services of a man as a guide who had only been as far as Beaver Lake. He was willing to go and run the risk of finding the Indian band, if possible, although so far beyond the most northern point he had ever gone before. As I could do no better I hired him and another Indian, and away we went.

After several days of hard work (for the portages around the falls and rapids were many, and several times we had to wade through muskegs up to our knees for miles together, carrying all our load on our heads or backs) we at length reached Beaver Lake. Here we camped for the night and talked over our future movements. We had come two hundred and forty miles through these northern wilds, and yet had about sixty miles to go ere we expected to see human beings, and were all absolutely ignorant of the direction in which to go.

We spent the night on the shore of the lake, and slept comfortably on the smooth rocks. Early the next morning we began to look out for signs to guide us on our way. There were several high hills in the vicinity, and it was decided that we should each ascend one of these, and see if from these elevated positions the curling smoke from some distant Indian camp fire, or other signs of human beings, could be observed.

Seizing my rifle, I started off to ascend the high hill which had been assigned me, while the Indians went off in other directions. This hill was perhaps half a mile from our camp fire, and I was soon at its foot, ready to push my way up through the tangled underbrush that grew so densely on its sides. To my surprise I came almost suddenly upon a creek of rare crystal beauty, on the banks of which were many impressions of hooves, large and small, as though a herd of cattle had there been drinking. Thoughtlessly, for I seemed to have forgotten where we were, I came to the conclusion that as the herd of cattle had there quenched their thirst, they and their owner must be near. So I hurried back to the camp, and signalled to the men to return, and told them what I had seen. There was an amused look on their faces, but they were very polite and courteous men, and so they accompanied me to the creek, where, with a good deal of pride, I pointed out to them the footprints of cattle, and stated that I thought that they and their owners could not be far off. They listened to me patiently, and then made me feel extremely foolish by uttering the word "Moose." I had mistaken the footprints of a herd of moose for a drove of cattle, much to their quiet amusement.

We looked around for a time, and, getting no clue, we embarked in our canoe, and started to explore the different streams that flowed into or out of this picturesque lake. After several hours of unsuccessful work we entered into the mouth of quite a fine river, and began paddling up it, keeping close to one of its sandy shores. Suddenly one of the Indians sprang up in the canoe, and began carefully examining some small tracks on the shore. A few hasty words were uttered by the men, and then we landed.

They closely inspected these little footprints, and then exclaimed, "We have got it now, Missionary. We can take you soon to the Indians!"

"What have you discovered?" I said, "I see nothing to tell me where the Indians are."

"We see it very plain," was the reply. "You sent word that you were coming to meet them this moon. They have been scattered hunting, but are gathering at the place appointed, and a canoe-load of them went up this river yesterday, and the dog ran along the shore, and these are his tracks."

I examined these impressions in the sand, and said, "The country is full of wild animals; these may be the tracks of a wolf, wolverine, or some other beast."

They only laughed at me, and said, "We can see a great difference between these tracks and those made by the wild animals."

Our canoe was soon afloat again, and using our paddles vigorously, we sped rapidly along the river. With no other clue than those little footprints in the sand, the men confidently pushed along. After paddling for about twenty miles we came to the camp fire, still smoldering, where the Indians had slept the night before. Here we cooked our dinner, and then hurried on, still guided by the little tracks along the shore. Towards evening we reached the encampment, just as my canoe men had intimated we should.

The welcome we received was not very cordial. The Indians were soured and saddened by having lost many of their number, principally children, by scarlet fever, which for the first time had visited their country, and which had been undoubtedly brought into their land by some free traders the year before. With the exception of an old conjurer or two, none openly opposed me, but the sullen apathy of the people made it very discouraging work to try to preach or teach. However, we did the best we could, and were resolved that having come so far, and suffered so many hardships to reach them, we would faithfully deliver the message, and leave the results to Him who had permitted us to be the first who had ever visited that land to tell the story of redeeming love.

One cold, rainy day a large number of us were crowded into the largest wigwam for a talk about the truths in the great Book. My two faithful Christian companions aided me all they could by giving personal testimony to the blessedness of this great salvation. But all seemed in vain. There the people sat and smoked in sullen indifference. When questioned as to their wishes and determinations, all I could get from them, was, "As our fathers lived and died, so will we."

Tired out and sad of heart, I sat down in quiet communion with the Blessed Spirit, and breathed up a prayer for guidance and help in this hour of sore perplexity. In my extremity the needed assistance came so consciously that I almost exulted in the assurance of coming victory. Springing up, I shouted out, "I know where all your children are, who are not among the living! I know, yes, I do know most certainly where all the children are, whom death has taken in his cold grasp from among us, the children of the good and of the bad, of the whites and of the Indians. I know where all the children are."

Great indeed was the excitement among them. Some of them had had their faces well shrouded in their blankets as they sat like upright mummies in the crowded wigwam. But when I uttered these words, they quickly uncovered their faces, and manifested the most intense interest. Seeing that I had at length got their attention, I went on with my words: "Yes, I know where all the children are. They have gone from your campfires and wigwams. The hammocks are empty, and the little bows and arrows lie idle. Many of your hearts are sad, as you mourn for those little ones whose voices you hear not, and who come not at your call. I am so glad that the Great Spirit gives me authority to tell you that you may meet your children again, and be happy with them forever. But you must listen to His words, which I bring to you from His great Book, and give Him your hearts, and love and serve Him. There is only one way to that beautiful land, where Jesus, the Son of the Great Spirit, has gone, and into which He takes all the children who have died; and now that you have heard His message and seen His Book, you too must come this way, if you would be happy and enter in there."

While I was thus speaking, a big, stalwart man from the other side of the tent sprang up, and rushed towards me. Beating on his breast, he said, "Missionary, my heart is empty, and I mourn much, for none of my children are left among the living. My wigwam is very lonely. I long to see my children again, and to clasp them in my arms. Tell me, Missionary, what must I do to please the Great Spirit, that I may get to that beautiful land, that I may meet my children again?" Then he sank at my feet upon the ground, his eyes filled with tears, and was quickly joined by others, who, like him, were broken down with grief, and were anxious now for religious instruction.

To the blessed Book we went, and after reading what Jesus had said about little children, and giving them some glimpses of His great love for them, we told them "the old, old story," as simply and lovingly as we could. There was no more scoffing or indifference. Every word was heard and pondered over, and from that hour a blessed work began, which resulted in the great majority of them deciding to give their hearts to God; and they have been true to their vows.

CHAPTER XIV

On the trail to Sandy Bar — Sleeping on the ice — Thieving Eskimo dogs — Narrow escape of Jack — Joyous welcome — Society formed — Benjamin Cameron, once a cannibal, now a lay helper — Plumpudding — A striking instance of honesty.

In December 1877, I made a journey to the Indians living at Sandy Bar. As there were some experiences quite different from those of other trips, they shall here be recorded.

Sandy Bar, or White Mud, as some call it, is over a hundred miles south of Beren's River, where we then resided. We made the usual preparations for our journey, getting sleds loaded with supplies for ourselves and fish for our dogs, with all the cooking arrangements necessary for a month's absence from home.

As the people among whom we were going were poor, we ever felt that, Paul-like, for the furtherance of the gospel, the wisest course among those bands who had not fully accepted salvation was to keep ourselves as far as possible from being burdensome to them. So my good wife cooked a generous supply of meat and buns, made as rich with fat as possible. Fortunate indeed were we in having supplies sufficient for this to be done. It was not always so. At this very Mission, all we had one morning for breakfast was a hind quarter of a wild cat!

All our preparations were completed, and we were ready to start at one o'clock in the morning. To our great regret a fierce storm arose, and so we were obliged to wait until the day dawned, ere we could harness our dogs and venture out. When we had gone about twenty miles, the storm swept with such power over the great Lake Winnipeg, driving the recently fallen snow before it, with such a stinging, blinding effect, that we were forced to give up the struggle, and run into the forest and camp.

We cleared away the snow from a space about eight feet square. At one side of this we built up our fire, and over the rest of the cleared space we spread some evergreen boughs, on which we placed our beds. We unharnessed our dogs, and thawed out for them some frozen fish. As this was one of my short trips, I had with me but two dog trains and two Indians. We melted snow in our kettles, made tea, and cooked some meat. This, with the bread, of which we were on this trip the happy possessors, constituted our meals. About sundown we had prayers, and then, as we had been up most of the previous night, we wrapped ourselves in our robes and blankets, and went to sleep to the lullaby of the howling tempest.

About ten o'clock that night I woke up, and uncovering my head, found that the storm had ceased. I sprang up and kindled the fire, but my fingers ached and my body shivered before I succeeded in getting it to blaze brightly. I filled the tea kettle with snow, and while it was melting I called up my two travelling companions, and also a couple of young natives, who with their dog trains, had joined us. The Indians can tell with marvelous accuracy the hour of the night by the position of the Great Bear in the heavens. This is their night clock. I saw by their puzzled looks, as they gazed at the stars, that they wanted to tell me I had made a great mistake, if I thought it was near morning. But I did not give them the opportunity, and only hurried up the breakfast. After prayers we harnessed our dogs, tied up our loads of bedding, food, kettles, and other things; and then throwing the boughs on which we had slept on the fire, by the light which it afforded us, we made our way out through the forest gloom to the frozen lake.

Taking the lead with my splendid dogs, we travelled at such a rate that, before the sun rose up to cheer us, over forty miles of Winnipeg's icy expanse lay between us and the snowy bed where we had sought shelter and slept during the raging storm. After stopping at God's

Head, where a few Indians, under the eccentric chief, Thickfoot lived, we travelled on, crossing the lake to what is called Bull's Head, where we camped for the night. The face of the cliff is here so steep that we could not get our heavy loads up into the forest above, so we were obliged to make our fire and bed in the snowdrift at the base of the cliff. It was a poor place indeed. The snow, from the constant drifting in from the lake, was very deep. There was no shelter or screen from the fierce cold wind, which, changing during the night, blew upon us. We tried to build up the fire, but owing to our peculiar position, could not change it. In the woods, at our camps, we build the fire where the smoke will be driven from us. If the wind changes, we change our fires. Here at the base of this cliff we could do nothing of the kind. The result was, we were either shivering in the bitter cold, or blinded by the smoke.

While in this uncomfortable plight, and trying to arrange our camp beds on the snow, for we could not get any balsam boughs here to put under us, we were joined by several strange Indians, who, coming down the lake, saw our campfire. They had a number of thin, wild, wolfish, half starved Eskimo dogs with them. They made a great fuss over me, which here meant I had to give them some tea and food. I treated them kindly, and fearing for our supplies, and even our dog harness, and the other things for which the terrible Eskimo dogs have such an appetite, I politely informed them that I thought they would be more comfortable if they travelled on a little further. This hint was met with loud protestations that they could not, under any circumstances, think of denying themselves the pleasure of at least stopping one night in the camp of the missionary, about whom they had heard so much as the great friend of the Indian.

Of course, I could not go back on my record, or resist such diplomacy; but I saw trouble ahead, and I was not disappointed. In order to save something, I gave to their wolfish dogs all the fish I had, which was sufficient for my eight for several days. These the Eskimo dogs speedily devoured. I made the men bring the dog harness into the camp, and with the sleds, to save the straps and lashings, they built a little barricade against the wind.

In addition to the food supplies for the trip, I had a bag of meat, and another of buns, for my use when I should reach the village, where I was going to preach and to teach. I gathered a pile of clubs, which I cut from the driftwood on the shore, from which we had also obtained that for our fire. Then, putting the bag of meat, which was frozen hard, under my pillow, and giving the bag of buns to one of my companions, with orders to guard it carefully, I lay down and tried to go to sleep. Vain effort indeed was it for a long time. No sooner were we down than in upon us swarmed the dogs. They fought for the honor of cleaning, in dog fashion, our meat kettle, and then began seeking for something more. Over us they walked, and soon, by their gathering around my head, I knew they had scented the meat. Up I sprang, and, vigorously using my clubs, a number of which I sent among them, I soon drove them out into the darkness of the lake. Then under my robes again I got, but not to sleep. In less than ten minutes there was an encore, which was repeated several times. At length my supply of clubs gave out. My only consolation was that the dogs had received so many of them that they acted as though they were ready to cry quits and behave themselves. As it looked as though they were settling down to rest, I gladly did the same. Vain hope, indeed! I went to sleep very quickly, for I was very weary, but I woke up in the morning to find that there was not an ounce of meat left in the bag under my head, nor a single bun left in the bag which the Indian had orders so carefully to guard.

Our condition the next morning was not a very pleasant one. The outlook was somewhat gloomy. Our camp was in an exposed snowdrift. We had no roof over us. The fire was a poor one, as the driftwood with which it was made was wretched stuff, giving out more smoke than heat, which, persisting in going the wrong way, often filled our eyes with blinding tears. Our generous supply of meat, that we so much needed in this cold climate, and our rich buns, so highly prized, were devoured by the dogs which, with the most innocent looks imaginable, sat around us in the snow and watched our movements. Fortunately one of the Indians had put a few plain biscuits in a small bag, which he was taking, as a great gift, to a friend. These were brought out, and with our tea and sugar were all we had, or could get, until we were sixty miles further south. No time for grumbling, we prepared ourselves for the race against the march of hunger, which we well knew, by some bitter experiences, would, after a few hours, rapidly gain upon us.

After the light breakfast we knelt down in the snow and said our prayers, and then hurried off. My gallant dogs responded to my call upon them so nobly that before that short wintry day in December had fled away, and the lake was shrouded in darkness, the flying sparks from the tops of the little cabins of the friendly Indians told us we had conquered in the race, although not without some narrow escapes and scars.

While crossing a long traverse of at least twenty-five miles, my largest dog, Jack, went through a crack in the ice up to his collar. These ice cracks are dangerous things. The ice, which may be several feet thick, often bursts open with a loud report, making a fissure which may be from a few inches to several feet wide. Up this fissure the water rushes until it is level with the top. Of course, as the cold is so intense, it soon freezes over, but it is very dangerous for travellers to come along soon after the fissure had been made. I have seen the guide get in more than once, and have had some very narrow escapes myself. On this occasion I was riding on the sled. The two foremost dogs of the train got across the thinly frozen ice all right, but Jack, who was third, broke through into the cold water below. The head dogs kept pulling ahead, and the sled dog did his work admirably, and so we saved the noble St. Bernard from drowning, and soon got him out. The cold was so intense that in a few minutes his glossy black coat was covered with a coat of icy mail. He seemed to know the danger he was in; and so, the instant I got the sled across the ice crack, he started off direct for the distant forest at such a rate that he seemed to drag the other dogs as well as myself most of the time. We were about twelve miles from the shore, but in a little more than an hour the land was reached, and as there was abundance of dry wood here, a good fire was soon kindled, before which, on a buffalo skin, I placed my ice covered dog. He turned himself around when necessary, and, before the other sled arrived, Jack was himself again. As two of the Indians behind us had fallen into this same fissure, we were delayed for some time in getting them dry again.

We boiled our kettle and had some more tea, and then on we hurried. I met with a very warm welcome from the people. The greater part of them were Indians I had met in other years. Many were from Norway House. To this place they had come, attracted by the stories of its valuable fisheries and productive soil. So rapidly had the Mission at Norway House increased that fish and game were beginning to fail. Hence a large number emigrated to this and other places.

To this place they had come late in the summer, and so the little houses they had built were small and cold. Then, to make matters worse, the fisheries had not proved to be what they had been represented. They crowded round me as I drove into their village, and told me of their "hungering often," and other hardships. As some sleds were ready to start for Manitoba, I hurried into one of the little homes to pencil a note to my

Chairman, the Rev. George Young, but found it to be almost an impossibility, as the four fingers of my right hand were frozen. These, and a frozen nose, reminded me for several days of that sixty mile run on short rations.

I found, in addition to the Christian Indians, quite a number of others who had been attracted to this place. I spent eight days among them. They had about a dozen little houses, in addition to a large number of wigwams. For their supplies they were depending on their rabbit snares, and their nets for fish, which were obtained in but limited quantities. As my food had been stolen from me by the dogs, I had nothing but what they gave me; but of their best they supplied me most cheerfully, and so I breakfasted, dined, and supped on rabbit or fish, and fared well.

I preached, as was my custom, three times a day, and kept school between the services. I organized a class of thirty-five members, ten of whom for the first time now decided for Christ, and resolved henceforth to be His loyal followers. It was a great joy to be gathering in these decided ones, as the result of the seed sown amid the discouragements of earlier years. I was very fortunate in securing a good leader, or spiritual overseer, for this little flock in the wilderness. Benjamin Cameron was his name. He had had a strange career. He had been a cannibal in his day, but Divine Grace had gone down into the depths of sin into which he had sunk, and had lifted him out, and put his feet upon the Rock, and filled his lips with singing, and his heart with praise. He was emphatically "a good man, and full of the Holy Ghost."

The hours I spent with the children were very pleasant and profitable. I was pleased to hear the older children read so well, and was especially delighted with their knowledge of the catechism in both Cree and English. I distributed a fresh supply of books which I had brought them, and also gave to the needy ones some warm, comfortable garments sent by loving friends from Montreal.

If the dear friends, into whose hearts the good desire to send these very comfortable garments had been put, could only have seen how much misery was relieved, and happiness conferred, they would have felt amply rewarded for their gifts.

In connection with one of the Sunday services I administered the sacrament of the Lord's Supper. We had a most solemn and impressive yet delightful time. The loving Savior seemed very near, and fresh vows and covenants were entered into by all, that to Him they would be true.

I spent Christmas among them, and as one of them had succeeded in getting some mink in his traps, and for the skins had obtained from some passing "free traders" some flour and plums, they got up in honor of my visit a plum pudding. It haunts me yet, and so I will not here describe it.

As beautiful weather favored us on our return, we took the straight route home, and arrived there in two days, rejoicing that the trip, as regarded its spiritual aspects, had been a great success.

One day an Indian came into my house and threw down a fine leg of venison upon the table. As we were poorly off for food, I was very much pleased, and said to him, "What shall I give you for this meat?"

"Nothing," he replied; "it belongs to you."

"You must be mistaken," I said. "I never had any dealings with you."

"But I had with you," he answered. "And so this meat is yours."

Being unacquainted with the man, I asked him to tell me who he was, and how he made it out that this meat belonged to me.

Said he, "Did you not go to Nelson River with dogs and Indians about two moons ago?"

"Yes," I replied, "I did."

"Well, I was out hunting deer, but I did not have much luck. The snow was deep, the deer were very shy, and I had no success. One day, when very hungry, for I had only taken a little dried rabbit meat with me from my wigwam, I came across your trail, and I found where your Indians had made a cache, that is, a big bundle of provisions and other things had been tied up in a blanket, and then a small tree had been bent down by your men, and the bundle fastened on the top, and let spring up again to keep it from the wolves. I saw your bundle hanging there, and as I was very hungry I thought, 'Now if the kind hearted missionary only knew the poor Indian hunter was here looking at his bundle of food, he would say, "Help yourself";' and that was what I did. I bent down the tree, and found the large piece of pemmican. I cut off a piece big enough to make me a good dinner, then I tied up the bundle again, and let it swing up as you had it. And now I have brought you this venison in place of what I took."

I was pleased with his honesty, and had in the incident another example of the Indian quickness to read much where the white man sees nothing.

The reason why we had made the cache which the Indian had discovered was, that we had taken a large quantity of pemmican for our food, as the people we were going to see were poor, and we did not wish to be a burden to them. But we had been caught in a terrible storm, and as the snow was very deep, making the travelling heavy, we were obliged to lighten our loads as soon as possible. So we left a portion, as the Indian had described, on the way.

When we returned to the cache, and my men pulled it down and opened the bundle, one of them quickly cried out, "Somebody has been at our cache."

"Nonsense," I replied, "nobody would disturb it. And then there were no tracks around when we reached here tonight."

Looking at the largest piece of pemmican, the Indians said, "Missionary, somebody has taken down our bundle and cut off a piece just here. That there are no tracks, is because there have been so many snow storms lately. All tracks made a few days ago are covered up."

As I knew they were so much quicker along these lines of education than white men, I did not argue any more with them. The coming of the old hunter with the venison was the proof of the cleverness of my men, and also a very honorable act on his part. I kept the old man to dinner, and among other things I asked him how he knew it was the missionary's party that passed that way. He quickly replied, "By your tracks in the snow. Indians' toes turn in when they walk, white men's toes turn out."

CHAPTER XV

An Indian love feast — Many witnesses — Sweet songs of Zion — The Lord's Supper — Memoir of William Memotas, the devoted Christian.

Our love feasts and sacramental services were always well attended, if it were within the range of possibility for the Indians to be present. To come in on Saturday from their distant hunting grounds sixty miles away, that they might enjoy the services of the Lord's house on His own day, was no unusual thing. Then on Monday morning we have seen them again strap on their snowshoes, and with glad hearts and renewed zeal start off to return to their lonely hunting camps in the distant forests.

They are able to express themselves clearly, and often quite eloquently. When their hearts are full of the love of God, and they are rejoicing in the blessed assurance of the Divine favor, they are willing to speak about it.

> "What they have felt and seen
> With confidence they tell."

Here are some of their testimonies. These are the living words of men and women who were once the slaves of sin and Satan. But on their hearts the blessed Spirit shone, and to His pleading voice they responded, and now, happy in the consciousness that they are the children of God, they love to talk about what wonderful things have been done for them and wrought in them. Timothy Bear said:

"It is such a joy to me, that I can tell you of great things done for me. Great is the joy I have in my heart today. I rest in the consciousness that He is my own reconciled heavenly Father, and so I feel it good to be here in the Lord's house, and with those that love Him. The good Spirit gives me to see how good and kind my heavenly Father is; and so I can say that the greatest anxiety of my heart and life is to serve God better and better as I grow older. To do this I have found out that I must have Divine help. But He is my helper for everything and so I need not fail. So I am encouraged that I shall love God more and more, and with that, I want to love His cause and people, and those who have not yet become His people, that they may soon do so, more and more. For the conversion of the unsaved, let us, who feel that Jesus saved us, pray more earnestly than ever, and may God help us to live our religion, that the lost around us may see in our lives what a wonderful thing it is."

Timothy's burning words produced a deep impression, and someone began to sing:

"Ayume-oo-we-nah,"
"The praying Spirit breathe."

Half a dozen were on their feet when the verses were sung, but Thomas Walker spoke first. He said:

"When I first heard the gospel long winters ago, as brought to us by Mr. Evans, I was soon convinced that I was a sinner and needed forgiveness. I found I could not of myself get rid of my sins, so I believed in Christ, and found that He had power to forgive. I was very wretched before I was forgiven. I was afraid I should be lost forever. I mourned and wept before God on account of my sins. In the woods alone, I cried in my troubles, and was in deep distress. But I heard of the love and power, and willingness to save, of this Jesus of the great Book, and so I exercised a living faith in Him; and as I believed, God's voice was heard, saying, 'My son, I have forgiven your sins. I have blotted them out. Go in peace.' I am sure I was not mistaken. I felt filled with peace and joy. I felt that I, Thomas Walker, was cleansed from my many sins, and clothed with the garments of salvation. That was a blessed day when the Spirit of God shone into my heart and drove out the darkness. Since then, my way in Him has been like the sunlight on the waters. The more waves, the more sunshine. I am happy in His love today. I am confident that, because He aids me, I am growing in grace.

"I rejoice at being spared to come to another celebration of the Lord's Supper. In view of partaking of the emblems of the dying, loving Jesus, I feel that my soul is feeding on Christ, the true Bread of Life."

Earnest yet suppressed words of praise and adoration quietly dropped from many lips as Thomas ended. Then dear old Henry Budd succeeded in getting a hearing. Henry was Mr. Evans' marvelous dog driver over twenty-five years before the date of this blessed love feast. He had many wonderful adventures and some narrow escapes. Once, when running ahead on a treacherous river, where in places the current was very rapid, and consequently the ice was thin, he broke through into the current underneath. He quickly caught hold of the edge of the ice, but it was so weak it would not hold him up. His only comrade could not get very near him as the ice was so bad, and so had to run about a mile for a rope. When he returned, so intense was the cold that both of Henry's hands, with which he had been holding on to the ice, were frozen. He was utterly unable to close them on the rope. George shouted to him to open his mouth. The rope was then thrown, lasso-like, so skillfully, that the poor half frozen man seized it in his teeth, and was thus dragged out, and rushed off to the nearest wigwam. He was literally saved by the "skin of his teeth."

Thus Henry Budd had, like many others, much for which to praise God. He spoke on this occasion as follows:

"I rejoice in God my Savior, who has done such

wonderful things for me. I feel very happy. I am His child. He is my reconciled Father. How can I help being happy?

"When I first began to get my poor blind eyes opened, and there came to me a desire to seek God, and to obtain salvation for my soul, I was troubled on account of my sins. My many transgressions rose up before me like a cloud. I was ignorant, and so my mind was full of doubts and fears. Yet with all my doubts there was the anxious desire to be saved. But the victory came at last. I was enabled to hear enough about the Almighty Friend, and so, as I had confidence in His power and love, and believed in Him, I was at last enabled to rejoice in the knowledge of sins forgiven through faith in the Lord Jesus Christ. From those sad doubts and fears I am now happily delivered. I feel I love God, and that God loves me. I am growing in grace, and in the knowledge of God my Savior. My hopes are brightening all the time. I am getting old, but not unhappy, for I am cheered with the blessed assurance of one day meeting in my Father's house in heaven, with many who are safely there, and many more who, like me, will soon enter in. That this may be a blessed certainty, I desire to be faithful unto the end, that no man take my crown."

When Henry sat down, before another one could be heard, the large congregation were singing:

> "Pe teh-na-mah-me cha-te yak
> Ke che ne-ka-mo-yak," etc.
> "O for a thousand tongues to sing
> My great Redeemer's praise."

The next to get the floor was one of the sweetest, purest Christians it was ever my lot to become acquainted with in any land. His name was William Memotas. He was a very happy Christian. As he was a lay preacher and a class leader, I was much in his society, and I can say, as many others have said, that William since the day of his conversion was never heard to utter an unkind word about anyone, or do anything that could give the enemies of the Lord Jesus an opportunity to scoff at his profession of loving the Lord with all his heart. He was never a very strong man physically while we knew him, and so was unable to go on the long tripping or hunting expeditions with his more vigorous comrades. He suffered much from inward pain, but was ever bright and hopeful. When he stood up to add his testimony, the sick, pallid face caused a wave of sympathy to pass over the audience, but his cheery words quickly lifted the cloud, and we seemed to look through the open door into the celestial city, into which he was so soon to enter. His obituary, which I wrote at the time of his death, is added at the close of this chapter. He said:

"For many years I have now been walking in this way, and proving this great salvation. It is a blessed way, and it is getting more delightful all the time. Every day on it is a day's walk nearer Jesus. It is not like the trails in our country, sometimes rocks, and then more often muskegs and quaking bogs; but it is the solid rock all the time, and on it we may always be sure of our footing, and it leads us up to Him who is the Rock of Ages. I am not now a strong man, as you know I once was. This poor weak body is like the old wigwam. It is breaking up. As each storm tears fresh rents in the old wigwam, so each attack of disease seems to tear me, and bring me nearer the time when what is immortal of me shall slip away from the worn body into the everlasting brightness of that land where the happy people never say, 'I am sick.' I am very glad and happy in the service of this Jesus, and will serve Him as long as He lends me health. But I do want to go home. I cannot do much more here. Our missionary, Mr. Young, said to me, 'William, don't talk so much about leaving us. How can we spare you?' I thank him for his love and friendship, but there is another Friend I am getting such a longing in my heart to see, and that is Jesus, my Savior, my Redeemer. I am praying for patience, but by and by I shall be with Him, with Him forevermore. There I shall have no pain, and I will praise my Jesus forevermore. So, while waiting, I ask God to be with me here, and to let me serve Him in some way every day."

With suppressed emotion, for many eyes were full of tears, the people sang,

>"Tapwa meyoo ootaskewuk,
> Ispemik ayahchik," etc.
>"There is a land of pure delight,
> Where saints immortal reign."

William was a sweet singer, and joined heartily with the rest in singing several verses of that grand old hymn. We had a presentiment that the end was not far off, but we little thought, as we looked into his radiant face, and heard his clear scriptural testimony, and his longings for rest and heaven, that this was to be the last love feast in which our dear brother was to be with us. Before another similar service was held, William Memotas had gone sweeping through the gates, washed in the blood of the Lamb.

James Cochrane, a class leader, said,

"I have great reason to bless God for the privileges and mercies I have had from Him. I am so glad to be with you today in His house. I try to arrange all my hunting and journeys so as to be present at all of these love feasts and sacraments. Since I decided, many years ago, to give up the old way and become a Christian, I have never missed one of these meetings, though sometimes I have had to take several days and travel hundreds of miles to get here. I only had to travel sixty miles on my snowshoes to be here today. It has paid me well to come. I rejoice that God has enabled me to be faithful all these years since I started in His service. When I first began, I had a great many doubts and fears. The way seemed very long ahead of me. I felt so weak and so prone to sin. It seemed impossible that such a weak, unworthy creature as I could stand true and faithful. But trusting in God, and constantly endeavouring to exercise a living faith in Christ, I have been kept to this day, and I can say I realize a daily growth in grace. I ask God to give me His Holy Spirit to help me to follow Christ's example and to keep all of God's commandments. May I, too, prove faithful."

Mary Cook, a very old woman, who has had to endure persecution for Christ's sake, spoke next. She said:

"I am very glad to be here once more. I have many unbelieving relatives who have no feeling of friendship towards me, because I am a follower of Jesus. But He is my Friend, so it is all right. I have been very sick, and thought that God was going to take me home to heaven. That thought made me very happy in my sickness. My poor little room often seemed light with the presence of my Lord. I love to dwell with God's people. It is my chief joy. I refused to go and live with my relatives in the woods, even though I should be better off, because I love the house of God, and because I so love to worship with God's people."

Mary Oig said:

"I feel very happy down in my heart today. My heart is filled with His love. I know I love Him and His people; and His service is a great delight to me.

Once, like many others, I was in the great darkness, wandering in sin. But God sought me by His Holy Spirit, and convinced me of my lost condition, showed me Himself as my only hope, and enabled me to rejoice in His pardoning mercy through faith in the atonement. May God keep me faithful, that with you I may join around the Throne above."

Thomas Mamanowatum, generally known as Big Tom on account of his almost gigantic size, was the next to speak. He is one of the best of men. I have used him to help me a good deal, and have ever found him one of the worthiest and truest assistants. His people all love and trust him. He is perhaps the most influential Indian in the village. Tom said:

"I, too, desire to express my gratitude to God for His great blessing and mercy to me. I am like David, who said, 'Come, all ye who fear the Lord, and I will tell you what He hath done for my soul.' He has taken me out of the pit of sin, and set me on the rock. So I rejoice, for I have felt and tasted of His love. When I think of what He has done for me, and then think of what I have been, I feel that I am not worthy even to stand up in such a place as this. But He is worthy, and so I must praise Him. I have a comfortable assurance that He, my good Father, is contented with me. But it is only because the grace of God is sufficient to keep me. I am growing in grace, and I desire more than ever to glorify God in all I think, or speak, or do. I have been helping our missionary at Beren's River in the good work among the people there. I often felt happy while endeavouring to point my heathen brethren to Jesus Christ, who takes away the sins of the world. My first consecration was of myself, when converted to Christ. My second was of my family to Him. My third is of my class. I am often very happy while trying to lead them on in the way to heaven. Today I renew my vows of consecration. I offer the sacrifice of thanksgiving, for He is my God and my portion forever. As He is the Source of Love and Light and Safety, I want to be continually drawing nearer to Him."

Very appropriate was the hymn which was next sung:

> "Ke-se-wog-ne-man-toom
> Ke-nah-te-tin," etc.
>
> "Nearer, my God, to Thee."

After three verses of this beautiful hymn were sung, we had a large number of short testimonies. Some of the people beautifully expressed themselves by quoting passages from their Indian Bibles. For example, one said; "The joy of the Lord is my strength." Another: "The Lord is my shepherd; I shall not want." Another: "Beloved, now are we the sons of God, and it doth not yet appear what we shall be: but we know that, when He shall appear, we shall be like Him; for we shall see Him as He is."

Thus delightfully passed away two hours. Perhaps fifty or sixty gave their testimonies, or quoted passages of Scripture. The speaking was up to the average of a similar gathering among white people, as these examples we have given would indicate. They were faithfully translated by two of our best interpreters, and then compared. And yet many of the beautiful Indian images are lost in the translation into English.

The best of all must be left out. The Divine power, the holy emotions, the shining faces, the atmosphere of heaven, cannot be put down on paper. Many of my readers know what I mean as thus I write, for they have been in those hallowed gatherings where "they that feared the Lord spoke often one to another."

Then followed the sacrament of the Lord's Supper. To the Christian Indians this service is, as it ever should be, the most solemn and impressive in the Church. Our custom was to hold four Communion services during the year. In addition, we sometimes gave a dying devoted member this sacrament, if so desired. Here there were a few other very important occasions, when we celebrated in this way the dying of the Lord Jesus. As, for example, when several scores of our people were going off on a dangerous trip in a plague infected district with but very poor prospects of all returning home again.

William Memotas

William Memotas was converted from the darkness of spirit worship to the light of the gospel soon after the introduction of the glad tidings of salvation among the Cree Indians by that most useful and godly man, the Rev. James Evans. William's conversion was so clear and positive that he never had any doubts about it. His progress in the divine life was marked and intelligent, and soon he became a useful and acceptable worker in the Church. He was a class leader and lay preacher of great power and acceptability.

He was pre-eminently a happy Christian. His face seemed full of sunshine. There was a genial sweetness about him that caused his very presence to act as a charm. His coming into our Mission home was like the sunshine, in which even our little ones basked with great delight. He was an everyday Christian. Although I was often in his company, and was thrown into contact with him on some occasions calculated to severely test him, yet I never heard from him an improper word, or heard of his having in any way gone contrary to his Christian profession during the thirty years that he had professed to be a follower of the Lord Jesus.

His greatest aim in life seemed to be to get to

heaven. Next to that he strove to induce others to follow in the same course.

When some of the Indians were getting excited about their lands, and the treaties which were soon to be made with the government, William, in writing to a friend, said, "I care for none of these things; they will all come right. My only desire is to love Jesus more and more, so as to see Him by and by."

He was a useful Christian. Possessing a good knowledge of the roots and herbs of his native forests, and also having had some instruction given him in reference to some of the simpler medicines of the white man, he was often called our "village doctor." Although seldom remunerated for his services, he was always ready to listen to the calls of the afflicted, and with heaven's blessing, was instrumental in accomplishing some marvelous cures. He believed in using a good deal of prayer with his medicine. His skill in dressing and curing gun shot wounds could not be excelled.

Yet, while doing all he could to cure others, his own health was very poor for several years. He suffered frequently from violent headaches that caused intense pain. Yet he was never heard to murmur or complain, but would say to us, when we tried to sympathize with him, "Never mind, by and by I shall get home, and when I see Jesus I shall have no more pain." About nine days before his departure he caught a severe cold that settled upon his lungs, which seemed to have been diseased for a long time. He had from the beginning a premonition that his sickness was "unto death," and never did a weary toiler welcome his bed of rest with greater delight than did William the grave. The prospect of getting to heaven seemed so fully to absorb his thoughts that he appeared dead to everything earthly. In life he had been a most loving and affectionate husband and father, but now, with a strong belief in God's promises of protection and care over the widow and fatherless, he resigned his family into the Lord's hands, and then seemed almost to banish them from his thoughts.

Being very poor on account of his long continued ill health, which had incapacitated him for work, he had, when his severe illness began, nothing to eat but fish. We cheerfully supplied him with what things our limited means would allow, to alleviate his sorrows and poverty. One day, when my beloved Brother Semmens and I had visited him, we had prayer and a blessed talk with him. As we were leaving him, after giving him some tangible evidences of our love, Brother Semmens said, "Now, Brother William, can we do anything else for you? Do you want anything more?" The poor sick man turned his radiant face towards us and said, "O no, I want nothing now, but more of Christ."

He often conversed with us about his glorious prospects and the joy and happiness he felt as the pearly gates of the golden city seemed to be opening before him. Here are some of his dying words whispered either to my beloved colleague or to myself. Would that we could portray the scene, or describe the happy, shining face of the dying man, lying there on a bed of blankets and rabbit skins in his little dwelling!

He said, "While my body is getting weaker, my faith is getting stronger, and I am very happy in Jesus' love. I am very glad that I responded to Mr. Evans' invitations, and gave my heart to Him who has saved me and kept me so happy in His love. I am so glad I was permitted to do some little work for Jesus. He used to help me when I tried to talk about His love and recommend Him to others. I used to get very happy in my own soul when thus working for Him. I am happier now than ever before. I am resting in His love."

Thus would the happy man talk on as long as his strength permitted. It was ever a blessing to visit him. It wonderfully encouraged and strengthened us in our work. One day, as we came from one of these blessed visits, Brother Semmens burst out in almost ecstatic delight,

> "O may I triumph so
> When all my warfare's past!"

When we administered to him the emblems of the broken body and spilt blood of the Redeemer, he was much affected, and exclaimed, "My precious Savior! I shall soon see Him. That will be joy forevermore."

Once, when conversing with him, I happened to say, "I hope you will not leave us. We want you to remain with us. We need you to help us to preach. We need you in the Sunday School and in the Prayer Meetings. Your sixty class members are full of sorrow at your sickness. They think they cannot spare you. Do not be in a hurry to leave us, William. We want your presence, your example, your prayers."

He listened patiently while I talked, and then he looked up at me so chidingly, like a weary, homesick child, and exclaimed, in a voice that showed that earth had lost all its charms, "Why do you wish to detain me? You know I want to go home."

Shortly after, his heart's desire was his in actual possession. Triumphantly he went home. While we felt that our Mission was much the loser by his departure, we knew it was better for him, and an ascension to heaven's glorious company of one who was worthy to mingle with the white robed throng around the throne of God.

There is nothing that more roots and grounds us in this blessed gospel, and more stimulates us to labor on even amid hardship and suffering, than the consistent lives and triumphant deaths of the Indian converts.

Unaware as many of them are of the non-essentials of our religion, yet possessing by the Spirit's influence a vivid knowledge of their state by nature, and of the Savior's love for them, they cling to Him with a faith so strong and abiding, that the blessed assurance of His favor abides with them as a conscious reality through life; and when the end draws near, sustained by His presence, even the valley of the shadow of death is entered with delight.

The missions among the Indians of North America have not been failures. The thousands converted from different tribes, and now before the throne of God, and the many true and steadfast ones following after, tell us that although many of the toilers among them, as they went with the seed, literally went forth weeping, yet the harvest has been an abundant one, and has more than compensated for the tears and toils of the sowers.

CHAPTER XVI

Varied duties — Christianity must precede civilization — Illustrations — Experimental farming — Ploughing with dogs — Abundance of fish — Visits from far off Indians — Some come to disturb — Many sincere inquirers after the truth — "Where is the missionary?" — Beren's River Mission begun — Timothy Bear — Peril on the ice.

Very diversified were our duties among these Indians. Not only were there those that in all places are associated with ministerial or pastoral work, but there were also many others, peculiar to this kind of missionary toil. Following closely on the acceptance of the spiritual blessings of the gospel came the desire for temporal progress and development. Christianity must ever precede a real and genuine civilization. To reverse this order of proceedings has always resulted in humiliating failure among the North American Indians.

Sir Francis Bond Head, one of the early Governors of Canada, took a great interest in the Indians. He zealously endeavoured to improve them, and honestly worked for their advancement. He gathered together a large number of them at one of their settlements, and held a great council with them. Oxen were killed, and flour and tea and tobacco were provided in large quantities. The Indians feasted and smoked, and listened attentively to this great man who represented the Queen, and who, having also supplied them with food for the great feast, was worthy of all attention.

The Governor told them that the great object of his coming to see them, and thus feasting with them, was to show his kindness to them, and interest in their welfare. Then, with much emphasis he told them how the game was disappearing, and the fish also would soon not be so plentiful, and, unless they settled down and cultivated the soil, they would suffer from hunger, and perhaps starve to death. He got them to promise that they would begin this new way of life. As they were feeling very comfortable while feasting on his bounties, they were in the humor of promising everything he desired. Very much delighted at their docility, he said he would send them axes to clear more of their land, and oxen and ploughs to prepare it for seed; and when all was ready he would send them seed grain. Great was their rejoicing at these words, and with stately ceremony the council broke up.

In a few days along came the ploughs, oxen, and axes. It was in the pleasant springtime, but instead of going to work and ploughing up the land that was cleared in their village, and beginning with their axes to get more ready, they held a council among themselves. These were their conclusions: "These axes are bright and shine like glass. If we use them to cut down trees, they will lose their fine appearance. Let us keep them as ornaments. These oxen now are fat and good. If we fasten them up to these heavy ploughs, and make them drag them through the ground, they will soon get poor and not fit for food. Let us make a great feast." So they killed the oxen, and invited all of the surrounding Indians to join them, and as long as a piece of meat was left the pots were kept boiling.

Thus ended, just as many other efforts of the same kind have ended, this effort to civilize the Indians before Christianizing them.

We found that almost in proportion to the genuineness of the Indian's acceptance of the Gospel was his desire to improve his temporal circumstances. Of course, there were some places where the Indians could not cultivate the land. We were four hundred miles north of the fertile prairies of the great western part of the Dominion of Canada, where perhaps a hundred million people will yet find happy times. From these wondrously fertile regions the Nelson River Indians were at least six hundred miles north. As hunters and fishermen, these men, and those at Oxford Mission, and indeed nearly all in those high latitudes, must live. But where there was land to cultivate, the Indians had their gardens and little fields.

I carried with me four potatoes when I came. I did not get them in the ground until the 6th of August. Yet in the short season left I succeeded in raising a few little ones. These I carefully packed in cotton wool and kept safe from the frost. The next year I got from them a pail full. The yield the third year was six bushels, and the fourth year one hundred and twenty five bushels; and before I left the Indians were raising thousands of bushels from those four potatoes. They had had some before I came, but there had been some neglect, and they had run out.

One summer I carried out, in a little open boat from Red River, a good Scotch iron beam plough. The next winter, when I came in to the District Meeting, I bought a bag of wheat containing two bushels and a half; and I got also thirty-two iron harrow teeth. I dragged these things, with many others, including quite an assortment of garden seeds, on my dog-trains all the way to Norway House. I harnessed eight dogs to my plough, and ploughed up my little fields. After making a harrow, I harrowed in my wheat with the dogs. The first year I had thirty bushels of beautiful wheat. This I cut with a sickle, and then thrashed it with a flail. Mrs. Young sewed several sheets together, and one day, when there was a steady gentle breeze blowing, we winnowed the chaff from the wheat in the wind. There were no mills within hundreds of miles of us; so we merely cracked the wheat in a hand coffee mill, and used some of it for porridge, and gave the rest to the Indians, who made use of it in their soups.

Thus we labored with them and for them, and were more and more encouraged, as the years rolled on, at seeing how resolved they were to improve their

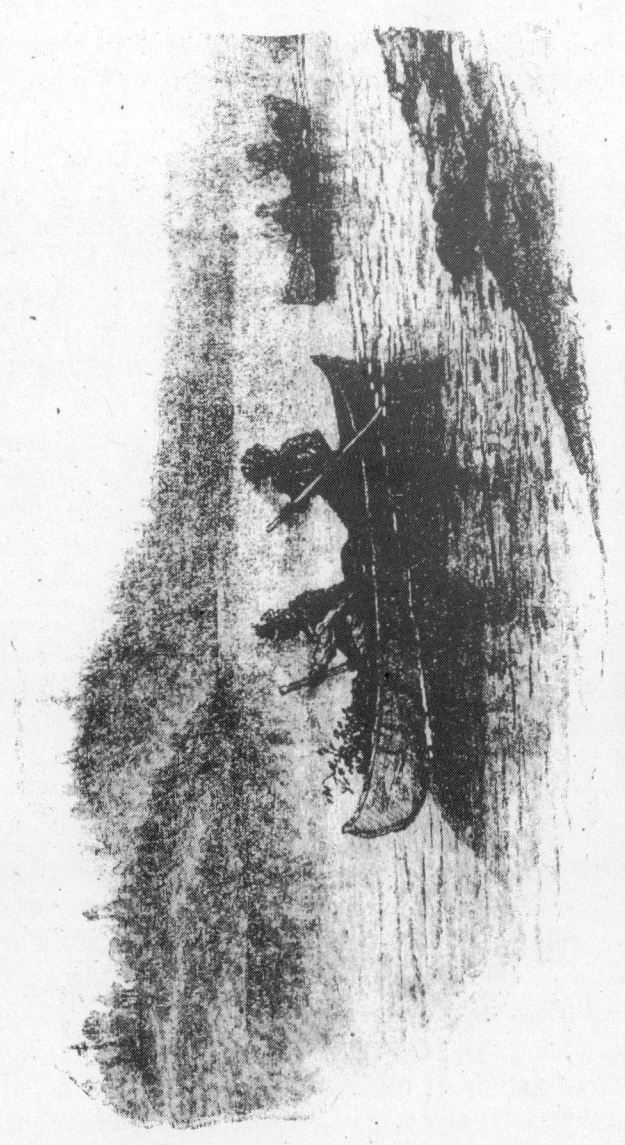

"Some came in their small canoes"

temporal circumstances, which at the best were not to be envied.

The principal article of food was fish. The nets were in the water from the time the ice disappeared in May until it returned in October; and often were holes cut in the ice, and nets placed under it, for this staple article of food.

The great fall fisheries were times of activity and anxiety, as the winter's supply of food depended very much upon the numbers caught. So steady and severe is the frost at Norway House, and at all the Missions north of it, that the fish caught in October and the early part of November, keep frozen solid until April. The principal fish is the whitefish, although many other varieties abound.

Each Indian family endeavoured to secure from three to five thousand fish, each fall, for the winter's supply. For my own family use, and more especially for my numerous dogs, which were required for my long winter trips to Mission appointments, I used to endeavour to secure not less than ten thousand fish. It is fortunate that those lakes and rivers so abound in splendid varieties of fish. If it were not so, the Indians could not exist. But providentially,

> "The teeming sea supplies
> The food the barren soil denies."

Deer of several varieties abound, and also other animals, the flesh of which furnishes nutritious food. But all supplies of food thus obtained are insignificant in comparison with the fish, which the Indians are able to obtain except in the severest weather.

As with the natives, so it was with the missionaries; the principal article of food upon their tables was fish. During the first Riel Rebellion, when all communication with the interior was cut off, and our supplies could not as usual be sent out to us from Red

River, my good wife and I lived on fish twenty one times a week, for nearly six months. Of course there were times when we had on the table, in addition to the fish, a cooked rabbit, or it may be a piece of venison or bear meat. However, the great "stand by," as they say out in that land, was the fish.

Every summer hundreds of Indians from other places visited us. Some came in their small canoes, and others with the brigades, which in those days travelled vast distances with their loads of rich furs, which were sent down to York Factory on the Hudson Bay, to be shipped to England. Sometimes the Indians remained several weeks between the trading post and the Mission. We had frequent conversations with these wandering men about the Great Spirit and the Great Book.

Some, full of mischief, and at times unfortunately full of rum, used to come to annoy and disturb us. One summer a band of Athabasca Indians so attacked our Mission house that for three days and nights we were in a state of siege. Unfortunately for us, all the able bodied Indian men were away as trip men, and the few at the Mission village were powerless to help. Our lives were in jeopardy, and they came very near burning down the premises.

Shortly after these Athabasca Indians had left us I saw a large boat load of men coming across the lake toward our village. Imagining them to be some of these same disturbers, I hastily rallied all the old men I could, and went down to the shore, to keep them, if possible, from landing. Very agreeable indeed was my surprise to find that they were a band of earnest seekers after the Great Light, who had come a long distance to see and talk with me. Gladly did I lead them to the Mission house, and until midnight I endeavoured to preach to them Jesus. They came a distance of over three hundred miles; but in that far off district had met in their wandering some of the Christian Indians from Norway House, who, always carrying their Bibles with them, had, by reading to them and praying with them, under the good Spirit's influence, implanted in their hearts longing desires after the great salvation. They were literally hungering and thirsting after salvation. Before they left for their homes, they were all baptized. Their importunate request to me on leaving was the same as that of many others: "Do come and visit us in our own land, and tell us and our families more of these blessed truths."

From God's Lake, which is sixty miles from Oxford Lake, a deputation of eleven Indians came to see me. They had travelled the whole distance of two hundred and sixty miles in order that they might hear the gospel, and get from me a supply of Bibles, hymn books, and catechisms. One of them had been baptized and taught years ago by the Rev. R. Brooking. His life and teaching had made the others eager for this blessed way, and so he brought these hungry sheep in the wilderness that long distance that they might have the truth explained to them more perfectly, and be baptized. As it had been with the others who came from a different direction, so it was with these. Their earnest, often repeated entreaty was, "Come and visit us and ours in our far away homes."

A few weeks after, another boat load of men called to have a talk with me. They seated themselves on the grass in front of the Mission house, and at first acted as though they expected me to begin the conversation. I found out very soon that they were Saulteaux, and had come from Beren's River, about a hundred and fifty miles away. After a few words as to their health and families had passed between us, an old man, who seemed to be the spokesman of the party, said, "Well, Ayume-aookemou" ("praying master," the missionary's name), "do you remember your words of three summers ago?"

"What were my words of three summers ago?" I asked.

"Why," he replied, "your words were that you would write to the Keche-ayumeaookemou" (the great praying master, the missionary secretary) "for a missionary for us."

When I first passed through their country, they with tears in their eyes had begged for a missionary. I had been much moved by their appeals, and had written to the Mission House about them and for them, but all in vain. None had come to labor among them.

For my answer to this old man's words I translated a copy of my letter, which had been published, and in which I had strongly urged their claims for a missionary. They all listened attentively to the end, and then the old man sprang up and said, "We all thank you for sending that word, but where is the missionary?" I was lost for an answer, for I felt that I was being asked by this hungering soul the most important question that can be heard by the Christian Church, to whom God has committed the great work of the world's evangelization.

"Where is the missionary?" The question convicted me, and I went down before it like the reed before the storm. I could only weep and say, "Lord, have mercy upon me and on the apathetic Christian Church."

That was the hardest question a human being ever asked me. To tell him of a want of men, or a lack of money, to carry the glad tidings of salvation to him and his people, would only have filled his mind with doubts as to the genuineness of the religion enjoyed by a people so numerous and rich as he knew the whites were. So I tried to give them some idea of the world's population, and the vast number yet unconverted to Christianity. I told him the churches were at work in many places and among many nations, but that many years would pass away before all the world would be supplied with missionaries.

"How many winters will pass by before that time comes?" he asked.

"A great many, I fear," was my answer.

He put his hands through his long hair, once as black as a raven's wing, but now becoming silvered, and replied: "These white hairs show that I have lived many winters, and am getting old. My countrymen at Red River on the south of us, and here at Norway House on the north of us, have missionaries, and churches, and schools; and we have none. I do not wish to die until we have a church and a school."

The story of this old man's appeal woke up the good people of the churches, and something was soon done for these Indians. I visited them twice a year by canoe and dog-train, and found them anxious for religious instruction and progress.

At first I sent to live among them my faithful interpreter, Timothy Bear. He worked faithfully and did good service. He was not a strong man physically, and could not stand much exposure. He had my large leather tent to live in, which was made of the prepared skins of the buffalo. One night a great tornado swept over the country, and Timothy's tent was carried away, and then the drenching rains fell upon him and his family. A severe cold resulted, and when word reached me several weeks after at Norway House, it was that my trusted friend was hopelessly ill, but was still endeavouring to keep at his duties.

So great was my anxiety to go and comfort him that I started out with my dog-trains so soon after the winter set in that that trip very nearly proved to be my last. The greater part of that journey was performed upon Lake Winnipeg. Very frequently on the northern end of that lake the ice, which there forms first, is broken up by the fierce winds from the southern end, which, being three hundred miles further south, remains open several days longer. I had with me two Indians. One was an old experienced man, named William Cochran; the other a splendid specimen of physical manhood, named Felix.

When we reached Lake Winnipeg, as far as we could judge by the appearance of the ice, it must have formed three times, and then have been broken up by the storms. The broken masses were piled up in picturesque ridges along the shore, or frozen together in vast fields extending for many miles. Over these rough ice fields, where great pieces of ice, from five to twenty feet high, were thrown at every angle, and then frozen solid, we travelled for two days. Both men and dogs suffered a great deal from falls and bruises. Our feet at times were bruised and bleeding. Just about daybreak on our third day, as we pushed out from our camp in the woods where we had spent the night, when we had got a considerable distance from the shore, Felix was delighted to find smooth ice. He was guiding at the time. He put on his skates and bounded off quickly, and was soon followed by the dogs, who seemed as delighted as he that the rough ice had all been passed, and now there was a possibility of getting on with speed and comfort.

Just as I was congratulating myself on the fact of our having reached good ice, and that now there was a prospect of soon reaching my sick Indian brother, a cry of terror came from William, the experienced Indian who was driving our provision sled behind mine.

"This ice is bad, and we are sinking," he shouted.

Thinking the best way for me was to stop I checked my dogs, and at once began to sink.

"Keep moving, but make for the shore," was the instant cry of the man behind.

I shouted to my splendid, well trained dogs, and they at once responded to the command given, and bounded towards the shore. Fortunately the ice was strong enough to hold the dogs up, although under the sled it bent and cracked, and in some places broke through.

We were very grateful when we got back to the

rough, strong ice near the shore. In quiet tones we spoke a few words of congratulation to each other, and lifted up our hearts in gratitude to our great Preserver, and then hurried on. If we had broken in, we could have received no earthly aid, as there was not even a wigwam within a day's journey of us.

That night at the camp fire I overheard William saying to Felix, "I am ashamed of ourselves for not having taken better care of our missionary."

We found Timothy very sick indeed. We ministered to his comfort, and had it then in our power so to arrange that, while the work should not suffer, he could have rest and quiet. His success had been very marked, and the old Saulteaux rejoiced that he and the rest of them were to be neglected no longer. He had made such diligent progress himself in spiritual things that I gladly baptized him and his household.

There were times when our supplies ran very short, and hunger and suffering had to be endured. During the first Riel Rebellion, when we were cut off from access to the outside world, we were entirely dependent upon our nets and guns for a long time. Our artist has tried to tell a story in three pictures.

At the breakfast table we had nothing to eat but the hind quarter of a wild cat. It was very tough and tasteless; and while we were trying to make our breakfast from it, Mrs. Young said, "My dear, unless you shoot something for dinner, I am afraid there will be none."

So I took down my rifle, tied on my snowshoes, and started off looking for game. See page 215. Pages 216 and 217 tell the rest of the story

I. Nothing but the hind quarter of a wildcat for breakfast. Off looking for game.

II. Six hundred yards is a long shot, but wildcat is poor food.
So we will try for something better.

III. Come, share with me our savoury venison.

CHAPTER XVII

Smallpox pestilence — Heroic conduct of Christian Indians — Whites supplied with provisions by Indians — The guide, Samuel Papanekis — His triumphant death — Nancy, the happy widow — In poverty, yet rejoicing.

We were very much shocked, during the early spring, to hear that the terrible disease, smallpox, had broken out among the Indians on the great plains of the Saskatchewan.

It seems to have been brought into the country by some white traders coming up from the State of Montana. When once it had got among them, it spread with amazing rapidity and fatality. To make matters worse, one of the tribes of Indians, being at war with another, secretly carried some of the infected clothing, which had been worn by their own dead friends, into the territory of those with whom they were at war, and left it where it could be easily found and carried off. In this way the disease was communicated to this second tribe, and thousands of them died from it.

Every possible precaution against the spread of this terrible destroyer was taken by the missionaries, Messers. McDougall and Campbell, aided by their Christian people. But, in spite of all their efforts, it continued cutting down both whites and Indians. To save some of his people Mr. McDougall got the Indians of his Victoria Mission to leave their homes and scatter themselves over the great prairies, where, he hoped, they would, by being isolated, escape the contagion. The other Indians, rendered desperate under the terrible scourge which was so rapidly cutting them off, and being powerless to check it, resolved to wreak their vengeance upon the defenseless whites. So they sent a band of warriors to destroy every white person in the country. The first place they reached, where dwelt any of the palefaces, was the Victoria Mission on the Saskatchewan River. They did not openly attack, but, leaving the greater number of their warriors in ambush in the long grass, a few of them sauntered into the Mission house. Here, to their surprise, they found that the smallpox had entered, and some of the inmates of the home had died. Quickly and quietly they glided away, and told their comrades what they had seen. A hasty consultation was held, and they decided that it could not have been the missionary who had control of the disease; for if he had, he would not have allowed it to have killed his own. They then decided it must have been the fur-traders, and so they started for the trading post. Here they pursued the same tactics, and found to their surprise that a Mr. Clarke, the gentleman in charge of that place, had fallen a victim. Another hasty council made them think that they had been mistaken, and so they quickly returned to their own country without having injured anyone.

But the missionary and his family were surrounded by perils. The Indians were excited and unsettled, and their old conjurers were ever ready to incite them to deeds of violence. The restraining power of God alone saved them from massacre. Once a missionary's wife and some of the family were at work in the garden, while secreted in the long grass not a hundred yards from them lay eleven Blackfeet, who had come to murder and pillage the place, but, as they afterwards acknowledged, were strangely restrained from firing. At another time some of the fierce warriors of this same tribe crawled through a field of barley, and for a long time watched the movements of a family, and then noiselessly retired, doing no harm to anyone. To hear the ping of a bullet as it passed in close proximity to the head was no rare event in the lives of several of the early missionaries among the Indians.

While the smallpox was raging in the great Saskatchewan country, strenuous efforts were made to prevent its spreading to other districts. Manitoba had now been formed into a province, and was filling up with white settlers. The old name, Fort Garry, had been changed to Winnipeg, and this place was rapidly growing into a prosperous town. From Fort Garry long trains of Red River carts had been in the habit of going for years with the supplies needed in the far off Saskatchewan country. These carts were made without having in their construction a single piece of iron. The Metis or Indian drivers never oiled or greased them, and the result was they could be heard about as far as seen, even on the level prairies. Each cart was drawn by one ox, and was supposed to carry from eight to twelve hundred pounds of supplies, in addition to the food and outfit of the driver, who was always expected to walk. This freighting by carts on the prairies is the counterpart of transporting goods by open boats or canoes in the northern rivers, to which we have elsewhere referred. The arrival of the brigade of carts with the supplies, and the news from the outside world, was the great event of the year in the early times of those lonely prairie settlements.

But stern measures had to be adopted in this year of the smallpox plague. A proclamation was issued by the Governor of the Province of Manitoba, absolutely prohibiting any trade or communication in any way with the infected district. Not a single cart or traveller was permitted to go on the trail. This meant a good deal of suffering and many privations for the isolated missionaries, traders, and other whites who, for purposes of settlement or adventure, had gone into that remote interior country.

As it was, only twice a year in many places did the lonely missionaries hear from the outside world.

Dog-train with mail

Then the mail carrier was very welcome, whether he came by canoe or dog-train.

Although there were still plenty of buffalo on the plains, it was well known that the ammunition was about exhausted, as well as all other supplies, including medicines, now so much needed. Some interested parties vainly urged the Governor to relent and allow some supplies to be sent in. But, conscious of the risks that would be run of the pestilence reaching the province over which he governed, he remained firm, while he felt for those who necessarily must suffer.

"What can be done to aid those unfortunate ones, who, in addition to their sorrows and troubles incident to the ravages of the smallpox among them, are now to be exposed to pinching famine and want?" was the question that sympathizing friends were asking each other. As a last resort it was decided to

Rev. Edward Papanekis and family

appeal to the Norway House Christian Indians, and ask them to form a brigade of boats, and take the much needed supplies up the mighty Saskatchewan River, where they could be reached by those needing them.

To me, as missionary to these Indians, Mr. Stewart, the highest official of the Hudson's Bay Company, came; and we talked the matter over, and the risks which the Indians, not one of whom had been vaccinated, must run in going on such a perilous journey. They would have to go hundreds of miles through the disease stricken land where hundreds had died. But it seemed essential that something must be done, and there were possibilities that the Indians, by acting very wisely, could escape infection; so we decided to call them together, and see what they would do in this emergency.

When the church bell was rung, and the people had assembled together in their Council house, wondering what was the matter, I described the sad circumstances to them, and then presented the request, that one hundred and sixty of them should take twenty boats loaded with supplies, and go up the Saskatchewan, to save these white people from starving. I said to the converted Indians, "I know your race on this continent has not always been fairly treated; but never mind that. Here is a grand opportunity for you to do a glorious act, and to show to the world and to the good Lord, whose children you are, that you can make sacrifices and run risks when duty calls, as well as the whites can."

We told them that there was a possibility that they, by keeping in the middle of the great river all the time, and never going ashore, might all escape. They would be provided with abundance of food; so they need not go ashore to hunt. Then we asked, "Are you willing to run the risk, and avail yourselves of this chance to do a glorious act?" Turning to one of the most trusted guides in the country, one of my best class leaders, I said: "Samuel Papanekis, you are to be the guide and leader of this party." He was a son of the old centenarian, and brother of the Rev. Edward Papanekis, now our missionary at Oxford House Mission.

He seemed at first a little startled by the responsibility of the position, and after a moment's thought quietly said: "Will you give us a little time to talk it over?" So we left them to discuss the matter among themselves. When they sent us word that they had their answer ready, we returned, and he said, "Missionary, we have talked it over, and have decided to go to take the supplies to our suffering white brothers and their families. But will you let us have one more Sunday at the church, and will you give us the sacrament of the Lord's Supper, before we start upon the dangerous journey?"

"Yes," I said, "it will take several days to get your loads and boats ready, and so we will have another blessed day of rest and hallowed worship together."

It was a memorable Sabbath. Every man, woman, and child who could come to church, seemed to be there. Some of the women wept as they thought of the risks their husbands, brothers, or sons were running. Others of them seemed to catch the spirit of the men, and felt proud that those they loved were willing to undertake so brave and noble a work.

At the close of the morning service we had the sacrament of the Lord's Supper. It was very solemn and impressive. As they came forward and partook of the emblems of their dear Lord's dying love, the recollection of His self-sacrifice and disinterested kindness seemed to come very vividly before us all, and there was in many hearts a kind of exultant joy that they were counted worthy to run some risks for the sake of doing good.

No foolish boastfulness, or desire to seek for

sympathy, characterized their utterances at the afternoon service, at which we met again in a testimony or fellowship meeting. Some made no reference at all to the work before them; others asked for our prayers for them, and others, well taught in the Word of God, with the hallowed influences of the morning sacramental service still resting upon them, thought that they ought to rejoice when there were chances for getting into this spirit, so as to be partakers of Christ's sufferings, or companions in tribulation with such a Friend, so that when His glory should be revealed, they also might rejoice, as He has taught us: "If we suffer with Him," we shall "also be glorified together."

Two or three days after this they started on their long, dangerous journey. They had twenty boats well loaded with supplies, each manned by eight Indians, and all under the guidance of Samuel Papanekis, whom they were expected to implicitly obey. They went up the Pine River that passes by Norway House, until they entered into Lake Winnipeg. From this place they skirted around the shore of this great lake, until they reached the mouth of the Saskatchewan River. Up this great river they had to row their boats against the current for many hundreds of miles. That summer was an exceedingly hot one, yet for weeks together these gallant fellows tugged away at their heavy oars. For a few short hours of rest during the night they anchored their boats in mid-stream, and then at first blush of morning they continued their journey. Wild beasts were sometimes seen walking on the shores or quenching their thirst in the river. The hunting instincts of the younger Indian boat men were so strong that they begged to be allowed to fire; but Samuel, ever on the alert, and seeing the danger, always positively refused.

When the Sabbaths came they anchored their boats as close together as possible near the middle of the river on some shoal or shallow spot, such as abound in this great river of shifting sand bars. Here they spent their quiet, restful days, having prayers and a couple of religious services each Sunday.

Before they reached the place where they were to deliver their precious cargoes, the river passed through many miles of the plague stricken country. They could see on the shores the deserted wigwams, in which all the inmates had fallen victims to the terrible destroyer, or had, panic stricken, fled away.

Very long seemed that summer, and great indeed was our concern, and many were our prayers for these noble men, from whom we did not hear a single word during the whole time of their absence. After being away for about ten weeks, they came back amid a doxology of thanksgiving and gratitude. All of them were happy and in vigorous health, with the exception of the guide. The strain and anxiety upon him had been too much, and he was never the same man after. The others said, "Samuel seemed to be everywhere, and to watch every movement with almost sleepless vigilance." Realizing how great the responsibilities were upon him, he determined, if untiring devotion to his work would enable him to rescue those suffering white, and then return with his large brigade uncontaminated by the disease, it should be done.

He succeeded, but at the price of his own life, for he only came home to linger a while and then to die. His indomitable will power kept him up until he saw the last boat safely moored in our quiet harbor, and witnessed the loving greetings between his stalwart crews and their happy families. He joined with us all in the blessed thanksgiving service in our overflowing sanctuary, where with glad hearts we sang together:

> "And are we yet alive,
> And see each other's face?
> Glory and praise to Jesus give
> For His redeeming grace:
> Preserved by power Divine
> To full salvation here,
> Again in Jesus' praise we join,
> And in His sight appear."

Then he began to droop and wither, and in spite of all that we, or the kind Hudson's Bay officials, who were very much attached to him, could do for him, he seemed almost visibly to slip away from us.

By and by the end drew near. It was a beautiful day, and as he had some difficulty in breathing, at his own request a wigwam was prepared, and he was well wrapped up and gently lifted out of his house and placed upon a bed of balsam boughs covered with robes. He seemed grateful for the change, and appeared a little easier for a time. We talked of Jesus and heaven, and the abundant entrance and the exceeding great and precious promises. Then he dropped off in a quiet slumber. Soon after, he awoke with a consciousness that the time of his departure had come, and laid himself out to die. Bending over him, I said, "Samuel, this is death that has come for you! Tell me how it is with you." His hearing had partly left him, and so he did not understand me. Speaking more loudly I said, "Samuel, my brother, you are in the valley of the shadow of death; how is it with you?"

His eye brightened, and his look told me he had understood my question. He lifted up his thin, emaciated arm, and, seeming to clasp hold of something, he said, "Missionary, I am holding on to God; He is my all of joy and hope and happiness."

Then the arm fell nerveless, and my triumphant Indian brother was in the better land.

Perhaps I cannot find a better place than here to refer to Samuel's widow and children, and an interview I had with them.

They moved away, shortly after his death, from his house in the village, and took up their abode with several other families up the river beyond the Fort, several miles from the village. We had visited them and substantially aided them up to the time of their moving away, but for a while I had not seen them, except at the services, and so did not know how they were prospering. When the cold winter set in, I arranged with my good Brother Semmens that we would take our dog-trains and go and make pastoral visits among all the Indian families on the outskirts, and find out how they were prospering, temporally and spiritually. It was ever a great joy to them when we visited them, and by our inquiries about their fishing and hunting, and other simple affairs, showed we were interested in these things, and rejoiced with them when they could tell of success, and sympathized with them when they had met with loss or disaster. Then they listened reverently when we read from the blessed Word, and prayed with them in their humble homes.

One bitterly cold day towards evening we drove up to a very poor little house. We knocked at the door, and in answer to a cheery "Astum," the Cree word for "Come in," we entered the little abode. Our hearts sank within us at the evidences of the poverty of the inmates. The little building was made of poplar logs, the cracks of which were filled up with moss and clay. The floor was of the native earth, and there was not a piece of furniture in the abode, not a table, chair, or bedstead. In one corner of the room was an earthen fireplace, and huddled around a poor fire in it, there sat a widow with a large family of children, one of whom was a cripple.

We said a few words of kindly greeting to the family, and then, looking round on the destitute home, I said sorrowfully, "Nancy, you seem to be very poor; you don't seem to have anything to make you happy and comfortable." Very quickly came the response, and it was in a very much more cheery strain than my words had been.

Fishing through the ice

"I have not got much, but I am not unhappy, Missionary."

"You poor creature," I replied, "you don't seem to have anything to make you comfortable."

"I have but little," she said quietly.

"Have you any venison?"

"No!"

"Have you any flour?"

"No!"

"Have you any tea?"

"No!"

"Have you any potatoes?"

When this last question of mine was uttered, the poor woman looked up at me, for she was the widow of Samuel Papanekis, and this was her answer: "I have no potatoes, for, don't you remember, at the time of potato planting Samuel took charge of the brigade that went up with provisions to save the poor white people? And Samuel is not here to shoot deer, that I may have venison; and Samuel is not here to catch mink and marten and beaver and other things to exchange for flour and tea."

"What have you got, poor woman?" I said with my heart full of sorrow.

She replied, "I have got a couple of fish nets."

"What did you do when it was too stormy to visit the nets?"

"Sometimes some of the men from the other houses visited them for me, and would bring me the fish. Then we sometimes get some by fishing through the ice."

"What about when it was too stormy for any one to go?"

She quietly said, "If nothing is left, we go without anything."

As I looked at her and her large family of fatherless children, and then thought of her husband's triumphant death, and his glorious transfer to that blest abode, where they shall hunger no more, neither thirst any more, and where God shall wipe away all tears from their eyes, the contrast between the husband and father in his dedication, and the sorrow of the widow and children in their poverty, so affected me that, to hide my emotion and keep back my tears, I hurried out of the room, following my loving Brother Semmens, who was, if possible, more deeply moved than I was. We had gone into that house to pray, but we could not. There must be tangible sympathy given before we could look to a higher source.

My brother had reached the cariole, which was a few yards away, and I was not far behind, when the word, "Ayumeaookemou," ("Praying master,") arrested my hurrying steps. I turned back, and there, just outside of the door was Nancy. With a woman's quick intuition to read the feelings of the heart from the face and voice, she had followed me out, and her words, as nearly as I can recall them, were these, "Missionary, I do not want you to feel so badly for me; it is true I am very poor; it is true, since Samuel died, we have often been hungry, and have often suffered from the bitter cold; but, Missionary," and her face had no trace of sorrow upon it, "you have heard me say that as Samuel gave his heart to God, so have I given God my heart, and He who comforted Samuel and helped him, so that he died so happily, is my Savior; and where Samuel has gone, by and by I am going too; and that thought makes me happy all the day long."

There came a blessed exultation into my soul, but I could find no answer then. So I hurried on and joined my weeping brother, and shouting, "Marche!" to our dogs, we were soon rapidly speeding over the icy trail to our Mission home.

That night our bed was a blanket thinner, and on our limited supplies there was a heavy drain. I told the Indians who were better off about her straitened condition, and she and hers were made more comfortable. Many of them gave very generously indeed to help her. The grace of liberality abounds largely among these poorer Christian Indians, and they will give to the necessities of those who are poorer than themselves until it seems at times as though they had about reached the same level.

The triumphant death of Samuel, and then

Nancy's brave words, very much encouraged us in our work. We could not but more than rejoice at the gospel's power, still so consciously manifested to save in the valley of the shadow of death, and also to make a humble log cabin a little heaven below. We pitied her in her poverty, and yet soon after, when we had thought it all over in the light of eternity, we could only rejoice with her, and in our spirits say, "Happy woman! Better live in a log hut without a chair, table, bedstead, without flour, tea, potatoes, entirely dependent upon the nets in the lake for food, if the Lord Jesus is a constant guest, than in a mansion of a millionaire, surrounded by every luxury, but destitute of His presence."

It is a matter of great thankfulness that not only spiritually but temporally thousands of the Indians in different parts of Canada are improving grandly. The accompanying picture (page 233) is from a photograph taken at the Scugog Lake Indian Mission. The fine barn, well filled with wheat, as well as all the surrounding vehicles and agricultural implements, belong to one of the Christian Indians.

Christian Indian's Barn, Scugog Mission

CHAPTER XVIII

A race for life in a blizzard storm — Saved by the marvelous intelligence of Jack — "Where is the old man, whose head was like the snowdrift?"

Blizzard storms sometimes assailed us, as on the long winter trails, with our gallant dogs and faithful companions, we wandered over those regions of great distances.

To persons who have not actually made the acquaintance of the blizzard storms of the Northwest Territories, or wild northland, it is almost impossible to give a satisfactory description. One peculiarity about them, causing them to differ from other storms, is that the wind seems to be ever coming in little whirls or eddies, which keep the air full of snow, and make it almost impossible to tell the direction from which the wind really comes. With it apparently striking you in the face, you turn your back to it, and are amazed at finding that it still faces you. Once, when on Lake Winnipeg, we saw one coming down upon us. Its appearance was that of a dense fog blowing in from the sea. Very few indeed are they who can steer their course correctly in a blizzard storm. Most people, when so unfortunate as to be caught in one, soon get bewildered, and almost blinded by the fine, dry, hard particles of snow which so pitilessly beat upon them, filling eyes, nose, and even ears and mouth, if at all exposed.

Once, when crossing Lake Winnipeg, to visit some Indians, whom we found on our arrival in the midst of the ceremonies of a dog feast, I got caught in a terrible storm. My men had gone on ahead with all the dogs, to have dinner ready in the camp on the distant shore, leaving me miles behind, tramping along on snowshoes. Down from the north, with terrific fury, came the gale. I tramped on as rapidly as possible, until I got bewildered. Then I took off one of my snowshoes, and, fastening it in a hole cut in the ice, I got ready to tramp in a small circle around it to keep from freezing to death, when fortunately I heard the welcome whooping of my companions, who, seeing my danger, had quickly turned round, and risking their own lives for mine, for they could have reached the woods and shelter, aided by the dogs, had fortunately reached me. There we stopped for hours, until the blizzard had spent its fury, and then on we went.

I had a remarkable experience in a blizzard, which I will more fully describe, as our escape was under Providence so much indebted to my wonderful dog, Jack.

I had started on one of my long winter trips to visit the few little bands of Indians who were struggling for an existence on the eastern coast of Lake Winnipeg, and who were always glad to welcome the missionary, and to hear from him of the love of the Great Spirit, and of His Son, Jesus Christ. Their country is very wild and rough, very different from the beautiful prairie regions. To keep down expenses, which in those northern Missions are very heavy, I had started out on this long trip with only one young Indian lad as my companion. But as he was good and true, I thought we could succeed, since I had been several years in that country, and had faced many a wintry storm, and slept many nights in the snow.

We had with us two splendid trains of dogs. My leader was a lively, cunning Eskimo dog, as white as snow. His name was Koona, which is the Cree word for snow; and he was well named. The other three dogs of my train were my favorites from Ontario. Two of them were gifts from Senator Sanford, of Hamilton; the other was kindly sent to me by Dr. Mark, of Ottawa. The other train, driven by Alec, was composed of some sagacious St. Bernards

Indian ceremonies at a dog feast.

obtained for me by the kindness of Mr. Ferrier, of Montreal. The largest and most enduring of the eight was Jack, from Hamilton, whose place was second in my train, and who is to be the hero of this adventure.

We had left our campfire in the woods early in the morning, and turning our faces towards the north, had hoped that before the shadows of night had fallen around us, at least sixty miles of the frozen surface of Lake Winnipeg would have been travelled over. For a time we were able to push on very rapidly, keeping the distant points of headlands well in view for our guidance. Lake Winnipeg is very much indented with bays, and in traveling we do not follow the coast line, but strike directly across these bays from point to point. Some of them run back for many miles into the land, and several of them are from ten to thirty miles wide. The dogs get so accustomed to these long trips and to their work, that they require no guide to run on ahead, but will, with wonderful intelligence, push on from point to point with great exactness.

On and on we had travelled for hours; the cold was very great, but we could easily jump off our dog sleds and run until we felt the glow and warmth of such vigorous exercise. After a while, we noticed that the strong wind which had arisen was filling the air with fine dry snow, and making traveling very difficult and unpleasant. Soon it increased to a gale, and we found ourselves in a real northwest blizzard on stormy Lake Winnipeg, many miles from shore.

Perhaps our wisest plan would have been, at the commencement of the storm, to have turned sharply to the east, and got into the shelter of the forest as quickly as possible. But the bay we were crossing was a very deep one, and the headland before us seemed as near as the other end of the bay; and so we thought it best to run the risk and push on. That we might not get separated from each other, I fastened what we call the tail rope of my sled to the collar of the head dog of Alec's train.

After Alec and I had travelled on for several hours, no sign of any land appearing, we began to think that the fickle blizzard was playing us one of its tricks, and that we had wandered far out into the lake. We stopped our dogs out there in the blinding, bewildering storm.

"Alec!" I shouted, "I am afraid we are lost."

"Yes, Missionary," he replied, "we are surely lost."

We talked about our position, and both had to confess that we did not really know where we were or which way we ought to go.

The result of our deliberation was that we could do no better than trust in the good Providence above us, and in our dogs before us.

As it was now after midday, and the vigorous exercise for the last few hours had made us very hungry, we opened our provision bag, and taking out some frozen food, made a fairly good attempt to satisfy the keen demands of appetite. We missed very much the good cup of hot black tea we should have had if we had been fortunate enough to reach the shore, and find some wood with which to make a fire.

After our hasty meal we held a short consultation, in which the fact became more and more evident to us, that our position was a very perilous one, as we were becoming blinded by the driving particles of fine snow that stung our eyeballs and added much to our bewilderment. We found that we did not know east from west, or north from south, and would have to leave the dogs to decide on their own course, and let them go in any direction they pleased.

I had a good deal of confidence in my dogs, as I had proved their sagacity. To Jack, the noblest of them all, I looked to lead us out of our difficulty; and he did not disappoint our expectations. I suppose I acted and talked to my dog in a way that some folks would have considered very foolish. When traveling regularly, the dogs are only fed once a day, and that when the day's work is done. However, I was different that day, as in the blinding gale Alec and I tried to eat our dinner. As Jack and the others crowded around us, they were not neglected, and with them we shared the food we had, as there was a great uncertainty whether another meal would ever be required by any one of us.

As usual in such emergencies, Jack had come up close to me, and so, while he, Alec and I, and the rest of us, men and dogs, were eating our dinners, I had a talk with him.

"Jack, my noble fellow," I said, "do you know that we are lost, and that it is very doubtful whether we shall ever see the Mission home again? The prospect is that the snow will soon be our winding sheet, and that loving eyes will look in vain for our return. The chances are against your ever having the opportunity of stretching yourself out on the wolf rug before the study fire. Rouse up yourself, old dog, for in your intelligence we are going to trust to lead us to a place of safety."

The few arrangements necessary for the race were soon made. Alec wrapped himself up as comfortably as possible in his rabbit skin robe, and I helped him to ensconce himself securely on his dog sled. I tied a rope from the end of my sled to the collar of his leader dog, so that our trains might not get separated. Then I straightened out the trains, and wrapping myself up as well as I could on my sled, I shouted "Marche!" to the dogs.

I had as leader dog the intelligent white Eskimo dog, Koona. As I shouted the word for go, Koona turned his head and looked at me, as though bewildered, and seemed to be waiting for "Chaw" or "Yee." the words for right and left. As I did not know myself, I shouted to Jack, who was second in the train, "Go on, Jack, whichever way you like, and do the best you can, for I do not know anything about it." As Koona still hesitated, Jack, with all the confidence imaginable, dashed off in a certain direction, and Koona with slackened traces ran beside him, very willing in such an emergency to give him all the honor of leadership.

For hours the dogs kept bravely to their work. The storm raged and howled around us, but not for one moment did Jack hesitate or seem to be at fault. Koona had nothing to do but run beside him; but the other two splendid dogs in the traces behind Jack seemed to catch his spirit, and nobly aided him by their untiring efforts and courage. The cold was so intense that I had grave fears that we should freeze to death. We were obliged so to wrap ourselves up that it was impossible with so much on us to run with any comfort, or to keep up with the dogs while going at such a rapid rate. Frequently would I shout back to my comrade, "Alec! don't go to sleep. Alec, if you do, you may never wake up until the Judgment morning." Back would come his response, "All right, sir; then I'll try to keep awake."

Thus on we travelled through that wintry storm. How cold, how relentless, how bitter were the continuous blasts of the north wind! After a while the shadows of night fell upon us, and we were enshrouded in the darkness. Not a pleasant position was that in which we were situated; but there was no help for it, nor any use in giving way to despondency or despair. A sweet peace filled my soul, and in a blessed restfulness of spirit my heart was kept stayed upon God. While there is life there is hope; and so, with an occasional shout of warning to Alec to keep awake, and a cheering call to the dogs, who required no special urging, so gallantly were they doing their work, we patiently hung on to our sleds and awaited the result. We were now in the gloom of night, dashing along I knew not where, and not even able at times to see the dogs before us.

About three hours after dark the dogs quickened their pace into a gallop, and showed by their excitement that they had detected evidences of nearness to the shore and safety, of which as yet I knew nothing. Soon after they dragged us over a large pile of broken ice and snow, the accumulations of ice cut out of the holes in the lake, where the Indian families had for months obtained their supply of water for cooking and other purposes. Turning sharply on the trail toward the shore, our dogs dashed along for a couple of hundred yards more. Then they dragged us up a steep bank into the forest, and, after a few minutes more of rapid traveling, we found ourselves in the middle of a little collection of wigwams, and among a band of friendly Indians, who gave us a cordial welcome, and rejoiced with us at our escape from the storm, which was the severest of the year.

We had three days of religious services with them, and then went on our way from encampment to encampment. Very glad were the poor people to see us, and with eagerness did they receive the word preached.

I felt that it was very slow work. My circuit or mission field was larger than all England. I was the only missionary of any church in this large field. By canoe or dog-train I could only get around to all my appointments or out stations twice a year. Six months the poor souls had to wait for the messenger and the message.

At one of these Indian encampments on one of these visits I had the following sad experience. Before

I closed the first service I asked, "Where is the old man whose head was like the snowdrift?" for I had missed a white haired old man, who had ever been at all the services, and had from the time of his conversion manifested the greatest anxiety to hear and learn all he could about this great salvation. At first he had opposed me, and was annoyed at my coming among his people. Ultimately, however, he became convinced of the error of his ways, and was an earnest, decided Christian. When I arrived at his village, whether by canoe in summer, or dog-train in winter, I was always received by this venerable old man with great delight. Not satisfied with attending all the services held, and being at hand whenever I taught the syllabic characters, that the Indians might be able to read the blessed Word, he used to follow me like my shadow, and listen very attentively to all I had to say. It was rather startling, indeed, when one night, after a hard day of preaching, teaching and counselling, I kneeled down to pray, before I wrapped myself up in my camp bed to get a little rest, to hear whispered in quiet tones beside me, "Missionary, pray in Cree, and out loud so that I can hear you." In the morning prayers there came into my ears from this old man the pleading words again, "Missionary, please pray in Cree, and pray out loud, so that I may hear what you say."

Is it any wonder that I became very much attached to my old friend with the snow white hair, who was so hungering and thirsting for the teachings of the Word? Only twice a year could I then visit him and his people. I used to remain a few days at each of these visits, and very busy ones indeed they were. For six months these poor sheep in the wilderness had been without the gospel, and as soon as I left they would have to get along as well as they could on what they had heard. Now that they had, under the Spirit's influence, a longing desire to receive the truth, can any one wonder at their anxiety to learn all they could from the missionary during his short stay among them? This intense desire on their part filled my heart with thankfulness, and amply compensated for all the sufferings and hardships of the long, cold, dangerous journeys.

On my arrival at this place, as usual, the Indians had crowded around to welcome me. I was disappointed at not seeing my old friend. So it was that at our first meeting, held as soon as possible after my arrival, I asked the question, "Where is the old man whose head was like the snowdrift?"

To my question there was no response, but every head was bowed as in grief and sorrow.

Again I asked, "Tell me, what have you done with the old man with the snow white hair?"

Then there was a little whispering among them, and one of them, speaking out softly, said in the Cree language, "Non pimmatissit," the English of which is, "He is not among the living."

These poor Indians, who have not as yet come to understand that death is a conquered foe, never like to use the word; and so, when speaking of those who have gone, they say they are "not among the living."

When in this expressive way I learned that my old friend was dead, my heart was filled with sorrow, as I saw also were theirs. After a little pause I said, "Tell me how he died."

At first there was a great deal of reluctance to answer this question; but when they saw I was not only anxious but resolved to know all about it, they took me into a wigwam where most of his relatives were, and there a young man, a grandson, got up and told me this pathetic story.

He said: "Missionary, you had not been long gone with your canoe last summer before Mismis (the Cree word for grandfather) got very sick, and after some weeks he seemed to know that he was going to leave us. So he called us all around him, and said a great many things to us. I cannot remember them all, as he spoke many times; but I do remember that he said, 'How I wish the missionary would soon come again to talk to me and comfort me! But he is far away, and my memory is bad, and I have forgotten what he used to say to me. My body is breaking up, and so also is my memory getting bad. Tell him his coming was like the sunlight on the waters; but it was so seldom that he came that all in my mind has got so dark, and my memory is so bad, that I have forgotten all he used to say to me. The good things he used to tell us about the Good Spirit and His Son, and what we ought to do, have slipped away from me. O that he were here to help me! Tell him, as long as I was able, I used to go up to the point of land that runs out into the lake, and watch if I could see his canoe returning. But it came not. Tell him I have, since the winter set in, listened for the sound of the bells on his dog-trains. But I have not heard them. O that he were here to help me! He is far away; so get me my old drum and medicine bag, and let me die as did my fathers. But you, young people, with good memories, who can remember all the missionary has said to you, listen to his words, and worship the Great Spirit and His Son, as he tells you, and do not do as I am doing!'

"Then, as we saw his mind was weak, or he would not have asked for his old things, we got him the old drum, and put it before him where he was sitting upon the ground. We also hung up a medicine bag before him in the wigwam, and he drummed. As he drummed he fell, and as he fell he died. But his last words were to the young people with good memories to be sure and listen to the missionary, and to give up all their old sinful ways."

When the young man ceased and sat down again, a deep silence fell upon us all, as there we were huddled that cold, stormy day in that little bark tent. An occasional sob from some sorrowing relative was the only sound heard for several minutes.

My own heart was deeply affected when they told me these and other things, which I cannot now call up, about the old Indian's death. After a while I broke the silence by saying, "Where have you buried him?"

They showed me the place. It was where his wigwam had stood. So terrible is the power of the Frost King in that land in winter, that to dig a grave out in the open places is like cutting through a granite rock. And so in his tent, where burned his fire, thus keeping the ground unfrozen, there they dug his grave and buried him. The wigwam was removed, and soon the fierce storms swept over the place, and the snow fell deeply upon it, and there was nothing to indicate that there, so shortly before, had been a human habitation.

When they had pointed out the place where, underneath the snowdrift, rested all that was mortal of my old friend, I lingered until the Indians had sought the shelter of their wigwams from the bitter cold, and then all alone, except with Him who hears His people's cry, I knelt down in the snow and prayed, or tried to pray. But I could only weep out my sorrow as I thought of this old man's precious soul passing into eternity under such strange circumstances. With his waning strength he exhorted his loved ones to be Christians, and yet he himself was performing some of the useless rites of the old ways, not because he had much faith in them, but because there was no missionary or teacher to keep in his memory the story of Jesus and His wondrous love!

Never before did the wants and woes of the weary, waiting, wailing multitudes of earth's perishing ones rise up so vividly as I knelt there in the snow. Before me, through my blinding tears, I seemed to see them pass in dense array, a dark world, to be illumined; an enslaved world to be set free; a sinful world, to be made holy; a lost world, to be saved.

In a spirit that perhaps showed too much unbelief I cried out, "How long, O Lord, how long? Why do Thy chariot wheels delay?"

Saving me from further gloom, came some of the sweet promises of the Word, and so I prayed for their speedy fulfillment. Earnestly did my feeble petitions ascend, that the time would soon come when not only all the Indians of the great north west, but also all the unnumbered millions of earth's inhabitants who are going down from the darkness of sin and shame to the darkness of the grave, might soon have faithful teachers to whisper in their ears the story of the Cross, and point them to the world's Redeemer.

Making all the visits we had arranged for that trip, we returned home. Months after, when the packet arrived from Manitoba, the sad news, that had so filled the Church with sorrow, of the death of the heroic George McDougall reached us. Out on the wide prairies he had been caught in a blizzard storm. Horse and man seem to have become bewildered, and there the noble missionary to the Indians on the great plains laid himself down to die, and his frozen body was not found until after fourteen days of diligent search. After my dear wife and I had read the story, and talked and wept about his death, so sad, so mysterious, so inscrutable, she said to me, "Where were you during that week?" The journal was searched, and we were not a little startled at finding that the race for life we have earlier in this chapter described, was in all probability on the same day as that on which the Rev. George McDougall perished.

CHAPTER XIX

Work outside the pulpit — Polygamy and its evils — Family re-arrangements — Dangerous work at times — Practical pastoral duties — A fish sermon — Five men won to Christ.

While the blessed work of preaching the glorious gospel of the Son of God was ever recognized as the most important of our duties, and we were permitted to rejoice that, as in Paul's time, still "it pleased God by the foolishness of preaching to save them that believe," yet there was a great deal to be done outside of the pulpit before the Indians could shake off the fetters of the old religion with all its evils.

The fear of the old conjurers deterred some from openly declaring themselves as willing to accept the truths of Christianity. Others were polygamists, and were unwilling to comply with the scriptural requirements. To have several wives is considered a great honor in some of the tribes. For a man to separate from all but one is to expose himself to ridicule from his friends, and also to the danger of incurring the hostility of the relations of the discarded wives. Some of the most perplexing and trying duties of my missionary life have been in connection with this matter of re-organizing, on a Christian basis, the families of polygamists, who, desirous to do what was right, have left the matter entirely in my hands. At first my convictions and views were that the first wife should always be the one to remain with the man, and the others should go away. Like all the other missionaries in the country, I had to modify these ideas, and decide differently in some peculiar cases.

For example, a man came to me who was much impressed by the truth, and desired to be a Christian. I questioned him closely, and found him very sincere and earnest in his resolves. The Spirit was undoubtedly working in his heart and conscience. He told us he had two wives, but was willing to put one away. Which one should go, he said he would leave to the missionary to decide. His first wife was much the older woman, but she had no children, while the younger wife had quite a family of little ones around her. So poor are they in this cold northern land that it is hard for the best of them at times to get along. Very sad is the condition of the widow, or those women who have no able bodied men as husbands, fathers, or sons, to hunt and work for them. Worse still is it if they have helpless little children to be cared for. So the decision we came to was, that the wife with the family of little ones should remain with the man, and the one who had no children should leave him.

We tried to arrange that a certain quantity of help should be rendered to the wife, or wives, put away by the husband. But we found that there was a certain amount of danger in this, the nature of which will be evident to the reader; and so, while we insisted on the one or more who left receiving as large a share as possible of the man's worldly goods, we endeavoured to make the separation complete and final. To help those who for conscience' sake thus acted was often a very heavy tax upon our limited means.

Often the women themselves were the first to insist on a change from the old polygamous style, which, they were quick to see very soon after the gospel was proclaimed to them, was against its teachings.

There was one most thrilling case that moved our hearts, and yet caused us to rejoice, for it showed us the depth of the religious convictions which impelled them to have the matter set right, even though one must be cast out and exposed to the ridicule of her unsaved friends, and to the loss of a fairly good natured husband, considering his surroundings.

Two women came to our Mission house, and asked to have a talk with my good wife and myself. After talking about different things, at length they told us, with much trepidation, that they had attended our services, and had a great desire in their hearts to become Christians. We found they were the two wives of an Indian whose wigwam had been pitched in our vicinity a few weeks before. These women and others had quietly come to our services at the church, and their hearts and consciences had been touched by the truth.

We had had some experiences on these lines, and so with entire strangers we had learned to be a little cautious. In that country, as well as in civilized lands, it is sometimes a dangerous matter to interfere in the domestic affairs of other people. So we questioned them closely, and found that they were resolved to have the matter settled. I asked them if they had spoken to their husband about it, and they answered in the affirmative. He had left it to them to settle which should go, as he likewise had begun to think they ought to live as the Christian Indians did. We asked them what they wanted us to do, and they said that they had decided that they would leave the matter to the missionary and his wife. Whichever we thought ought to leave, would go away, and try to get her own living.

They returned to their wigwam, and with the consent of their husband made an equal division of the few things which constituted their possessions, such as nets, traps, blankets, kettles, and axes. Then accompanied by their children, they came again to our house, and sat down apart from each other, and patiently awaited our decision. My wife and I deeply felt the responsibility of deciding; yet, as it had come to us because of the awakening of their hearts to desire a better life, we could not do otherwise than accept the situation, and do the best we could.

We had talked the matter over, and had asked Divine guidance. So now, when summoned to give our decision, we quickly but kindly said to the woman with five children, "You are to stay with your husband," and to the other woman, who had four children, we said, "You are not to return to the wigwam, but must be from this hour as an entire stranger to it."

The first woman sprang up, her eyes flashing with joy, and gathering her children and property around her she uttered her hasty words of farewell, and was gone. For a few moments the other woman, who had drawn her blanket over her head, remained perfectly still, with the exception of a suppressed sob, which seemed to make the whole body quiver. Soon, with that wonderful will power which these Indian women, as well as the men, possess, she appeared to have obtained the mastery over herself again, and uncovering her head, she began to make preparations for leaving. As she turned her large black eyes dimmed with tears towards us, while there was no malice in them, there was a despairing sorrow that pierced us like a knife. She seemed to see the lonely, neglected, condemned, suffering life before her; but she had counted the cost, and had taken the step for conscience' sake, and she would not flinch now. We entered into conversation with her, and it seemed almost cruel that we, who had given a decision that had shut up against her the only home she had, should begin to talk to her about where she would go and what she would do.

She told us she did not know where to go or what to do. Her husband had bought her from her father, but he was dead. As her girlhood home was far away, and she had not been there since her husband took her away, she knew nothing about any of her relatives. But even if she did, and could find some of them, it was very likely they would treat her with contempt, and perhaps persecute her. So she had not the slightest idea as to the future.

Need I write that our hearts were full of sorrow, and we saw that this was a case which must have help, no matter how straitened might be our financial circumstances?

We had but lately read the story of the little oil in the cruse, and the handful of meal in the barrel; and so this woman and her children must be helped. While Mrs. Young fed them and talked kindly to them, I went out and got some of the Christian Indians together, and we talked the matter over, and then took off our coats and went to work, and made her a wigwam for the present, as it was in the pleasant summer time. A canoe was obtained for her, and her nets were set where white fish could be caught readily. She was an industrious woman, willing to do everything she could; and so, with the help we gave her and the tangible sympathy manifested by the Christian Indians, she took heart and got along very well, and became a good Christian woman.

As the result of the looseness of the marriage tie in their old way of living, we found many strange complicated tangles, some of which it was impossible to straighten. To deal with some of them would have caused endless difficulty, without any possibility of improving matters. To refuse to interfere gave offence to some, who, I am afraid, were more pharisaical than wise. Here, for example, was one case. A couple had been married years ago. After living together for several years and having three children, the man went off to Red River as a boatman for the Hudson's Bay Company. Delayed there for a time, he married a wife in the Indian settlement, and made that place his home, only returning with this second family about the time I went there. His first wife, a year or two after he left, not hearing from him, married another man, who supposed she was a widow, and they had several bright, interesting children. As the result of the faithful preaching of the Word, these families were converted, and became good Christians. They felt keenly their position, but after pondering it over and listening to many solutions, I gave it up. As the two families were living happily, I left them as I had found them. Sin, not Christianity, was responsible for the difficulty.

At Nelson River I was accosted one day by an old man, who said he had listened carefully to what I had said, and wanted to become a Christian and be baptized. I was very much pleased with his talk, but suspecting him to be a polygamist, I asked him as to the number of his wives. His answer was that he had four. I had a long conversation with him as to our views, and explained to him the teachings of God's Word, and candidly told him that I could not baptize him until he put three of them away.

He seemed grieved at my decision, and said that he did want to be a Christian, but he and his wives were getting old, and they had got along fairly well; and now if he went and told them what he would have to do, he was afraid there would be trouble. As I saw the man was really in earnest, and it was evident that the Spirit was working upon his heart, I encouraged him to make the effort, and I told him everything would work out all right.

He went to his large tent, and getting his large family around him, for three of these wives had stalwart sons, he told them of his desire to become a Christian, and what he would have to do before the missionary would consent to baptize him. At once there was a "row." The women began to wail, and the sons, who generally treated their mothers with neglect and indifference, now declared, with a good deal of emphasis, that their mothers should not be sent away, and thus degraded in the eyes of the people. From what I afterwards learned, there must have been a rough time.

At length one of the sons spoke up and said, "Who is causing us all this trouble?"

The answer was, "Why it is the missionary, whom we have all heard, and who refuses to baptize our father unless he puts away all of his wives but one."

"Let us go for that missionary," said several of them, and seizing their weapons, they came for me.

Fortunately for me I was outside of the trading post on the green, and saw them coming. Not liking their suspicious movements, and imagining the cause, I speedily decided on my course of action. Calling one of my reliable Christian Indian friends, I went quickly towards them, and ignoring their angry looks, I began talking to them as though we were the best of friends. Something like the following were my words to them:

"Men, you have heard me talk to you out of the great Book. You have listened attentively. You are thinking about what I have said to you. I wish we could do something, or find out some way, by which you and your mothers and father could all resolve together to give up the old bad life, and accept the new one, and become Christians together. I have been thinking it over since I had a little talk with your father, and I have a plan that I think will work well."

While I went on in this way, they listened attentively. When I came to mention a plan by which the difficulty could be overcome, the wicked looks began to fade from their eyes, for they were not anxious to kill me if any other solution of the difficulty could be found.

They were eager to know what I had to suggest, and listened very attentively when I told them it would not be humiliating to any one. I told them I was pleased to find some young men who were willing to stand up for their mothers, while the great majority treated them worse than they did their dogs. My suggestion was, that the sons of each mother should form a wigwam of their own, and take their own mother with them and care for her. They were good hunters and strong men, and could do well. Then I added, "Let your father remain with the wife who has no children, no strong sons or daughters. Do this, and the Great Spirit will be pleased, and when you are further instructed there will be nothing to prevent you all being baptized and becoming Christians together."

They were much pleased with the suggestion, and went away to talk it over. I did not succeed in getting the scheme immediately carried out, but my successor, the devoted and heroic Rev. John Semmens, was so successful in following up the work thus begun, that these Indians, with many scores of others, have become sincere, consistent Christians.

Various were the plans adopted by my zealous, devoted wife and myself to help the people up to a better and happier life. In their old ways there were but few efforts made by the women to keep their homes neat and tidy, and their children or themselves clean. They had no encouragements to do anything of the kind. Kicked and cuffed and despised, there was left in them no ambition to do anything more than would save them from the rough treatment of those who considered themselves their lords and masters. The result was, when they became Christians, there was a great deal to learn before their simple little homes could be kept decently and in order. Fortunately, with a great many of them there was a desire to learn. A novel plan that we adopted, as one among many that did much good, was occasionally to go and dine with some of them. Our method was something like this. On the Sabbath from the pulpit I would announce that on Monday, if all was well,

Mrs. Young and I would dine with such a family, mentioning the name. On Tuesday we would dine with someone else, and on Wednesday with some other family, and so on for the week. This was, of course, the first intimation any of these families had received that, without waiting for an invitation, the missionary and his wife were coming to dine with them.

After service they waited to ask us if they could believe their own ears.

"Yes, certainly," I replied.

"Why, we have nothing to set before you but fish," they would say.

"Never mind if you have but little. We will see to the food. All we are anxious for you to do is to have your little house as clean as you can possibly make it, and yourselves and children as clean and nice as possible."

In this way we would talk to the half-frightened women, who were at first really alarmed at the prospect of having to entertain us. However, our words comforted them, and they went off delighted.

Our plan was generally as follows. I would start off after breakfast and make several pastoral visits, or attend to some other matters, and so arrange my forenoon work that I should be able to reach the Indian home, where that day we had announced to dine, about noon. Mrs. Young would have her own train of dogs harnessed up about ten o'clock. In her cariole she would put dishes, tablecloth, and provisions, with everything else needed for a comfortable dinner considering our limited circumstances. A faithful young Indian acted as her dog-driver, and soon she and her load were at the home of the expectant family, who were all excited at the coming of the missionary and his wife.

Very clean and tidy looked the little house and

family. The floor had been scrubbed and rubbed until it could not be made whiter, and everything else was similarly polished up. As but very few of the houses had tables in those days, the floor was used as the substitute. On it the tablecloth was spread, and the dishes and knives and forks were arranged in order, and the dinner prepared. If the family had fish and potatoes, some of them would be cooked; but if not, sufficient was always taken in the cariole. We found it best to let them contribute to the dinner if they had abundance of either fish or potatoes.

About the time I arrived dinner would be ready, and after cheering words of greeting to all, even to the fat baby in the board cradle, we sat down, picnic style, on the floor to dinner. It would be called in other lands a plain dinner, and so it was; yet it was a feast to them, a banquet to us. Cheery conversation added to our enjoyment, and a very happy hour was thus spent. Then the Bible and hymn books were brought out, and together we sang and read and talked about the blessed truths of that glorious Book. Then together we kneeled down, and "by prayer and supplication with thanksgiving" made our requests known to God; and to us came the sweet fulfilment, "the peace of God, which passes all understanding," filled our hearts.

I generally hurried off to other duties. Mrs. Young directed in the washing of the dishes and in putting them away, and then helped the woman of the house in some things about which she was longing for assistance. Perhaps it was a dress to be cut for herself, or some garments fitted on some of the girls, or other similar things too intricate or difficult for my male mind to be able to grasp.

Thus from house to house we would go, and by our presence and cheery words encourage them to become more industrious and tidy. Those families never forgot these visits. With many of them there was a marked change in their homes, and with many also, there was a marked improvement in their religious life.

Once, in preaching from the text, "Behold, I stand at the door, and knock: if any man hear My voice, and open the door, I will come in." I tried to describe the blessed Redeemer coming to our hearts and knocking for admittance. I told them, all He wanted was a welcome to come in. As they made their little houses so clean, and gave the missionary and his wife such a welcome, so the Savior asked us to drive all sin out, and give Him all the place.

"Some of you said, 'We cannot entertain the missionary. We have no food, so there will be no dinner.' But the missionary and his wife brought abundance, and there was a good dinner. Better far is it when Jesus comes. He spreads out the feast, and He invites us to sit down and feast with Him. O let Him in!"

Such talks as these, with such practical illustrations, opened many hearts to the heavenly guest.

So many and importunate had been the pleading calls for visits to different places, to tell the wonderful story of the Great Spirit and His Son, and to teach the people to read His Book, that one year my canoe trip to Oxford House Mission had to be delayed until the summer was nearly ended. But my comrades were splendid fellows, and we started off in good spirits, anticipating a successful visit. We were not disappointed.

We preached several times to the Indians, and baptized a large number of children. Some young couples were married, and we had a solemn and blessed time when celebrating the dying of the Lord Jesus. The sacrament of the Lord's Supper is very much prized by the Indians, and the greatest reverence is always manifested during the service. The fellowship meeting was a very good one, and some of the testimonies given by the men and women, so happily rescued by the gospel's power, were of great interest.

When travelling, if the weather was good, we generally rose with the first blush of morn, and so were often on the way by four o'clock. Sometimes our route was across fine lakes, or along majestic rivers; and then we were in narrow, sluggish streams, that were destitute of beauty or interest. One morning our way was down a large river, on the shores of which the fog had settled, completely hiding us from land. The early morning air was invigorating, and so in unison we were plying our paddles vigorously, and rapidly speeding along. We had seen no signs of human beings for days, and so were surprised and startled when several reports of firearms in quick succession sounded sharp and clear through the fog on our right. Nothing was visible through the gloom, but we quickly turned in the direction from which the *feu-de-joie* had sounded. As we approached the shore human forms began to appear in ghostly outline, more and more distinct, until they resolved themselves into a company of Indians, who were delighted to see us, and had been on the look out for days. They had come sixty miles from the interior, and had camped on that point jutting out into the river, for the purpose of having a visit from us as we passed.

The fact that they detected us as we were passing was another evidence of the marvellous education, in certain lines, of these Indians. It was very early in the morning; our canoe was some hundreds of yards from the shore; a dense fog hid us completely from each other. All the noise we made was the dip of our paddles in the water. Yet these wide awake, alert Indians heard that sound, and by the rapid firing of the guns drew us to them.

We shared their hospitality, as they had abundance of game. We had a service with them, married a young couple, baptized several children, and had a pleasant time. Then on we hurried, since the time of open navigation was drawing to a close, and we did not wish to be caught in the ice, and have to walk perhaps scores of miles with our bedding, provisions, kettles, axes, and other things strapped on our backs.

We made the greater part of the return trip all right, had reached Harry Lake early in the forenoon, and were rapidly paddling out of the river which entered into it, when again we heard the report of guns. So anxious were we to get on that we hesitated about stopping. It was now later in the season than often in some other years. Fierce storms had raged, and the ice had formed on the lakes and rivers. We were dreading these fierce fall storms, which come down very suddenly, and stir up these northern lakes, so that in a very short time where all was calm and still, great foam crested waves go rushing madly by.

The lake before us, into which we had just entered and which was several miles in diameter, was now as placid as a pond.

To cross it now, as in wondrous beauty it spread before us, would be but a pleasure jaunt. The poetry of motion is to be found in the Indian's birch canoe, when the water is calm and the sky is clear. Cold hearted prudence said, "Go on, and never mind those Indians' signals for you to land." Our better natures said, "They may be in need, and have good reason for asking you to stop. Perhaps you can do them good." So we turned the head of our canoe to the shore, and were soon alongside the rock on which we saw them standing. They were five hunters. Without getting out of the canoe, we asked why they had signalled to us to come ashore. Their answer was one we had often heard before. They were hungry, and wanted help. Finding they had only been a few days away from the Fort, where they had got supplies, I asked how it was that they were so badly off. Their reply was that they had unfortunately left their powder, which they were carrying in a canvas bag, out on the rock a few nights before. While they slept the rain came down upon them and ruined it, and so they could not shoot anything. I quickly said to one of my men, "How much food have we?" He examined our limited supply, and then said there was about one square meal.

We found these men were unbelieving Indians, whom I had met before, and had talked with about becoming Christians; but all I could get from them was the characteristic shrug of the shoulders, and the words, "As our fathers lived, so will we." Our dinner was the last of a bear we had shot a few days before. While it was cooking the storm which we feared began to gather, and before our dinner was finished the lake looked very different from what it was an hour before. If we had not stopped, we could have easily got across it. As it was now, it would have been madness to have ventured out upon it. So we had to pull up our canoe, and there, as contentedly as possible, wait for the storm to cease. It raged furiously all that day and the next. The third day it began to moderate. What made it worse for us was the scarcity, or rather the entire absence, of food. We were unfortunately storm-bound in about the worst part of that country for game. It was so late in the season that the ducks and geese had gone south, the beaver and muskrats were in their houses, and we could find nothing. On some of our trips we carried fishing tackle, but this time we had nothing of the kind. Fortunately we had some tea and sugar.

Without breakfast, dinner, or supper, we had to live on as best we could. Before we lay down to sleep there had to be a considerable tightening of the belts, or there would be no sleep at all, so keen was the gnawing of hunger. I found it helpful to sleep to roll up my towel as hard as possible, and then crowd it under my tight belt over the pit of my stomach. Nearly three days without food was no pleasant ordeal even in missionary work.

We held several religious services, even though our congregation was a small one. We also found out that it was not at all helpful to piety to try to worship on an empty stomach, and have been ever since in great sympathy with those who would feed the poor first, and then preach to them.

The third day one of the Indians, while walking along the shore, found the old bleached shoulder-blade of a bear. With his knife he carved out a rude fishhook, and, taking the strings of his moccasins and others', he formed a line. A piece of red flannel was used as bait, and a small stone served as a sinker. With this primitive arrangement he began fishing. His method was to stand on a rock and throw the hook out as far as his line would permit, and then draw it in rapidly, like trolling.

Strange to say, with this rude appliance he caught a fish. It was a pike weighing six or eight pounds. Very quickly was it scaled, cleaned, and put in the pot. When cooked, about a third of it was put on my tin plate, and placed before me with these words, "Please, Missionary, eat." I looked at the hungry men around me and said, "No, that is not the way." I put back the third of the fish with the rest, and taking out my hunting knife, I counted the company, and then cut the fish into eight pieces, and gave each man his eighth, and took an equal portion myself. It was right that I should thus act, and it seemed to be a little thing to do, but it was a sermon that led those five men to become Christians. As soon as they had finished their portions they lit their pipes, and as they smoked they talked. As near as I and my men could make out, here is what they said:

"We must listen with both ears to that missionary. He is here without food, suffering from hunger, because he stopped to share with us his last meal. We caught a fish, and when we offered him a large piece he refused it, and divided equally with us all. He has been anxious to do us good and to have us to listen to his words. He has not once scolded us for asking him to stop, although he could have got across the lake before the storm arose, and as the rest of the way is in the river, he could have gone on home. He has shown himself to be our friend, and we must listen to what he has to say." Thus they went on, and I must confess I paid but little attention to what they were saying. After a few hours more the storm went down, and we gladly embarked that evening in our canoe and pushed on.

The next day we reached the Mission village of Rossville, making our last portage at Sea River Falls, near Norway House; and as we saw the fish and venison hanging on the stages around the houses of the people, my patient fellows cried out, "We should like to laugh at the sight of food, but we are too empty altogether."

We paddled the last mile as quickly as we had any other, and kept up our courage until we were home. As I entered the house, a strange faintness came over me, and all the welcome words I could give to my loved ones were, "My dear, we are starving; please get us some food." Then I sank down exhausted. Loving care from one of the best and bravest of wives quickly brought me round again, and I was soon ready to be off on another trip.

The long winter passed away, and the welcome summer came at last. We have really very little of spring in that northern land. The transition from winter to summer is very rapid. With the disappearance of the ice from the lakes and rivers came the Indians in their birch canoes, from various quarters

Sea River Falls, near Norway House

where they had spent the winter in trapping the fur-bearing animals. As usual they came to see the missionary in goodly numbers. Among those who thus honored us were five big men, who, after a few words of greeting, said, "We hope you have not forgotten the fish; we have not, and we want to have a talk with you."

"Fish?" I said, "Why, we have fish twenty-one times a week: boiled, baked, fried, salt, dried, good, bad, and indifferent. I have seen so many fishes, I cannot think of any one in particular."

Then they told me about the long delay by the storm, when I had stopped and fed them, at the time when they had not kept their powder dry; and how, when one of them caught a fish and offered me a good sized piece, I divided it equally among them. As they brought the incident back to my memory, for there were so many strange adventures occurring in the wild life that this one had partly faded, I said: "Yes, I now remember there did happen something of the kind."

Very earnestly spoke up one of them and said, "We have never forgotten it, and all through the moons of the winter we have talked about it and your lessons out of the great Book. And while up to that time we had decided not to be Christians, but to die as did our fathers, we have changed our minds since that time you divided the fish, and we want you to teach us more and more of this good way."

They were intensely in earnest and fully decided for Christ. So five more families settled down in the Christian village, and are giving evidence by their lives and conversation that the change wrought in them was real and abiding. Their conversion in this peculiar way was very cheering to us, and it was another lesson to be "instant in season, out of season."

CHAPTER XX

Exploring new fields — The gospel before treaties — Big Tom's noble spirit of self sacrifice.

In 1873 I received a most urgent request from a deputation of Indians to go and visit a band of their countrymen who lived on the western side of Lake Winnipeg at a place called Jack Head. They were getting unsettled and uneasy in their minds in reference to their lands. Treaties were being made with other tribes, but nothing as yet had been done for them; and as surveyors and other white men had been seen in their country, they were suspicious, and wanted to know what they had better do.

So, after many councils among themselves, they decided to send over into the land of the Crees for their missionary to come and give them advice, in order that they too might make a treaty with the Government of the Queen.

I felt much pleased on receiving this deputation; and as it would give me a grand opportunity to preach the gospel to a people who had not as yet heard it, I consented to go. With two dog-trains, and accompanied by a couple of trusty Indians, we left the eastern side of the great Lake Winnipeg about sunrise. We dug a hole in the snow at Pigeon Point, and there made a fire of some dry young willows, and enjoyed our breakfast. From that point we struck out in a south west direction across the great lake. The day, although cold, was a very bright one. The ice was good, and our dogs were magnificent fellows; and so we sped along at a rapid rate. We reached a chain of little islands out in the middle of the lake early in the afternoon. On the shore of one of them we gathered some dry wood, cleared away the snow, made a fire, melted some snow, and made ourselves a good kettle of tea. This, with some pemmican and flat cakes, made us a great dinner.

From this island the western shore of the lake was just visible, over thirty miles away. Towards it we pushed as rapidly as possible, considering that one of our party was quite an old man. When within about three miles of the shore, the report of fire arms reached our ears, telling us that the Indians had observed our coming. Our noble dogs seemed to rejoice at the sound as much as ourselves, and, well knowing that their day's journey of over sixty miles was nearly ended, changed their swinging trot into a gallop; and very soon we were at Jack Head, received in a most extraordinary manner.

At some other places where I have gone as the first missionary who ever visited them, I have had two or three hundred men, women, and children trying to see who could be the first to kiss me; but here the reception was very different. Night was just falling upon us as we drew near the shore, but there was light enough to observe that the narrow trail, up from the lake into the dark recesses of the forest, along which we must pass with our dog-trains, was lined with men armed with guns.

When we were about a hundred yards from them, the foremost ones began firing. This *feu-de-joie* continued until we had reached them and had dashed through the lines of fire, for they continued loading and firing as rapidly as possible. Our ears were almost deafened with the continuous reports, and our nerves were somewhat tried, as the younger braves especially consider it great fun to fire off their heavy charges of powder as close to their visitors' heads as possible. But a well singed fur cap was the only evidence of harm having been done.

To increase the welcome, they courteously brought out for our special benefit the few English

Indian Council

and French words of which they were masters. Some of them were most ludicrously out of place. It did require a good deal of nerve to keep my face straight when a grave and dignified chief, who wished to inquire politely as to my health, for the moment dropped his own language, and in good English said, "Does your mother know you're out?" I found out afterwards that a roguish fur trader had taught him the expression, as a very polite one to use to distinguished strangers.

We quickly unharnessed and fed our faithful dogs. We hung up in the trees our sleds and harness beyond the reach of the village dogs, which in large numbers prowled around. If they could get the opportunity, they would make short work of the deer skin and rawhide fastenings of the sleds, and the harness would entirely disappear, with perhaps the exception of the buckles. We waited until our big dogs had given a few of the most impudent and saucy of these brutes a good thrashing, so that there was some prospect of peace; and then, feeling that our outside work was attended to, and that the Indians had had time to get arranged in their council room, we went to the door, and were ceremoniously ushered in. The council house was a large square log building of much better construction than I had expected to see. It was without partitions, and was lighted by the brilliant council fire, and a number of fish oil lamps hanging from the walls. At the places of honor were seated the chiefs of the band. Their "thrones of state" were curiously woven mats of rushes made by the Indian women. Their head dresses were gorgeous masses of feathers, and their costume was very picturesque. Some of them had not yet adopted trousers, but wore instead the scant leggings of native manufacture.

From the chiefs on either side, and extending around the room in circles, were the old men, warriors and hunters, ranged according to their rank and standing. Behind these were the young men and boys. All were seated on the ground, and all were silent, as I entered. The chiefs were fine looking men, and there was that indescribable hautiness now so rarely seen among these interesting people. Crowded out behind the men and boys, and in many places packed against the walls of the house, were the women and girls. While the men were in many instances well and often brilliantly dressed in their finery, the women and girls were wretchedly clothed, and miserable in appearance.

The house was filled, with the exception of a small space reserved at the right hand of the principal chief for the visitors. With a good deal of ceremony we were escorted to our seats. For me they had obtained a little box, on which a fur robe was placed, as they said afterwards, that they had heard that white men cannot sit comfortably on the ground. On this I seated myself next to the chief, and my attendant Indians ranged themselves beside me. During the profound silence that lasted for several minutes after our entrance, I had a good opportunity to grasp the situation. I breathed an earnest prayer to God for the much needed wisdom, and that I might here preach the gospel in such a way that it might be understood and accepted by this people, the majority of whom had not as yet heard the glad tidings of salvation.

Then I rose up, and addressing the chief, I said: "I have come at your request from across the great Lake Winnipeg, to visit you and to meet you at your council fire. I will preach to you and discuss treaty matters with you, and will help you all I can with the government. I want to find out your views about giving up your old religion and becoming Christians. I also want to know how many children you have among you, and if you desire a school for them. So I am here for these reasons."

When I sat down, the calumet, the pipe of peace, was gravely lit, and after the chief had puffed away at it, he handed it to me. As I have not as yet acquired the art of smoking, I adopted the plan of taking hold of the long stem, which is over a yard in length, by the middle. The result was that when my hand was near my mouth, the mouthpiece of the pipe was a foot or so behind my head. As previously arranged, one of my obliging Indian friends was always on hand to do my smoking.

After the pipe ceremony was over, the chief began his address of welcome. He said a good many kind things, and told me of their anxieties as to their future and that of their children. The fire canoe (steamboat) was rushing through the waters, destroying their fisheries. The white hunters, with their fire guns and steel traps, were fast killing off the game. The surveyor was driving his lines of stakes into the ground, and the white people, more numerous than mosquitoes, were crowding in on the prairies. They had nothing but peace in their hearts, but still he could not help thinking that a treaty ought to be made with them before the fire canoe or the surveyor came. They were powerless themselves to speak before the Queen's representative, the Governor. They had heard of the missionary's love for the Indian, and so they had sent across the great Lake Winnipeg for him, and their hearts were glad that he had come. With their right hands they had fired off their guns, which all said, "Welcome!" With his left hand he had handed the pipe of peace, which also from the heart again said, "Welcome!" Their hearts were all glad that with their eyes they saw the missionary among them. Their ears were now open to hear what he had to say about their future, and what he thought the Queen's men would do for them.

Then he sat down on his mat, and I rose up and in reply said, "Before I dare talk to you about treaties, and lands, and your future for this life, and that of your children, I must speak about something more important."

This seemed to astonish them, and they said, "What has he got to talk about that is more important than the treaty?"

"Yes," I answered, "I have something more important than the treaty, and something to say about One greater than the Queen, or the Governor she sends; for I must first talk about our great God, Whom the Queen and we all must love if we would be happy. The Great Spirit, our good Father in heaven, wants to make a treaty with us; and if we will be willing to comply with His conditions, it will be the best treaty ever made, for it will bring us joy and happiness for this life and the life to come."

Loud were their words of approval that I should thus speak to them; and so I preached to them, making use of my trusted and careful interpreter, Timothy Bear, who is as thorough a master of the Saulteaux language as he is of the Cree. Considering that it was the first sermon they had ever heard, and that their ideas of our worship were very crude, they behaved remarkably well, seeing they were a crowd of plumed and painted Saulteaux. They kept up a constant smoking through all the service, except when we were singing or at prayer. Men, women, and children were all at it, and it seemed as though they were always at it.

Before I got through my sermon I was almost suffocated by the smoke. The cloud, not that for which we had prayed, overwhelmed us, blinded us, and nearly smothered us. As well as I could I talked to them of God and His love, and of the way of salvation, and the blessings which would come to them if they would cheerfully and heartily accept Him. We than sang the Jubilee hymn,

"Blow ye the trumpet, blow."

This hymn has been translated into their language. The tune we used was "Lennox," and I urged them to help us to sing. I gave out the hymn verse by verse, and said, "Sing as well as you can." Some followed very well, and others, while trying to follow the words, seemed to have substituted for the tune one of their own chants. After the religious service was over, we hastily boiled our kettles, made tea, and had our suppers, for we had travelled far, and were very hungry. The Indians had nothing themselves but tea, fish, and tobacco. I never saw such smokers. Even little unweaned children were adept in the use of the pipe.

After tea the ceremonious speeches were delivered. The head chief was of course the first to speak again. His address was very complimentary. He said he had been gazing all day long across the great lake watching for my coming. Although it was several moons since, I had promised that in this one, if possible, I would be on hand. My coming just at the time I did, showed that I was a man of my word, and could be depended upon.

"We feel," he said, "that we Indians are but children in the presence of the whites. Great changes are taking place. The buffalo and deer once so abundant are fast disappearing. Our fathers told us long ago that the buffalo was the special gift of the Great Spirit to the Indian, and that when it disappeared the Indian must go also. But in your words you tell us good things about the Great Spirit, and we are thankful that you have come. We wish you could live among us and thus talk to us."

Thus he and others talked for a long time.

We went over the business of the approaching treaty, and I told them all I knew about the matter, and assured them that they need have no fear or alarm. The Dominion Government would treat them honorably and fairly. More tobacco was smoked, and extra kettles of tea were made and drunk, and then I was told that as an additional mark of their thankfulness to me for thus coming with these assuring and quieting words, they now wished to give me the tribal ceremony of the greatest welcome, which was only given at rare intervals, and then only when the best of news came to them.

The room was quickly rearranged for the ceremony. The crowd in the centre of the room was moved back, much to the discomfort of the women and girls, some of whom were roughly ejected to make room for their masters. Then some drums were brought in, and between twenty and thirty of the most active and agile young men, dressed, or rather undressed, in their picturesque way, seated themselves closely around the men who were to act as drummers. The first part of the ceremony was supposed to be a kind of concert, part musical and part pantomime.

To describe it with its monotonous drumming and shrill songs, which they said were words of welcome, is altogether beyond my powers. At certain places in the songs, ten or twenty of the young men would spring up in their places, and without moving their feet from the ground would go through such strong, undulating, graceful motions, and yet all in such perfect unison with each other and with the music, that I was almost fascinated by the strange weird beauty of the scene.

Then their program changed, and rapidly they glided around in simple and intricate movements, but all in perfect time to the songs and drums.

Not satisfied with giving me the welcome of their own tribe, they also gave me the still more exciting

A young Indian with his canoe
at the foot of the rude water slide

Sioux welcome, and also that of the Crees in the Saskatchewan. Until long after midnight these scenes were being enacted. Then word was passed round that the supply of tobacco devoted to the welcome ceremonies was exhausted, for through all of these scenes the pipes were only out of the mouths of the performers. All the rest of the crowd smoked without apparent cessation.

This intimation of the exhaustion of the supply of tobacco abruptly closed the ceremony. Such is their custom. Some more tea was made and drunk by the chiefs. Then the missionary's hand was shaken, and the people quickly flitted away to their wigwams. A supper, consisting of beautiful fish, called "gold eyes," which are caught by the young Indians in the rapid river at the foot of the rude water slide, was then much enjoyed.

One of my faithful Indian companions brought in my camp bed, and unrolled it near the council fire. I rolled myself up in a blanket and buffalo robe, and there on the ground I soon fell asleep, for I was very weary. At daybreak we arose, and had our breakfast cooked at the council fire. While eating it, many of the Indians crowded in to see us before we left for our home across Lake Winnipeg. With them we held another religious service. I talked kindly and faithfully to them, and urged them to decide speedily to forsake their old religious habits and become Christians; telling them that now, as they were making treaties and entering upon a new way of obtaining a living, they should adopt the religion of the great Book.

With them we sang a hymn, and then kneeled down and prayed. Devoutly and reverently did they bow with us at the mercy seat. When we rose up from our knees, a young man spoke up on behalf of the young people. He said they were glad I had come, and hoped I would come again. Their minds were dark; would I soon come back and bring in the light?

I said all I could to encourage them to seek after the great Light, and promised to come again. We harnessed up our dogs, and in company with my attendant Indians, I started for home. A wild blizzard storm came down upon us from the north when we were far out from land. We toiled on through it as well as we could, although at times unable to see a dozen feet ahead of us. Often we got bewildered by its fury, as it seemed to circle an eddy around us; but Jack was in the foremost train, and so we safely reached the other shore, and did not for many a day cease to think about some of the strange features of this adventurous trip, and which in after years we found much real good had been done.

As we have been referring to treaties and the excitement there was in the minds of the Indians in reference to the new relationship they would have with the government, it may be well here to put upon record the noble spirit of one of our Indians, on whom honors were desired to be conferred by his people.

When the Dominion Government of Canada took possession of the territories so long held by the Hudson's Bay Company, they began to make arangements for treaties with all the Indian tribes. Word came out to us at Rossville Mission house, that the government wished the Indians to elect one of their number as chief, with whom they could make a treaty, and whom they could confer with if difficulties arose in the future. They wished the people to select a wise, judicious man, in whom all confidence could be placed.

Naturally the Indians were very much excited at this new order of things, and so there were many councils and much speech making. A good deal of curiosity was expressed to know what benefits would result, and how much money would be received by each of them. While there was still much uncertainty about these things, it had become well known that the one selected to be chief would fare very well. He would have more money and presents than any other. He would be presented with a silver medal with the face of the "Great Mother," the Queen upon it, and would be honored with the personal friendship of the Governor, and with other honors naturally dear to people.

After many councils the people came to the almost unanimous conclusion that Big Tom should be their chief. In a full council, with much ceremony, they offered him the position. Instead of seizing the proffered honors with avidity, his face became very grave, and it was evident he was full of suppressed emotion. When he arose, as all supposed, to indicate his acceptance of the position, and to express his thanks, they were very much surprised to hear him quietly say that he could not answer fully now, but desired a day to think it over. So he asked the council to adjourn until the following morning.

Of course this request was complied with, and full of curiosity, the people thronged the building the next day. I had naturally taken a deep interest in the matter, as next to their spiritual interests, I was anxious to do all I could for their temporal welfare. So I attended many of their meetings. The council was opened in due form, and then Big Tom rose to give his answer. He began quietly and slowly, but warmed up a good deal before he ended.

He spoke, in substance, as follows:

"Long ago, when the missionaries came and preached to us, for a time we refused to listen to them, and would not become Christians. Then, after a while, many of us who had been in the darkness began to feel in our hearts that what they told us was for our good; and so we accepted these things, and they have done us good. When I got the assurance in my heart that I was a child of God, and had a soul that should live forever, I found that in working out its salvation I had something great to live for. To do this was the great object of my life. By and by I married, and then, as my family increased and began to grow up around me, I found I had another object for which to live. To help them along in the way to heaven, as well as to work for their comfort here, was my second great work. Then, after a while, the missionary gave me the charge of a class. I was to meet with them, and we were to talk together about our souls and God's love to us, and to do all we could to help each other on to the better land. To do my duty as the leader was a great and important work. While attending to these duties, I found I had another object for which to live. These three things, 1. My own soul's salvation; 2. The salvation of my family; and 3. To do all I can to help and encourage the members of my class to be true and faithful to Him Who died for us, that we may see Him by and by, are the uppermost things in my heart.

"I am thankful for your confidence in me in asking me to be your chief. I know it is a great honor, but I see it will have many responsibilities, and that whoever has the position will have to attend to many other things than those which I have my mind set upon. So you must appoint someone else, for with those three things I cannot let anything else interfere. I thank you, my brothers, and love you all."

In this strain he went on for a long while, and then sat down. No one thought any the less of the noble Christian man; and David Rundle, who was appointed, found in Big Tom a wise and judicious counsellor and friend. I was thrilled by the address and the spirit manifested. How few white men in like circumstances would have had grace and self denial enough to have acted in a similar manner!

CHAPTER XXI

The Mission among the Saulteaux established — Nelly's death — Missionary anniversaries attended — Rev. Thomas Crosby — Traveling adventures — More working with dogs — Our new home — Visit from a chieftainess — Closing words.

After a great deal of correspondence it was decided that I should begin the work at Beren's River among the Saulteaux Indians who lived there, and in little bands scattered along the eastern shores of that great lake, and in the interior, most of them in extreme poverty and without Christ. A few of them, as the result of acquaintance with the Christian Indians of other places, were groping after the great Light, and trying to lift themselves up socially in life.

The Rev. John H. Ruttan was appointed to Norway House, the Rev. Orrin German to Oxford House, and I was put down for Beren's River.

As it was advisable that I should remain at Norway House until my successor, Brother Ruttan, arrived, and as there was only one opportunity for Mrs. Young and the children to return to Red River, they availed themselves of it, poor and miserable as it was.

With loving farewells, I wished them success on their journey, and saw them off. Sandy Harte, our adopted Indian lad, and I sailed down to the old Norway House, about twenty miles from our home, and there saying goodbye, we returned to our lonely home.

Mrs. Young had with her our three darling children, Eddie, Lilian, and Nelly. All were well and full of the best of spirits as the sail was hoisted, and we saw them glide away before the favoring gale. Precious Nelly we never saw again. So terrible was the heat, and so miserable were the accommodations in that little open boat, without deck, awning, or cabin, that the child sickened and died.

As we have referred to this sad event in an earlier chapter, we need not dwell upon it here. What the poor mother felt and suffered as, sick herself, she saw her beautiful child attacked by brain fever, and then droop and die amid surroundings so sad and trying, can be realized by but few. God knows all about it. As mentioned, the venerable Archdeacon Cowley's sympathy did much to raise up Mrs. Young's crushed spirits and dry her bitter tears.

I remained at Norway House until Brothers Ruttan and German arrived; and then, after having spent a Sabbath with them, and seen Mr. Ruttan and his noble young wife cheerfully and hopefully entered upon their blessed work among the people, to whom I had become very much attached, I started off for Beren's River. Sandy Harte, the Nelson River lad, went with me as far as my first camping place, and spent the night with me. We read the sacred Word together, and then, after singing a hymn, we bowed in prayer. We lay down together, but we had so much to say, that hours passed away before we slept.

Early the next morning we were aroused from our slumbers by the cry of "Fair wind," and so no time must be lost. I was very much surprised to find that during the night some scores of Indians had come in their canoes from the Mission, although it was many miles away, to shake hands with their missionary once more, and say a final farewell.

After a hasty breakfast we assembled on the shore for prayers. We sang in Cree a favorite hymn:

> "Jesus, my all, to heaven is gone,
> He Whom I fix my hopes upon.
> His path I see, and I'll pursue
> The narrow way till Him I view."

We closed by singing the Doxology, and then, after prayers, I sadly said goodbye, and shook hands again with them all. I found it hard to break away from them. Many of them were in tears, who seldom wept before. Coming to my beloved Sandy last, I put my arm around his neck and kissed him as there he stood, weeping as though his heart would break. With a "God bless you all," I sprang into the boat, which was quickly pushed off from the shore, and then the long journey to the land of the Saulteaux was begun.

After some of the usual incidents of travel I reached Beren's River, and was most enthusiastically received by the Indians. The man who had said, "Our eyes were dim from long watching," now said that they were dim with tears of joy that he had lived to see the day when a missionary of their own lived among them. As I was to leave before the lake froze up, every day was precious. I pitched a canvas tent, and in it lived for several weeks. All assembled once every week-day for religious worship, and then, when that was over, the missionary and men took off their coats and went to work. The spot for the Mission was decided upon, and then acre after acre of the forest from this place, and also from where each Indian had decided to build, was rapidly being cleared of the forest trees. We held three services every Lord's day, and saw that the school for the children was faithfully kept up.

Getting everything in good shape, and leaving Martin Papanekis, a devout and trusty Christian Indian from the Norway House Mission, in charge, I started in a birch canoe, with Big Tom as principal canoe man, for Red River.

Of our adventures and dangers I need not write, although there were several on that long journey in such a frail craft. One complete upset chilled me most thoroughly, as the water was about down to freezing point. At one place, where we tried to push on all night, we were tantalized by some most brilliant "Will-o'-the-wisp" lights, which the experienced Indians thought were decoy signals put out by wicked people to bewilder or injure us. Canoe traveling on this great lake is risky business. The storms come up with surprising rapidity, and the waves rise up like those of the ocean. However, we had a good canoe, and Big Tom was in charge; and He who holds the winds and the waves in His fists was our Father and our Friend.

At Red River I called on the Rev. Archdeacon Cowley at his Indian Mission home. Very cordial and sympathetic was he, as I introduced myself, and told him I had come to accept of his kind offer, and seek in some part of the quiet graveyard of his Mission Church a little place where I could bury the body of my darling child. He at once went with me and showed me all kindness and help, as also did Mr. Flett and his family, of the Hudson's Bay Company's Service. As we laid away the beautiful child, and the solemn words, "Earth to earth, dust to dust," were uttered, we felt that there was now an additional tie holding us to that country and work.

In due time I reached Toronto, and there met the Missionary Secretaries, and obtained from them an outline of the work before me. Here it was my great joy to meet for the first time the Rev. Thomas Crosby, the energetic and successful missionary from British Columbia, who has been wonderfully owned of God in his glorious work. Uncalled by any Church, but impelled by the good Spirit, shortly after his conversion he made his way to British Columbia at his own expense, and offered himself to one of the missionaries there as a volunteer teacher among the poor, neglected Indians, who, uncared for by anyone, were prowling around the cities and towns of that new province, living lives of shame and sin. Great indeed was his success.

He has also established flourishing Missions at Fort Simpson and elsewhere in the north of that land, and through his labors a blessed work began among the Indians in Alaska. Some of them, hearing wonderful stories about the black-coated man and his mysterious Book, came hundreds of miles, that they might have their curiosity satisfied. They returned with more than they anticipated. They reached the Mission, and from Mr. Crosby, and also from some of their own tribes who lived there, they heard the "old, old story" for the first time in their lives. It was indeed wonderful news to them, but they accepted it with a simple faith that was pleasing to God, and brought into their hearts the consciousness of His smile and benediction. Rejoicing in this new found treasure they returned to their own land, and there they published the glad tidings of God's love, and added the testimony of their own personal experience that they had a new joy in their hearts, the result of their having accepted this Savior. Great indeed was the excitement among the people. Some mocked, and some opposed and tried to persecute, but many were affected by what their companions had brought them, and believing their testimony entered into their joy.

Of course the new converts could give but little instruction; and so, as the work proceeded, it was decided that a deputation must go for the missionary and bring him into their land. Mr. Crosby responded, and went over to Alaska, and spent some time among them. God blessed his labors, and many of the Indians gave up their old ways and became Christians. Convinced that a grand opening was here for missionary triumph, Mr. Crosby wrote to the Methodist Episcopal Mission Rooms, New York, urging the officials there to enter this open door and begin work here. The answer was that it was impossible; that their other fields absorbed all their income, and so there was no prospect of their being able to respond to his appeal.

Not to be discouraged very easily, Mr. Crosby next wrote to the Presbyterian Board at Philadelphia, and told of these poor sheep in the wilderness; and here, thank God, he met with success, and there was a glad response; and the successful Presbyterian Missions and Indian Schools in that land today are the out growth of that work.

In company with this heroic Brother Crosby, who had so much to tell, I spent several months in attending missionary meetings. We had blessed times. Immense crowds came out to hear us, and if I am not mistaken, the increase in the missionary income that year was the greatest in its history. In all, we attended eighty-nine Missionary Anniversary Services in different Canadian towns and cities between Sarnia and Quebec.

A very happy week was spent with my family at "Oaklands," Toronto, the beautiful residence of the Honorable Senator Macdonald, the Lay Treasurer of our Missionary Society. Of Senator Macdonald's great kindness, and tangible evidences of sympathy, neither few nor slight, if I should here write, I should only be mentioning what scores of ministers and missionaries could say had been their own fortunate experiences with this large hearted philanthropist. Eternity alone will be able to reveal the full measure of what, with a glad heart, he has been constantly and without show doing for many of Christ's ambassadors, and among the different churches.

As soon as the season for holding missionary meetings ended, I returned to my Indian work. I left the province of Ontario on the 6th of April, and reached Beren's River after twenty three days of continuous traveling. On the railroads in Minnesota and Dakota we were detained by snowdrifts, which so blocked up our way that we had some very unpleasant experiences. After leaving the railroad I had to travel two hundred and fifty miles in a stage on runners over the snowy prairies. We had some blizzards to encounter, and one night, when we were fortunate enough to have reached one of the stopping places, the storm raged like a hurricane. The house was built of logs, and not well finished, and the snow sifted in through the wide cracks between these logs and on to our beds. My experiences in wintry camps served me a good purpose now, and so pulling up the hood of my overcoat, and then completely covering myself up under the bedclothes, I slept soundly through the raging storm and driving snow. When we were called up to eat a hasty breakfast and resume our journey, I found several inches of snow on the top of my bed, but I had suffered no inconvenience from it. With my traveling companions in the other beds it was very different. The upper story, in which our beds were placed, was all one room, and so the snow had equally assailed us all. But, not being able to sleep with their heads completely covered up, they had suffered much, and were in anything but an amiable mood when we resumed our journey.

At Winnipeg I was cordially welcomed by my beloved Chairman, the Rev. George Young, who had ever taken the deepest interest in my work, and done all he could to add to our comfort and efficiency in its prosecution. Fortunate indeed were we, missionaries of the interior, whether it was north or west, that we had such a man to look after our supplies, and see that we were not cheated or swindled by those who once a year sent them out to the poor toilers in their lonely fields. For years we had no money in our northern Missions. Our plan was, once a year to receive from Winnipeg all that our salary would purchase for us in the shape of supplies that were needed in our own home, and also with which to pay teacher, interpreter, guides, canoe men, dog drivers, and others who might be employed in the prosecution of the work.

As all the work of purchasing and packing these things depended very much upon the Chairman, fortunate indeed were all of us, who had Dr. Young as our Chairman.

My dogs and Indians were waiting for me, having come down from the north to meet me, as arranged months before. We purchased our supplies, loaded our sleds, and away we started by dog-train on the last part of the long journey. We had left Toronto in a splendid railroad carriage; we ended the trip of over twenty days duration with dog sleds.

Very quickly did I come back to the wild life of the north after the six months of incessant pleading the cause of the Indians before the large and enthusiastic audiences in our towns and cities. The days of hard and rapid traveling over the frozen surface of Lake Winnipeg, the bitter cold that often made us shiver in spite of the violent exercise of running, the intense and almost unbearable pain caused by the reflection of the brilliant rays of the sun upon the snowy waste, the bed in the hole in the snow with no roof above us but the star decked vault of heaven, were all cheerfully endured again and successfully passed through.

Very cordial was my welcome by the Saulteaux at my new field. I was very much gratified to find that they had had a successful winter, and that those left in charge had worked faithfully and well. A little log house, twelve by twenty-four feet, had been put up, and in one end of it I was installed as my present home. My apartment was just twelve feet square, but

Toiling along on snowshoes through the woods.

to me it was all sufficient. It was kitchen, bedroom, dining room, study, reception room, and everything else. Two of my grandest dogs, Jack and Cuffy, shared it with me for months, and we had a happy and busy time. With several hard working Indians, two of them being Big Tom and Martin Papanekis from Norway House, we toiled hard at getting out the timber and logs for our new church, school house and parsonage. We had to go a distance of twelve or fourteen miles over the frozen lake before we reached the large island on which we found timber sufficiently large for our purpose. Here we worked as hard as possible. Often we had to go in miles from the shore to find what we wanted. To make our work more difficult, we found but few large trees growing close together. So, for nearly every large stick of timber, we had to make a new trail through the deep snow to the lake. The snow was from three to four feet deep. The under brush was thick, and the fallen trees were numerous. Yet under these discouragements we worked. We cut down the trees, measured them, squared them, and got them ready for their places. Then we hitched one end on a strong dog sled, and attached one dog train to this heavy load. How four dogs could drag these heavy sticks of timber was indeed surprising. The principal pieces were thirty six feet long and ten inches square. Yet my gallant St. Bernards and Newfoundlands would take these heavy loads along at a rate that was astounding. We had thirty-two dogs at work, and rapidly did our piles of timber and logs accumulate.

Dressed as one of the natives, with them I toiled incessantly for the material building up of the Mission. We had delightful services every Sabbath. Nearly every Indian within some miles of the place attended, and good results were continually cheering our hearts. Although it was so late in the season when I arrived, yet there was not, for weeks after, any sign of the spring, except in the lengthening days and increasingly brilliant sun. For a long time the vast snowy wastes remained crisp and hard. Very glorious was the atmosphere, for there was no fog, no mist, no dampness. The sky seemed always cloudless, the air was always clear.

Nearly every morning during these weeks of hard toil we were treated to the strange sights which the beautiful and vivid mirage brought to us. Islands and headlands, scores of miles away, were lifted up from below the horizon, and shown to us as distinctly as though close at hand. With but few exceptions our nights also were very glorious, especially when the Northern Lights, taking this vast Lake Winnipeg as their field of action, held one of their grand carnivals. Generally beginning in the far north, with majestic sweep they came marching on, filling the very heavens with their colored bars, or flashing, ever changing, yet always beautiful clouds of brightness and glory. Sometimes they would form a magnificent corona at the zenith, and from its dazzling splendor would shoot out long columns of different colored lights, which rested upon the far off frozen shores. Often have I seen a cloud of light flit swiftly across these tinted bars, as if a hand were sweeping the strings of some grand harp. So startling was the resemblance, that there was an instinctive listening for the sound that we used to think ought to come. Sometimes I have suddenly stopped my dogs and men, when we have been traveling amid these fascinating and almost bewildering glories of the heavens above us, and we have listened for that rustling sound of celestial harmony which some Arctic travelers have affirmed they have heard, and which it seemed to me so evident that we ought to hear. But although for years I have watched and listened, amid the death stillness of these snowy wastes, no sounds have I ever heard. Amid all their flashing and changing glories these resplendent beauties ever seemed to me as voiceless as the stars above them.

When spring arrived, and with its open water came our first boats, we brought out from Red River a quantity of building material and two experienced carpenters. Then actively went on the work of building a Mission house, and also a large school house, which for a time was to serve as a church also. We called it "the Tabernacle," and for a good while it served its double purpose admirably.

Leaving the carpenters and Indians at work, I went into the then small village of Winnipeg for Mrs. Young and our two little children, who were now returning from Ontario, where they had remained among friends, until I, who had so long preceded them, should have some kind of a habitation prepared for them in the wilderness. For weeks we had to live in my little twelve by twelve log cabin. It was all right in cold or dry weather, but as its construction was peculiar, it failed us most in times of rain and wet. The roof was made of poplar logs, laid up against the roof pole, and then covered very thickly with clay. When this hardened and dried, it was a good roof against the cold; but when incessant rains softened it, and the mud in great pieces fell through upon bed or table, stove or floor, it was not luxurious or even comfortable living. One morning we found that during the night a mass, weighing over five pounds, had fallen at the feet of our youngest child, as she, unconscious of danger, slept in a little bed near us. However, after a while, we got into our new house, and great was our rejoicing to find ourselves comfortably settled, and ready for undivided attention to the blessed work of evangelization.

While there was a measure of prosperity, yet the Mission did not advance as rapidly as I had hoped it would. My hopes had been that the surplus population at Norway House would have settled there, and that many from the interior directly east would, as they had stated, come out and help to build up the Mission.

Opposition in various quarters arose, and the Norway House Crees preferred to go farther south; and finally seventy families preferred that place, and there they have formed a flourishing additional Mission. Thus the work advanced, although not all along the lines which some of us had marked out. With patient endurance my noble wife and I toiled on. There was room for the exercise of the graces of courage, hope, faith, and patience; but a measure of success was ever ours, and we saw signs of progress, and had every now and then some clear and remarkable cases of conversion from the vilest into a clear and conscious assurance of heaven's favor and smile.

One summer there came from the east to visit us a chieftainess with several of her followers. Her husband had been the chief of his people, and when he died she assumed his position, and maintained it well. Her home was several days journey away in the interior, but she had heard of the missionary who had come to live among the Saulteaux and teach them out of the great Book. Was not she a Saulteaux, and had not she a right to know of this new way, about which so much was being said? With these thoughts in her mind she came to see us. When she came to the Mission, we saw very quickly that here was an interesting woman. We had several interviews, and Mrs. Young and myself did all we could to lead this candid, inquiring mind into the right way. Before she left I gave her a sheet of foolscap paper, and a long lead pencil, and showed her how to keep her reckoning as to the Sabbath day. I had, among many other lessons, described the Sabbath as one day in seven for rest and worship; and she had become very much interested, and promised to try to keep it.

As she pushed out in her canoe from our shore, her last importunate request was, that as soon as possible I would visit her and her people in their own land. So many were my engagements that I could not take up this additional one until about the middle of the winter following. When, with a couple of Indian attendants, with our dog trains, we dashed into her village, great indeed was her joy at seeing us, and very demonstrative was the welcome given. She had put up on a stage outside in the cold a couple of caribou heads, keeping them there preserved by the frost until I should arrive. Very quickly were they taken down to cook. The hair was singed off, and then they were cut up with an axe into pieces weighing about two pounds each. Soon they were in the pot, boiling for our dinner. I furnished some tea, and while everything was being got ready by a few, the rest of us sat down and talked. They were indeed anxious for instruction in spiritual things. I read, and through my interpreter, explained truth after truth, to which they gave the most earnest attention. Then we stopped a little while, that we might have dinner. As I and my men were the guests of this chieftainess I did not get out my tin plates and cups and knives and forks, but sat down beside her in her wigwam with the rest of the people, completing a circle around the big wooden dish, in which the large pieces of cooked caribou heads had been thrown. I asked a blessing on the food, and then dinner began. The plan was for each person to help himself or herself to a piece of the meat, holding it in the hand, and using hunting knife or teeth, or both together, to get off the pieces and eat them.

I am sorry to say my lady friend on the right, the chieftainess, had very dirty looking hands, and long, strong, brilliant teeth. She took her piece of meat, and turning it over and over in her hands, began tearing and cutting at it in a way that was not very dainty, but extremely otherwise. After biting off a few mouthfuls, she threw it down on the dirty ground of the wigwam before her, and inserting one of her greasy hands in the bosom of her dress, she pulled out a large piece of soiled paper, and unfolding it before me, she began in excited tones to tell me how she had kept the tally of the "praying days," for thus they style the Sabbath. Greatly interested in her story, and in her wild joyous way of describing her efforts to keep her record correct, I stopped eating and looked over her paper, as she talked away. Imagine my great delight to find that through the long months which had passed since I had given her that paper and pencil, she had not once missed her record. This day was Thursday, and thus she had marked it. Her plan had been to make six short marks, and then a longer one for Sunday.

"Missionary," she said very earnestly, "sometimes it seemed as though I would fail. There were times when the ducks or geese came very near, and I felt like taking my gun and firing. Then I remembered that it was the praying day, and so I only put down the long mark and rested. I have not set a net, or caught a fish, or fired a gun, on the praying day since I heard about it at your house so far away."

Of course I was delighted at all this, and said some kind words of encouragement. Then we resumed our dinner. I had my piece of meat in one hand, and with the knife in the other was endeavouring to cut off the pieces and eat them. The good woman replaced the precious paper and pencil in her bosom, and then picked up her piece of meat from the dirty ground, and, after turning it over and over in her hands, began with her strong teeth to tear off the large mouthfuls. All at once she stopped eating, and looking intently at my piece, she said, "Your piece is not a very good one, mine is very fine," and before I could protest, or say a word, she quickly exchanged the pieces; and from her portion, which she put in my hand I had to finish my dinner. As what she did is considered an act of great kindness, of course I would not grieve her by showing my annoyance. So I quietly smothered any little squeamishness that might naturally have arisen, and finished my dinner, and then resumed the religious service. Soon after, she became a decided Christian.

The following extracts are from the last letter which I sent to the Mission Rooms, before, owing to the failure of Mrs. Young's health, we left the land of the Saulteaux for work in the Master's vineyard elsewhere. The Mission had now been fully established, a comfortable parsonage built and well furnished. A large school house had been erected, which answered also for the religious services until the church should be finished. Many had been our trials and hardships, and there had been a great deal of opposition, much of it from places not expected. But to be enabled to send such tidings from such a place, where I had gone as the first missionary, and among such a difficult tribe as were these Saulteaux, so different from the more peaceful Crees, caused my heart to rejoice, that He who had permitted me to go and sow the seed had also given me the honor of seeing some golden sheaves gathered in for the heavenly garner:

"Last Sabbath was perhaps the most interesting and encouraging one we have spent on the Mission. Our place of worship was crowded, and many had to remain outside. Some of the old Indians, who in spite of our pleading, had clung to their sin, renounced it on that day in a most emphatic manner. Seven of them, after being questioned as to their thorough renunciation of their old ways, and as to their present faith in Christ, were then and there baptized.

"At the afternoon service several more were baptized; among them an old man, perhaps seventy years of age, with his wife and grandchild. He had never been inside a Christian sanctuary before. He had just arrived from the vast interior eastward of this place, the country I visited under so many difficulties last April.

"The old man brought down with him the Bible and hymnbook which I had given him months ago. He stated that although he could not read them very well, yet he kept them close to him by day, and under his pillow by night, and tried to keep in his memory all he had heard of what was written in them, as I had told him.

"I have been teaching the school myself for

months, as my faithful teacher, Timothy Bear, is doing poorly. Among the scholars I have none more attentive than the old man and his wife. Seated on the ground with the Rev. James Evans' syllabic characters marked out with a pen on a piece of paper in their hands, and the open Bible on the grass before them, they are striving hard to read fluently in their own language the wonderful works of God.

"If this old man had presented himself for baptism a little better clothed, we should have been pleased. All he had on was a dirty cotton shirt and a pair of deer-skin leggings. However, as such fashions occur here, his appearance created no remark, but all were deeply moved at his coming forward and so emphatically renouncing his old ways of worship.

"The sacrament of the Lord's Supper on the same day was also a service of great interest, as several new members, baptized a few months ago, were admitted to the Lord's Table for the first time. In two instances the decided stand for Christ taken by the women has led to the conversion of their husbands. Until lately they were careless, reckless men; but they have now come and declared that they are convinced that the religion of their wives is better than the old, and they desire to have it too. Thus the work goes on; but how slowly! When shall the time arrive when 'nations shall be born in a day'? Haste, happy day!"

"We are toiling through the darkness, but our eyes behold the light
That is mounting up the eastern sky and beating back the night.
Soon with joy we'll hail the morning when our Lord will come in might,
    For Truth is marching on.

"He will come in glorious majesty to sweep away all wrong;
He will heal the broken hearted and will make His people strong;
He will teach our souls His righteousness, our hearts a glad new song
    For Truth is marching on.

is calling on His people to be faithful, prompt, and brave,
To uplift again the fallen, and to help from sin to save,
To devote themselves for others, as Himself for them He gave,
    For Truth is marching on.

"Let us fight against the evils with our faces toward the light;
God is looking through the darkness, and He watches o'er the flight,
And His joy will be our recompense, His triumph crown the right,
    For Truth is marching on."